EATING WHILE BLACK

EATING

WHILE

BLACK

FOOD SHAMING
AND RACE
IN AMERICA

Psyche A. Williams-Forson

THE UNIVERSITY OF NORTH CAROLINA PRESS

CHAPEL HILL

© 2022 The University of North Carolina Press

All rights reserved

Designed by April Leidig
Set in Minion by Copperline Book Services

Manufactured in the United States of America

The University of North Carolina Press has been a
member of the Green Press Initiative since 2003.

Cover images: hand and apple © LivDeco/Shutterstock; woman's profile
© WibbyDesigns/Shutterstock

Library of Congress Cataloging-in-Publication Data
Names: Williams-Forson, Psyche A., author.
Title: Eating while black : food shaming and race in America /
Psyche A. Williams-Forson.
Other titles: Food shaming and race in America
Description: Chapel Hill : University of North Carolina Press, [2022] |
Includes bibliographical references and index.
Identifiers: LCCN 2021060590 | ISBN 9781469668451 (cloth ; alk. paper) |
ISBN 9781469668468 (ebook)
Subjects: LCSH: African Americans—Food. | Blacks—Food—United States. |
Food habits—United States. | Food—Social aspects—United States. | Stigma (Social
psychology)—United States. | Racism against Blacks—United States.
Classification: LCC E185.89.F66 W55 2022 | DDC 394.1/23—dc23/eng/20211222
LC record available at https://lccn.loc.gov/2021060590

CONTENTS

ILLUSTRATIONS

EATING WHILE BLACK

INTRODUCTION

Worry about Yourself

When Food Shaming Black Folk Is a Thing

Worry about yourself.
—Female African American WMATA employee,
Washington Post

In May 2019, an unsuspecting female African American employee of the Washington, D.C., Metropolitan Area Transit Authority was photographed while in uniform, eating while riding an area Metro train. Natasha Tynes, a passenger on the train, took a photo of the employee and tweeted it with the comment, "When you're on your morning commute & see @wmata employee in UNIFORM eating on the train . . . I thought we were not allowed to eat on the train. This is unacceptable. Hope @wmata responds. When I asked the employee about this, her response was, 'Worry about yourself.'"[1]

Worry about yourself, indeed. That's it. That is actually what this book is about. But we need to dig down to understand. For example, what would possess Tynes, an author and World Bank employee in Washington, D.C., to take this picture and post this tweet? Why did anyone, other than those on the train, need to know what this employee was doing? And why did Tynes feel as if it were her duty to inform the world, via social media? What was the actual point of this communication? And could it only have been accomplished by shaming this Metro employee? Most of us who use the DMV (D.C., Maryland, Virginia) Metro system are familiar with this policy and almost equally as many applaud others when they subvert it. But challenging the policy was not, in fact, necessarily the issue at play here. Because while Metro forbids eating or drinking (among other infractions) on its buses, trains, or in its stations, apparently an email had gone out earlier in the month advising Metro transit police to stop issuing tickets for "fare evasion, eating, drinking, spitting and playing musical instruments without headphones until further notice."[2] The transit worker was obviously aware of the new policy; Tynes, perhaps, was not.

On its face, it would seem that the incident is run-of-the-mill, a necessary calling-out by Tynes of a socially disobedient employee who seemed to be breaking the rules that nonemployees have to follow. But, in our current cultural climate where Black people's lives are constantly being policed, surveilled, and regulated, this incident takes on a more insidious meaning. *Eating While Black: Food Shaming and Race in America* begins with this occurrence involving the female D.C. Metro employee particularly because of the way in which the shamed Metro worker responded: "Worry about yourself." Embedded in her plaintive response is the question, Who are you to regulate me?

This incident stands among a series of recent situations where Black people are publicly vilified and policed for "living while Black." These incidents have been and continue to be all too common and, even more, incredibly disturbing. From "BBQ Becky" calling the police on Black families grilling in an Oakland, California, park to "Starbucks Susie or Sam" calling police officers on two Black men in Philadelphia who were waiting for friends to join them in the coffee shop. Long before the present crisis of living while Black, I found myself thinking about what it means simply to eat publicly and privately as a Black person in America. So often, our food encounters—whether trying to get, prepare, consume, or enjoy food—are under fire. *Somebody* is always watching, waiting to tell Black people what they should and should not, can and cannot, eat. And why? Why do African Americans food cultures and eating habits elicit so much attention, criticism, and censure? The practices of shaming and policing Black people's bodies with and around food arise from a broader history of trying to control our very states of being, and this assumed stance is rooted in privilege and power.

Eating While Black looks at how Black people's food cultures are shamed and surveilled in even the most innocuous situations. I situate this discussion within a broader context of structural and systemic racism, violence, degradation, socioeconomics, and exploitation—conditions that have always been inflicted upon Black people in American society. I specifically discuss three sites—movement and displacement, cultural trauma, and formal/informal food spaces—as just a few of the many examples where these actions occur. Using food shaming and food controlling as central frames, I look at Black people's experiences, because our relationships to food are, and historically always have been, intricate—from criticism and scarcity to creativity and ingenuity. In addition to the beliefs that our food cultures are limited to a particular set of foods, our culinary histories are often rooted in continued misinformation. This distortion aids in the idea that Black people are in more general need of regulation, correction, and control.

The examples above, which took place in a coffee shop and at the park, are just two demonstrations of this belief. And while the food itself is not necessarily the central reason for this surveillance, the violence occurs within the context of a food event, so they are relevant to my discussion. Despite the burst of scholarship on African Americans and food, Black chefs, and Black-owned eateries and restaurants, it is often still believed (even by Black people) that African American food cultures derived almost solely from "scraps" or only the worst pieces of meat and offal (animal entrails).[3] There is also the inaccurate impression that all Black people primarily eat what is commonly known as soul food—foods such as fried chicken, fried fish, cornbread, collard greens, and macaroni and cheese.

Yet, as quiet as it might seem, not all Black people are the same. Nor do we eat the same foods, listen to the same music, wear the same kinds of clothes, and so on, despite most of us having ancestral roots from the South. No matter if we live in the Mississippi Delta, New Orleans, Seattle, Detroit, or Bangor, Maine, it is assumed we are all the same. And there is no regard for those who might "look" African American but come from other countries throughout the African Diaspora; hence, my use of both "Black" and "African American," sometimes interchangeably. The discourses that imply Black culinary sameness are fraught with mistakes, even though they circulate throughout society at lightning speed, infiltrating our lives. But, when you look below the surface of any food conversation and dig deeper, you find that these discourses are generally denser, more multilayered, and more complex than we realize, because they are informed by our gender, class, regions, levels of exposure, family dynamics, and more, even when we are from the same cultural group. Food conversations seem simple, because it is food and we all eat. The fun nature of reality television cooking shows, the fact that everyone eats so they are an expert on their own cuisine, and a general lack of reading leave many thinking that talking about food beyond a surface level is unnecessary. In fact, the subject is so taken for granted because food and eating seem simple— you get food, you prepare it (or not), and you eat it. Most people do not know or consider food is a potent conveyor of power.

But it is; food is used daily in power dynamics. I realized this long before I began studying the ways that food and culture can reveal influence and control. When I first began my academic career, I worked at a university in

New England. It was the eighties and vegetarianism, though widely prac-
ticed, was not necessarily known to be as popular a way of eating as it is
today. I participated in a major diversity assessment initiative that would
affect the university's strategic plan. The two to three of us women of color on
the committee often left the meetings feeling marginalized, silenced, and of
course, extremely frustrated. Throughout the months of meetings, it became
readily apparent to us that we were asked (or told) to be on the committee
to serve as window dressing, and little else. Rarely were our suggestions and
experiences further explored, though they were duly noted. Shortly after
the final report was submitted, we each received an invitation "to celebrate
our committee's work" by attending a cookout at the home of one of the
higher-ups who led the group. As a junior administrator, I felt my attendance
was more than requested—it was required. I responded affirmatively, and
when I followed the etiquette of my home training and asked what I could
bring, I was assured that I did not need to bring anything; the host would
take care of everything. On the day of the event, my sister and I traveled to
the hinterlands of the region to attend the cookout. We arrived at the sprawling home and were ushered into the backyard where we were greeted by our
colleagues. We were encouraged to enjoy the main dish—tofu kabobs! One
of the other women of color took me aside and asked, "What is this?" My
response was, in a word, "Power."

Each time I share this story, I think long and hard about it, applying what I
now know about food, eating, and power dynamics. It is entirely possible that
our supervisor simply cooked only what was familiar to her. On campus, we
all knew she was a vegetarian because she often told us so. And since so few
people on our campus were vegetarians at the time, it remained in our minds.
But then why not let those of us who were not vegetarian bring the foods that
we wanted to eat when we asked what we could contribute? It was astound-
ing, really, and as we sat around the table, amid ready-to-be-discarded paper
plates of half-eaten tofu, we were irritated by the lack of consideration. And
we were hungry. I did not know then what I know now, but as we munched
on baskets of rippled potato chips, we grew more and more angry that we
had been dragged into one more inhospitable space for the sake of our jobs.
Perhaps our day-party host thought she was exercising proper etiquette when
she suggested that we not bring anything. Yet the elephant in the room was
the obvious discomfort most of us felt at being forced into a situation where
we were supposed to eat the unseasoned bean curd. Did she consider at all
that many of us probably did not even know what tofu is? It was the late

1980s, so tofu was not necessarily eaten as much as it is now. Where were the hamburgers, hot dogs, potato salad, baked beans, bean salad, or whatever? Judging by the number of tossed-aside plates, it was not only the people of color who rejected the single available cookout food; it was all of us.

I summed up this event as "power" because the host made a lot of assumptions without consulting those of us whom she had invited. By not providing alternative foods, she decided it was that dish and nothing else. How was this hospitable? For the faculty of color, the food event was even more disconcerting, because in both the professional and personal settings, power was exercised. On the committee, members of the group left the meetings believing that no institutionalized processes of change around diversity would be forthcoming. While a lot of lip service was paid to inclusion and equity, few concrete examples of institutional accountability were mentioned in the final report (which we did not see but heavily questioned about its contents); nor did any substantive change emerge in the short time I worked at the campus. In fact, I left the job because I felt my safety, as an African American woman working and living in the residence hall with a majority of young white men, had been compromised. Nonetheless, the diversity box was checked, meetings were held, and people of color were in attendance. Short of this, little concrete action took place. Similarly, we went to the cookout and could check that box. However, we were offered one dish—half-cooked tofu—and we either ate it or went hungry. We chose the latter and left the event in search of a meal that would satiate our bodies as well as our souls.

We should be attentive to the subtleties of power and how they are exercised, especially in relation to privilege. Foods, like the tofu at the committee celebration, mark time, place, and circumstances by their absence as well as by their presence. And power and privilege often work in the silence(s) and the everydayness in which food resides. Sociologist Avery Gordon elaborates upon this point with regard to power when she plaintively states, "Life is complicated." Acknowledging the banality and truism of the statement, she goes on to tell us that sociologists have yet to really understand the meaning of this "in its widest significance" in part because of the ways in which power operates. Gordon explains how power relations in "any historically embedded society are never as transparently clear as the names we give to them imply." This is because power is "invisible," and "it can be fantastic," as much as it can also be "dull and routine." Gordon goes on to say that power "can be obvious, it can reach you by the baton of the police, it can speak the language of your thoughts and desires. It can feel like remote control, it can exhilarate like liberation, it can travel through time, and it can drown you in the present. It is dense and superficial, it can cause bodily injury, and it can harm you without seeming ever to touch you. It is systematic and it is particularistic and it is often both at the same time. It causes dreams to live and dreams to die." She concludes by admonishing readers, "We can and must call power by recognizable names, but so too we need to remember that it arrives in forms that can range from blatant white supremacy and state terror to 'furniture without memories.'"[4] On that day, at that cookout, power was delivered in the form of white, tasteless, spongey cubes on a stick. And it was served to us as unapologetically as was the bland, empty rhetoric contained in the final report from the committee on diversity and inclusion.

There is a richness in recognizing that even though foods do not speak, they do tell stories. One of the things I know from studying this topic is that one-dimensional conversations about food are as absurd as they are ineffective. Foods operate on multiple levels beyond merely satisfying our stomachs. There is a lot to know and to share about food interactions, traditions, memories, likes and dislikes, habits, and tastes. So it behooves us all to shift *how* we talk about food and culinary cultures—especially those involving Black people.

Shifting how we talk means we cannot simply rely upon mantras and slogans. Yet everywhere we look nowadays there is a farmers market, a bumper sticker, or a recyclable bag advocating that we "buy local," or touting some other hip and cool catchphrase. And everyone, from pundits to journalists, food scholars, enthusiasts and "foodies," seems to have some expertise on what is considered "fresh," "healthy," and "wholesome" food for all people. We are in the midst of food hysteria. Eating is no longer just about enjoying your food but about assigning labels: "organic," "sustainable," "healthy," "clean," and "local." And at the heart of this culinary madness is often an attitude of moral certitude that one person, or group of persons, is more knowledgeable on what everyone else should be eating, as well as when, where, and why. Furthermore, when we fail to adhere to this set of prescriptions, food shaming often occurs.[5]

Since 2007 and the publication of my first book, I have been traveling nationally and internationally, writing and discussing the intersections of gender, food, and power. I also have been observing how people engage food personally and professionally. Inevitably, people—most of them African American—tell me their stories. Young and old, people vehemently and excitedly share how they have been told and/or been made to feel that the foods they find comfort in, the foods they like, love, and are familiar with are unhealthy, unclean, and even harmful. These offenses against African American people are not isolated; rather, they are very widespread. They are being perpetrated in doctors' offices, social-services agencies, food banks, churches, schools, and of course in homes and at work. This behavior is not simply white-on-Black but also Black-on-Black, across different racial backgrounds, socioeconomic statuses, religious beliefs, and other cultural lines. As a result, this book's intended audience is fairly broad, from academics to laypersons, including anyone interested in conversations about food.

This book is shaped in large part by the personal stories and observations gathered over the years, and from feedback I have received on presentations I have given. These responses suggest that those who are inflicting harm sometimes are unaware of the pain they are causing. For example, what may be proffered in the name of "good intentions" often can land with a thud, having a more destructive impact. On the other hand, there are some people who absolutely intend to offend others with their comments and actions. I saw this firsthand when I attended a food bank workshop in the Washington, D.C., metropolitan area. I was the only African American and the only non–social worker in the room, as we established our identities at the outset of the event. As we moved through the activities, I listened to the ways some of the social workers chastised and criticized their clients for a range of "offenses": trying to get more food than they were allotted; not knowing what some of the foods are; rejecting food that was unfamiliar to them; asking for culturally familiar foods, and so on. I did not hear a single conversation that recognized or acknowledged cultural traditions, cultural familiarity, cultural sustainability, or empathy even in its broadest sense.[6] As I sat, listening to the complaints of the other attendees, I could not help but wonder how some of the clients could benefit from discussions that were more open and multifaceted as opposed to dialogues that were laced with ridicule, assumptions, and stereotypes.

The discussions that follow are designed to address these issues by opening up conversations rather than providing answers. The concepts here invite open dialogue and even disagreement. They are designed to provoke serious thought about the multipronged issues related to food shaming and food policing, or what Vivian Halloran calls "gastronomic surveillance." For Halloran, gastronomic surveillance refers to "the observation and policing of a person's eating habits to ensure conformity with an assumed norm."[7] Most often, this regulating, and surveilling—by other groups and even within a group—is frequently undergirded by xenophobia, racism, socioeconomic bias, and other prejudices. It may also stem from self-loathing and ignorance of cultural habits, be they one's own or those of others. Recognizing this, I come to this topic from multiple perspectives that center gender, race, and class. As always, I am interested in representations—how Black people see themselves and how we are characterized with regard to food. So, I use a multilevel approach that involves stories told to me, popular and material culture analysis, literary analysis, self-ethnography, and folklore, using a Black feminist lens as the portal.[8] Approaching the topic from these perspectives allows me to connect people to real-life experiences and in turn reveal the variations that inform African American people's lives. Also, using these narratives and the other strategies I employ highlights the translatability of food between and among people of the African Diaspora even as they reveal the dynamism of Blackness vis-à-vis the unstable signifier of food. I say "unstable" because food is vulnerable to the manipulative whims and joyful maneuverings of people. People use food to say, I am happy, I am sad, I am mad, I am tired, and so on.

Narratives about food told by Black women and girls are particularly dynamic for how they unveil the textures of interior lives. Their experiences unveil not only the ways women influence the food behaviors and traditions of others but also the powerful ways in which food communicates cultural norms and their aberrations. These tried-and-true approaches demonstrate how, as a womanist scholar of foodways, I understand the "sometimes thorny terrains of power, food, identity, place, and gender."[9] So, while this book is written for several different audiences it is also very intentionally geared toward African American communities. There is so little scholarship about this subject that, as Linda Tuhiwai Smith says in *Decolonizing Methodologies*, it is "written primarily to help ourselves."[10]

When I travel to provide scholarly discussions, workshops, and classes, I am introduced to different kinds of food scenarios. I learned a long time ago that it is difficult to enter a situation involving food and not be a participant-observer. Most of the time, my involvement is not extensive but takes place for only a few short days while I am with my host. These short interactions mean I have to quickly capture my experiences while they are fresh in my mind. My habit is to write them down as I recall them happening, think deeply about them, and then process them with different groups of people. So, most of the encounters reflected here are serendipitous, and they are plentiful. A perfect example of this kind of unanticipated scenario occurred during a conversation with an African American woman and friend of many years. When we first met, she was a vegetarian and remained so for most of the years we were in graduate school. Years later after we reconnected and while we were having dinner together, I noticed that she ordered a dish made with chicken. Later, I casually asked her about the change in her diet, and she explained that once she left the Northeast, her health changed. She noticed she was constantly sluggish, her breathing was difficult, and she experienced other physical and emotional pain. After a good while, and in concert with her physician's suggestion, she gradually began reincorporating some meat products into her diet. She went on to explain that, almost overnight, she experienced significant changes in her energy levels. To be sure, this is not everyone's situation. Many people are equally as healthy as vegetarians and vegans. There is no judgment or insinuation. The point here is that any number of factors can affect what, when, how, where, and why we consume certain foods.

Examples like this are used throughout this book to highlight the daily ways that foods are embedded with so much more meaning than we ordinarily consider. As we move about our lives, circumstances change, and these changes affect how we interact with our material world, from the choices we make as consumers to the ways in which we comment on the decisions made by others. And herein lies the tension between intent and impact. Throughout this book, we will explore how good intentions, aims, and ideas can land differently among various audiences. This is especially the case when the context has not been established to help ensure a successful delivery. In the example above, the context in which the conversation between my friend and me took place makes a difference. I was able to question my friend about her dietary choices because we have known each other for decades. We went to school together, so she knew me well enough to know my query was born out of curiosity and not with an intent to challenge or shame her. When these kinds of individual perspectives are not taken into account, our intentions can sometimes cause more harm than good. This is where an understanding of the material world and people's relationships to their objects is instructive.

Long before the violent intrusion by law enforcement into the home of Chicago resident Anjanette Young, who was left standing naked and handcuffed during a botched police raid in 2019, or the murder of twenty-six-year-old Breonna Taylor, who was shot and killed by Louisville police officers in March 2020, I would use the metaphor of "having your life violently disrupted without warning." I would do this to impress upon audiences how personal encroachments look and feel. Sadly, for many African Americans, these kinds of scenarios are not unfamiliar. Like Young and Taylor, Black people know the fear of invasion, violation, and disturbance all too well. A trip to the doctor, a major natural disaster, sitting in the lunchroom cafeteria, and even a trip to the corner store can all end with unsuspecting people feeling demoralized, deflated, or worse—dead. And please hear me: while food shaming is in no way comparable to the violence heaped upon either Young or Taylor, the point here is to emphasize that psychic and physical traumas are thrust upon Black people all the time. Even the most intimate space—the privacy of our homes—can be turned into spaces of intrusion and violent disruption.

Ashanté Reese and Hanna Garth discuss how food spaces can be places of violence—social, cultural, emotional, economic, and physical.[11] For most Black people, the food system is predicated on unequal distribution and so many other inequities that it appears "broken," when in fact it is operating exactly as it was intended. It is through our food that a central element of our expressive and non-expressive Black identity is called into question and even contested. The state—as represented by various government agencies and individuals including health, nutrition, extension, medical, and other welfare professionals—often comes into African American homes and spaces. When representatives of these agencies suggest removing long-standing food sources or insist on particular ways of being and eating, all while depriving us of food-distribution sites—new or old—the result may be a swift or a slow death. Generally speaking, homes and bodies are sacred spaces. People surround themselves with objects that are useful, beautiful, and comforting. Objects make up who we are because as humans our lives are closely tied to our things and belongings. How we behave toward others should honor the personal and social limits that people set for themselves. Close talkers (those who stand too close), loud and lewd talkers, uninvited huggers, and even smokers all can be viewed as boundary violators—and those violations can be either knowing or unconscious. People defend their personal limits, whether sensory, behavioral, or psychological. When personal and physical boundaries are violated, especially those involving taste, touch, smell, sight, or sound, we engage in a range of emotions, from anger, annoyance, irritation, and rebellion to avoidance. This is why I can appreciate the Metro worker's retort, "Worry about yourself!" She probably felt violated and thus defended her space—personal and culinary.

It seems to me people have thought little about the myriad relationships humans have with food. Food is intensely personal and is layered with meanings—historical, social, cultural, sexual, and physical—like any other objects we use. So in this discussion I consider food to be an object of material culture, something that grounds us. As social scientist Mihaly Csikszentmihalyi explains in his essay "Why We Need Things," objects are important to our self-identity for psychological as well as physical reasons. For certain, they help us do the things we need to do on a daily basis, but they also reflect our personal power and our place in the social hierarchy. Objects help us locate and identify ourselves and give us concrete evidence of our place in the world. Objects also reflect the organization of our lives over time even as they provide permanence and/or meaning. Foods we have consistently consumed since childhood or even as adults are connected to our memories and act as hallmarks of our place and being in the world. This is especially the case if you are a transmigrant or have been dislocated due to natural disaster. Lastly, our homes, clothes, cars, books, and technologies not only connect us to social relationships and networks, but they also help us feel as if we belong. So foods reflect relationships and connect us to others.[12] A special meal may be symbolic of an important moment in our lives with family and friends. A particular food may remind us of loving connections in our past and present. For example, I have a childhood friend who never fails to remember my mother with fondness for many reasons but primarily because of the number of times she ate at our house and had eggplant. My mom introduced her to the food, and every time she eats the vegetable, she associates it with the warmth and the welcoming love my mother showed her.

Foods, along with the habits and behaviors that accompany them, mean a great deal to people, as individuals and as groups. When we consider food from this point of view, then maybe we can understand why people feel as if they have been infringed on when their food is taken away and their foodways are disrespected, minimized, and ridiculed. This is one reason why changes to food habits and behaviors do not come easily. Culinary historian Vertamae Grosvenor long ago told us, "Although we may leave home, get rid of our accents, and change our names and diets, the aroma of certain foods will trigger warm memories and fill us with a longing and taste to return home."[13] Food is invested with our identities, so it is critical that we not be misinformed or, worse, remain completely ignorant of the histories of

African American culinary practices.[14] Like other racial and ethnic groups, one way African Americans self-define and reinforce group identities is through their expressive culture: food, clothing, dance, speech and language, games, and so forth. If food consumption and habits signify belonging, then more work has to be done to bring a person along when it is being suggested that their food practices must change. Insisting on such a directive is akin to interrupting and disrupting African American lifeways; this begs for more than simple instructions and sound bites.

Consider one incident that highlights an attempt at disrupting African American food cultures. During the question-and-answer period of a talk I gave to a group of graduate students studying food and culture, my then-fourteen-year-old daughter raised her hand. With slight hesitation, she said, "I have a question . . . or I have something to say about something that happened to me." Surprised that she wanted to share her experiences, I turned to hear her. She went on to tell a group of strangers that when she was in elementary school her health education teacher publicly asked her and her classmates to step on a scale, then read aloud their weight. When everyone had been weighed, the teacher told her and the other African American girls and boys that many of them would not live to see adolescence because they were already obese. There was a brief yet loud silence when she finished her reflection as the conference attendees stared at her in shock.

My daughter is not the only young person to have experienced such an assault on her body, mind, and soul. Indeed, it is an all-too-familiar attack. Sarah Katula, a psychiatric advanced practice nurse, states, "A major reason for an increase in eating disorders, poor body images, and dieting—all at an increasingly young age—has to do with what is in the media and social media. . . . Young girls are bombarded with ideas of beauty that are unrealistic, unattainable for most and often not even real."[15] For certain, social media has increased the spread of such attacks, but even without Katula's confirmation we have long since known this to be the case. A trained health educator, male to boot, should have known better than to publicly shame young people, especially girls, by asking them to step on a scale in front of everyone and then criticizing them. Moreover, if most of the children who attend the elementary school are African American, why would the teacher not consider a cultural connection rather than immediately say that the students are unhealthy and at risk of dying? My daughter concluded her account by telling the audience that this kind of public shaming was nothing short of a microaggression issued against Black and Brown children.

My daughter had shared the incident when it happened, and it had been immediately addressed with the principal. But the fact that my daughter said it out loud in front of strangers was new. She was bearing witness and testifying, speaking of the pain of having her body shamed and policed for how it filled out during her preadolescent years. Never mind that she had had pubescent curves like many African American girls or that, genetically, her body looked like that of her siblings and other members of her immediate family. None of this seemed to matter to her male Filipino health teacher. My daughter's anecdote mirrors another approach I use in the book: telling stories. Despite being heartbreaking and difficult to relive, these kinds of life experiences provide insights into how African Americans view themselves and their relationships to food. They are also a good way to find out how others view us. Children offer particularly insightful perspectives on food shaming. Their stories expose how some of the best advice, even (or especially) when given under the guise of health and nutrition education, can actually be examples of anti-Black racial aggression. The thoughts and comments of young people are often raw because they speak innocently about the intense pain of having been made to feel ashamed of themselves.

In addition to personal experiences, television and literature also offer windows into culinary shaming. Stories from the life of the fictional character Chalky White on the TV series *Boardwalk Empire*, for instance, are helpful because the food-related scenes are powerful. But these parts of the show are often seen as B-roll or background noise because they are not the central part of the narrative. Examples taken from folklore—oral histories, rumors, and traditions—are used in this book because they provide a gateway for understanding culinary cultures. Folklore reveals what the people in the community believe, what they say, and how they act, and it provides a ready understanding of cultural facts that have been passed down, often through generations and more often in the absence of written archives. Taken together, all of these approaches enable us to construct social histories that inform the contemporary moment and that highlight long-standing social mores and practices within Black communities that are and have been central to our survival.

When most of the examples provided throughout this book happened, the intention most likely was not to inflict harm. But food is big, "larger than life . . . highly charged with meaning and affect," and it does a lot of work.[16] Even as it is changed and altered when it is cooked, food itself is transformative. As anthropologist Jane Fajans says, food "can substantiate kinship; it can instill power or prestige; it can create social relations, it can affect social control; it can participate in the formation of the person or aspects of identity; and it can serve as an operator in rites of passage, feasts, and myths." To this I would add that food can be used to shame, surveil, and regulate. Fajans refers to these actions as forms of social control when she argues, "Only those who are successful producers and controllers of food can participate fully in these social and political activities." I tend to see participation and behaviors with food as variable; the ways we operate with and around food exist along a continuum. Sometimes we eat one way; sometimes we eat another way. Sometimes we participate in shaming; sometimes we are shamed. Myriad kinds of people are able to exercise social control and influence using food as a weapon.[17]

The notion that food choices exist along a continuum of options and the knowledge that Black people have always had agency when it comes to food are two primary tenets that undergird this study. Each individual engages life distinctly, despite belonging to particular racial or ethnic groups. Yes, we have cultural similarities, peculiarities, and patterns, but how we approach these are as different and varied as the people. This is yet another reason we have to be more broadly inclusive when we discuss culture and recognize not just "similarity" and "difference" but variation. Yes, Black people have been excluded when it comes to affordable and equitable food distribution centers. Yes, we have been ridiculed and have had our lifeways constantly surveilled and criticized and our foodways shamed and policed. Yes, we have been subjected to racism in farming and with agricultural subsidies. Yes, yes, yes; but Black people are not helpless pawns. We have always been creative when it comes to food. And we are as varied in those practices as anyone can be. We eat from fast-food chains, and we eat from Whole Foods. There are days that we eat from our own gardens, and there are days we eat from the dollar store. We eat fresh, frozen, and canned. We are carnivores, vegans, pescatarians, vegetarians, and maybe even breatharians. This is what I mean when I say we embrace a continuum of options and cannot and should not be defined by any one of them, alone.

Many Black people do not necessarily believe in being bounded by externally imposed rules of performance, habit, and ritual; but we communally make up our own, separate from those that govern others in society. One need only to turn to Twitter and other social media discussions to know that African Americans are the ones who decide "who can be invited to the cookout." In her article on "Black Twitter," Alexandria Lockett cites the

social media platform as "a text comprised of narratives about digitally me-
diated Black cultural preservation and expression." She says it is "a living
archive of collective memories of Blackness. It enacts and represents experiences of misidentification, disinformation, alienation, belonging, forget-
ting, and remembering. These stories represent various forms of testimony
that articulate different accounts of how one experiences being Black—the
ways we share joy, suffering, and survival as we move through a world that
exploits, overlooks, and tries to erase us."[18] These kinds of living archives,
cultural-preservation tools, and memory banks—digital or otherwise—are
what aids the Black community in our ability to keep on keepin' on. But well
before the current uses of technology we had word of mouth, oral histories,
and our own way of doing things. We do not need social media or anything/
anyone else to tell us what, how, and when to eat.

Almost all cultures of people experience food shaming as well as fat- and
body image–shaming. The literature on these topics is expansive. Because
of this, my treatment of these issues, along with obesity and nutrition, is not
exhaustive; it is selective but not reductive. In other words, I am not cherry-
picking arguments. My aim is to intervene in these ongoing discussions by
providing another point of view. Namely, my focus is on examining this form
of Black expressive culture and how African Americans often experience
this aspect of our material world. While the food itself is usually the focal
point, sometimes, as in the example that opens this book, it is not. In some
cases, what is key is the physical action of Black people consuming food and
being perceived as transgressing and misbehaving. In some cases, it is the
context or the event or space wherein food is consumed. From incendiary
and denigrating images of African Americans with chicken and watermelon,
to policies that suggest African Americans have the worst health records, to
arguments that food is the culprit in our early deaths, racist ideas are continuously contrived in order to try and convince us and society at large of
Black inferiority.[19] This is just one of the many ways that white supremacy
works to maintain power structures; it creates hysteria where no actual threat
exists in order to justify surveilling, controlling, and killing Black people
with impunity.

The chapters in this book are framed by one or more of the many food
encounters I have had and what I see as some of the important lessons we
can learn from each. Food shaming of African American people did not
begin yesterday or today. It is deeply embedded in the histories of our existence in the United States and their imbrication in anti-Blackness, gender

discrimination, class hierarchies, and the like. This is so much the case that some of us, as African American people, only know one history, and it is one that is only partially true: that Black people's food cultures are rooted in eating "scraps" or whatever enslavers could scrounge up, along with discarded animal entrails. In discussing some of the ways that this and other myths have taken hold in the African American psyche, I delve into our legacies with food traumas, including resistance to as well as internalization of shame. Oftentimes, these legacies are so normalized that it seems African American foodways need "saving," as gender and food studies scholar Kimberly Nettles-Barcelón discusses.[20] These beliefs, and others like them, are rooted in notions that attempt to infantilize Black people and thus trivialize the details of our lives. Understanding these beliefs as belonging to a set of racial projects may help make sense of this behavior and offer some possible meanings for why they persist and how we can stop this madness in food-centered contexts.

Sociologists Michael Omi and Howard Winant argue that racial projects generally frame how we operate with race throughout the world. These projects are so normalized that they permeate every facet of our lives, from daily incidents to the implementation of public policies.[21] It is a racial project that makes a barista believe she or he needs to call the police because a lone Black man is sitting in a coffee shop without having ordered. There is no need to ask him why he is sitting there because that would lead to the question of why anyone cares. People sit in coffee shops for hours on end without being questioned. No doubt, he was most likely on his phone or doing something else innocuous while he waited for the rest of his party to arrive. But none of this is relevant when it comes to Black people, and especially not Black men, who are always assumed to pose a physical threat. It is this same kind of racial project that empowers a woman to call the police because Black people are cooking out at a public beach or removing groceries from their car outside a rental home. And it is absolutely the same racial project that emboldens a random stranger to take a picture of a Black woman eating at her place of work and to post it on social media because the photographer assumed she was enforcing some policy she understood better than the actual employee. Within this framework, racism is so commonplace that it appears natural, and so the perpetrator feels it is normal to behave this way toward Black people. No, it is more than that. Many, if not most, white people believe it is their right to question the behaviors and actions of Black people. And if the answers are not satisfactory, these same white people believe they should take action. Yet when we call out this behavior as racial aggression, large or small, we are accused of "playing the race card" or "playing the victim." Because, after all, what is the big deal? Why are Black people getting upset or getting an attitude because others are trying to be "good citizens"?

Along with Derrick Bell and Kimberlé Crenshaw, the principal contemporary architects of critical race theory, Richard Delgado and Jean Stefancic identify several premises on which the theory is based—primarily, the idea that racism is "ordinary, not aberrational." Of equal importance to the theory is the argument put forward by Eduardo Bonilla-Silva that "racism is much more than individual prejudice and bigotry; rather, racism is a systemic feature of social structure. Given that racism is so deeply embedded in social structure . . . racial inequality often gets misrecognised as a natural process rather than a by-product of a system of racial domination . . . [or] a 'racialised social system.'"[22] To this point, I like how scholar-activist Keeanga-Yamahtta Taylor responds in a Twitter thread discussing how workshops on racism are praised and admired. While acknowledging there is "a market" for these kinds of meetings, Taylor argues, "The notion that we will end racism one workshop at a time, one white person at a time really undermines what structural racism really is. Racism in real estate, housing, employment and beyond isn't because there are not enough nice white people in the world. The entire point is that it doesn't matter if you are nice or not nice, capital relies on racism to extract, exploit, accumulate, and profit. Capital manufactures scarcity and sets different groups in competition for those scarce resources, creating an atmosphere where racism, xenophobia, nationalism and all other divisions thrive." By manufacturing narratives about the loss of social, culture, and economic power as well as by creating systems of lack and inequality and perpetuating ideas of Black criminality and inferiority, society cements structural differences that seem normalized because they are so widespread throughout every facet of our lives. This is the systemic part of racism. Racism is perpetuated between individuals, yes. But, more so, it is in the ways in which white people move about society assuming they have the right to do this or that. This is what is meant by "white privilege." I am willing to bet there are few people in world, white or otherwise, who would voluntarily swap places with a Black person, wealthy or otherwise. But there are many people who would willingly pass as white precisely because of the opportunities that come along with being perceived as superior. Taylor is right to point out, "To only focus on interpersonal relationships ignores the social and material world in which those relationships exist. This is just high liberal folly dancing around the idea that we can educate ourselves out of structures: that ignorance is at the root of inequality."[23]

Food is not left out of this phenomenon. From the lack of restaurant franchise ownership to the erasure of any acknowledgment that, historically and today, many Black women and men chefs have been culinary masters, from repeated uses of Black-faced caricatures in food advertising to the continued association of Black people with stereotypes, racism is embedded deeply and disturbingly in food.[24] These racial projects are often rendered invisible in their execution because they appear as commonplace single-story narratives reinforced as they are played and replayed throughout popular culture, in magazines, in the daily news, throughout social history, and through daily actions. Though often visibly displayed, the project of racially discriminatory thinking is entrenched and lodged deeply in food policies, leading to the practices wherein this insidious work is carried out. As I discuss later, these ways of thinking form the bedrock for discourses on food deserts, or communities where food apartheid—or the lack of good, affordable, and varied options—exists. Nigerian novelist Chimamanda Ngozi Adichie calls out this concern in "The Danger of the Single Story" when she says, "Show people as one thing over and over again, and that's what they become."[25] But, anticipating this moment, literary scholar Barbara Christian made a similar observation: "I have students, both black and white, who believe these [negative] images because it is become a thread throughout major fiction, film, popular culture, the songs, [and] even the jokes black people make about themselves. It is become a part of our psyche. It's a real indication that one of the best ways of maintaining a system of oppression has to do with the psychological control of people."[26]

So when society repeatedly tells you, through popular culture, social media, and other technology, that all Black people are criminals in need of being policed and incarcerated; or that we have no bodily control over our appetites—culinary or sexual—so we are like children and thus in need of regulating; or that we are perceived to be cheap and uncouth because we do not tip in restaurants in ways that society deems acceptable; then we are bound to have gross distortions about African American people's culinary patterns. These misrepresentations bolster ideologies that inform how we approach social issues and thus how we write policies about everything from health care to banking to voting—including food. From this vantage point, of course soul food is "bad" and "unhealthy," because it is primarily associated with Black people. Focusing on this idea and not on the ways that southerners more generally tend to heavily season their foods and often use sugar, pork (and now turkey) products, cream and other fatty ingredients because they form the template for tastiness, places the focus on supposed Black inferiority. Totally ignored is the culinary richness and diversity of the region. Furthermore, it is this standpoint that sees all fuller and rounder Black people's bodies as evidence of laziness and slothfulness rather than as attractive and Rubenesque.[27] This is also the perspective that sees the "best" and "healthiest" foods largely only as those that are fresh. And it is a perspective that might go so far as to see the best places from which to purchase said food as being farmers markets, organic groceries, locally sourced outlets, and the like. When it comes to food, most people, regardless of race or ethnicity, may not readily recognize these behaviors as part of the ubiquitous racial projects. Many people are apt to buy into these single narratives and beliefs about Black culinary cultures because, absent knowledge to the contrary, these mistruths seem plausible.

The above discussion partly explains why it may be difficult to see anti-Black racism in food interactions. When these sentiments are couched in offers of community improvement—such as building gardens, helping children reduce obesity, or embracing a particular way of eating to conjure a healthier lifestyle—they are difficult to identify as belonging to an anti-Black or a white-supremacist agenda. This obscurity is why many of the examples detailed throughout this book might not appear to fall into the category of a racial project, but they very much are, and they operate as such. Just because a situation is held up by class, regional, sexual, or religious differences does not mean it cannot also be considered a racial project ultimately serving the "psychic and material needs of whites."[28] Thusly, taken together and read through the lenses proposed here, Naa Oyo Kwate's warnings about restaurants and their racial underpinnings seem even more salient. In *Burgers in Blackface: Anti-Black Restaurants Then and Now*, Kwate considers the ways that restaurants embed racism in their marketing and branding, making "everyday consumption" a "marketable good." Kwate argues that these occurrences "ought not be seen as bizarre one-offs but rather as a deeply rooted exemplar of common-sense American racism."[29] Trading on African American stereotypes for the enjoyment of family dining is an age-old strategy of white-owned eating establishments. These strategies not only make it seem as if the stereotypes are accurate; they also suggest that using such labels and images makes for the most effective and most "natural" marketing approach available. In this, the approaches both reinforce the stereotypes and normalize racism.

But what happens when this way of thinking and doing business is also adopted by members of the Black community? When these racial projects are perpetrated by Black people and we buy into the misinformation that is primed by beliefs in white superiority, then that, too, is a form of anti-Black racism. And it operates in virtually the same way, though with potentially different results. Historian Ibram Kendi suggests that misinformation fueled by self-interests and beliefs about Black inferiority leads to racial ideas that are designed to legitimize racial inequality, racist policies, and divisions, because those who perpetuate this kind of misinformation most often benefit from its psychic and social power. According to Kendi,

> All these self-serving efforts by powerful factions to define their racist rhetoric as nonracist has left Americans thoroughly divided over, and ignorant of, what racist ideas truly are. It has allowed Americans who think something is wrong with Black people to believe, somehow, that they are not racists. But to say something is wrong with a group is to say something is inferior about that group. These sayings are interlocked logically whether Americans realize it or not, whether Americans are willing to admit it or not. Any comprehensive history of racist ideas must grapple with the ongoing manipulation and confusion, must set the record straight on those who are espousing racist ideas and those who are not. My definition of a racist idea is a simple one: it is any concept that regards one racial group as inferior or superior to another group in any way. I define anti-Black racist ideas . . . as any idea suggesting that Black people, or any group of Black people, are inferior in any way to another racial group.[30]

Oftentimes, the groups championing these ideas will argue their aims are noble and/or altruistic. They do not *mean* to suggest that all Black people love pork chops, chit'lins, chicken, and watermelon, or are lazy, fat, and dumb. But those who benefit from these kinds of beliefs—consciously or unconsciously—most often also produce and disseminate the narrative that "Black people [are] best suited or deserving of the confines of slavery, segregation, or the jail cell. And those who buy into these racist ideas have been led to believe Black people are the problem and not the policies, rules, and strategies that continue to ensnare Black people."[31]

We would be negligent to dismiss how this behavior functions in expressive culture. It is pervasive and perhaps most infused in material, visual, and popular cultures, which are some of the most deceptive and overt ways that messages are spread. Daily, we are inundated with messages of Black inferiority and have been since technology allowed for mass dissemination of information. Food has not been spared. Both written and visual ephemera have been used to circulate messages about African Americans eating chicken and watermelon and having limited knowledge about the preparation and flavors of food unless it is soul food.[32] Another example can be found in what culinary historian Toni Tipton-Martin calls "the Jemima Code," which she defines as "an arrangement of words and images synchronized to classify the character and life's work of our nation's black cooks as insignificant."[33]

Eating While Black explores the connections between racism and the shaming of Black people's food cultures. The primary focus is on African Americans, but people of the African Diaspora, more generally, have not been spared. The discussions presented in this book serve to ask people to examine their underlying motives in the perpetuation of such shaming and regulation and then encourage us all to create and tell new stories about Black culinary lives. This conversation begins where all discussions like this should begin: by looking at some elements of how Black people have been food shamed historically. Then I move on to provide some examples of how African Americans adhere to culturally sustainable traditions during times of displacement and dislocation. Using specific examples from Hurricane Katrina, I focus on particular moments in the storm's aftermath to examine how African Americans can and do reproduce systems of identities, relationships, and values using food. Next, I discuss cultural traumas and how they get overlooked in the practice of gastronomic surveillance. Racial and cultural stereotypes have substantially contributed to these discourses of food shaming, and it is often the physical bodies of Black women and Black girls that are most affected. This discussion argues that creating healthy bodies requires a redefinition of the food stories that define African American cultures. It also urges people to consider putting into practice a "both/and" way of thinking instead of narrowing the suggestions of how and what Black people should eat.

What seems to be lost on some is the recognition that people have to be able to eat "in the meantime." "Meantime" here refers to the time spent waiting for food inequalities to cease. It refers to the time spent watching some activists go into Black communities to start community gardens. It refers to the time spent waiting for "reputable" food outlets to be opened in our communities. And it refers to the time Black people spend receiving invitations to visit neighborhood farmers markets in order to be self-sufficient only to find themselves being shamed and judged by the very people who claim to want to assist. All of these real-life "meantime" situations are discussed in the final chapter to reveal how Black people actually survive in spite of the obstacles. I look at the ways Black people live despite the racial scripts that attempt to keep us off-kilter. There are a range of creative opportunities African Americans use to acquire and access food, from culinary collectives to corner markets, bodegas, dollar stores, container gardens, farmers markets, and supermarkets. All of these push back on the narrative that suggests Black people need other people to worry about our culinary lives.

A Black feminist tradition of storytelling, hearing, listening, and sharing encourages us to expand the dialogues about African American food cultures. It uses Black people's lives and experiences to illustrate the gravitas inherent in recognizing the numerous viewpoints and cultural differences that are embedded in our conversations about food. To be sure, there are multiple interpretations for all of these situations; the ones offered here are from one perspective, and they suggest in large that when it comes to Black communities and food, people need to worry about themselves.

CHAPTER 1

It's a Low-Down, Dirty Shame
Food and Anti-Black Racism

You're forgettin' something—all Black people ate scraps.
—Family friend, private conversation

In one study, subjects were placed in a crooked chair in a crooked room
and then asked to align themselves vertically. Some perceived themselves as
straight only in relation to their surroundings. . . . Some could be tilted by
as much as 35 degrees and report that they were perfectly straight, simply
because they were aligned with the images that were equally tilted. . . .
Some managed to get themselves more or less upright regardless
of how crooked the surrounding images were.
—Melissa Harris-Perry, "Crooked Room"

I t was a brisk February day when I went with my sorority sister to a contemporary soul food luncheon at an African American museum. Knowing
my work on African Americans and food studies, she had thought I might
be interested in the event, and going together would let us enjoy some sis-
terly bonding time. The event was held in a good-sized meeting room where
the tables were arranged in a U shape in preparation for the day's lecture.
Along with plasticware, at each place setting was a salad made of mixed red
and green lettuce, lightly topped with some kind of low-fat dressing, on a
purple paper plate. After sitting for a while, the twenty or so attendees were
advised to start eating the otherwise-naked lettuce appetizer. As we ate, a
young white woman welcomed us and explained that while the Black chef
prepared the rest of the meal, she would be speaking to us about the history
of soul food. She began by sharing that she and the chef were vegans and that
we would be introduced to a more modern and healthier way of cooking soul
food. After providing us with the background on our chef for the evening,
she launched into her lecture.

Our speaker began telling us about the transatlantic slave trade and how enslaved people arrived in North America. We listened as she then told us something to the effect that the enslaved were fed the poorest cuts of pork, and that that was how African Americans came to eat what is today known as soul food. I sat as patiently as I could. I did not want to interrupt her lecture, but it was filled with so many inaccuracies that I could not remain quiet for long. We had been invited to ask questions throughout the presentation, so eventually I gently interjected and asked where she had gotten her information. She responded that she had gotten it from the internet, though she did not mention any specific sites, nor did she cite any of the numerous credible scholars who had by this time written a great deal on the subject. As she continued, it became clear why most people—Black and non-Black—are wholly uninformed about African American food culture beyond stereotypes and myths.

Knowing a different set of stories about African American foods, my soror and I sat in unbearable tension throughout the remainder of her lecture, until the time came for the final course: a plate of greens. To our left sat an older, well-dressed African American couple. The woman offered the speaker a lot of head nods and took lots of notes, using a napkin as her improvised notepad. As she ate, she loudly complimented the chef by declaring something to the effect that while all the food was good, the greens were the best she had ever had. When the chef finally emerged from the kitchen at the back of the meeting room, she asked him how he had made the vegetables so tasty. She went on to explain that she needed a recipe to substitute for the one from her mother-in-law, since her elder in-law "always" cooked her greens with pork. She further indicated her exasperation with a short wave of her hand, a gesture of dismissal at the repeated culinary offense. After a short chuckle, the chef explained that what we were eating was only partly collard greens; also in the pot were several other leafy vegetables, like dandelion greens, kale, carrot greens, and more. All the greens had been soaked overnight with black truffles, which he had imported from France.[1]

There is a lot to unpack in this anecdote. In addition to the speaker's problematic presentation, there was the attendee's confession about cooking and eating, and some in-group food shaming. Let us begin with the African American woman who preferred the porkless greens. When she rejected her family's traditional way of cooking in favor of the mess of greens marinated with black truffles, she was clearly seeking a better taste but also seemingly trying to align herself with those in the room who might be described as eating "right" and "clean" (read, in this context, "vegan" and "white"). A large portion of the audience that day consisted of about twelve young women attending the luncheon as part of a tour group, eleven white and one Black, ranging in age from twenty to thirty. There were approximately six more of us—the African American couple seated beside my sorority sister and me and another set of well-dressed women, one Black and one white. Judging by our ages, attire, and speech, we all represented various professions. But on that day we were all fed from the same table of misinformation that led to food shaming both cross-racially and intraracially, even as we varied by multiple identity markers.

The experience reminds me of Melissa Harris-Perry's discussion of "the crooked room" experiment, in which participants sat in a crooked chair in a crooked room and then were asked to align themselves vertically. The contortions to which they subjected themselves in order to sit upright are synonymous with the ways in which some African Americans try to avoid being shamed by insisting to others that they themselves eat healthily. On the face of it, there is absolutely nothing wrong with changing how one eats to obtain better health. There is also nothing necessarily wrong with deciding to eat in ways that follow trends to signal a particular kind of cultural capital. There is, however, something slightly askew when participating in these choices means overthrowing and discarding cultural traditions and practices in favor of information derived from distortions, myths, and stereotypes. Writing in the context of African American women's political action, Harris-Perry explains, "African American women are standing in a room skewed by stereotypes that deny their humanity and distort them into ugly caricatures of their true selves. As they struggle to find the upright in this crooked room, they are beset by the emotional, physiological, and political consequences of race and gender shaming. This shaming has tangible, even disastrous consequences. . . . One way black women have demonstrated their agency under difficult circumstances is by crafting alternative images of themselves."[2]

That day (and maybe on other days as well), our African American luncheon companion seemed to be crafting an alternative image of herself as someone who strives to eat healthier and in a more modern way. After all, no one likes to be wrong or to feel like they have a shortcoming. And no one likes to feel like their knowledge of *anything* is subordinate to someone else's, especially when they are shamed into feeling this way. And yet, this is a part of the work done by shaming, whether deliberate or not. Psychologist June Price Tangney explains,

People feel shame and guilt for all manner of failures and transgres-
sions, but the difference is when people feel shame, they feel badly about
themselves; when people feel guilt, they feel badly about a specific behavior. So this shameful feeling about the self is associated with a sense
of shrinking, of being small, with a sense of worthlessness and pow-
erlessness and with a sense of being exposed. Feelings of guilt about a
specific behavior are more closely linked to a sense of tension and remorse and regret over the bad thing done, and feelings of guilt, this kind
of tension and remorse and regret, seems to prompt reparative action,
confessing, apologizing, undoing the harm that was done rather than
hiding and denying.[3]

We came to this event for a soul food tasting and a lecture from which we
had hoped to learn something new, but we were more or less sold a version
of the African American culinary single story: traditional soul food is bad.
Clearly, some attendees agreed that we should be eager and willing to try a
more modern way of cooking certain staple foods (which are still revered
and eaten by many in the South) in order to free ourselves from the failure of
bad eating. This is instructive when coupled with the fact that a young white
woman told the audience she was a vegan. It meant the stage was set for a
number of food-centered performances to emerge, denial and defensiveness
among them. Participants may have felt duped into feeling ashamed about
cooking with meat products, as if that were the ultimate culinary transgression. The speaker that day presented a distorted view of African American
foodways, and many in the audience bought into this illusion. Pork was vilified, and cooking with pork was made out to be similar to eating the scraps
discarded on plantations. I wish I could have told them how I once attended
a mostly white southern meeting that was themed "The Year of the Hog,"
wherein every part of the animal, including the ears, was served one way or
the other, on plates of delicate china.

But the African American attendee who wanted to change her ways of
cooking and eating is not alone. Over the years, I have had numerous encounters with professional women, some African American but many more white,
who make it a point to convey that they eat under the rubric of one label or
another—vegetarian, pescatarian, vegan—but rarely do they acknowledge
being carnivores. It is almost as if people are eager to say, "Look at me! I'm a
good person because I eat 'healthy' and 'clean.'" When I hear statements like
this, whether implied or overt, I have to resist asking if that means the rest of

us are "bad" because we "eat dirty."[4] This kind of bifurcated thinking comes out in the most interesting places. Take, for instance, the time Eric Schlosser, the noted journalist and author of *Fast-Food Nation*, visited the University of Maryland campus. During his lecture, he explained how his investigations into fast-food and meatpacking have put him in the crosshairs of some leaders in both industries. Schlosser suggested that it was merely his goal to encourage people to know where their food comes from and to be wise in choosing "food from providers who uphold ethical practices."[5] Overall, Schlosser's discussion was very interesting. But the part I found most compelling was the question-and-answer period. Several women went to the mic and gave testimonials on how the journalist's books and insights had prompted them to change their way of eating. At least three women were African American, and they ranged in age from around twenty to much older. They stated that as a result of being exposed to his ideas, they either became vegans or simply stopped eating meat. One of these women explained that prior to reading his book, she had frequently drunk strawberry milkshakes. After reading it, she decided she could no longer down a drink that contained artificial flavors and no actual strawberries. What was most interesting about this moment in Schlosser's discussion was his response. He not only registered surprise but also implied that her actions were extreme. He admitted that he himself did not "eat clean." Rather, he explained, he ate meat, including hamburgers, but he tried really hard to eat from restaurants that he knew engaged in ethical and responsible practices such as paying a living wage, offering health care to their workers, and so on.

Perhaps these points—Schlosser's response to the testimonials and his own admission—were lost on others in the audience, but I found this part of the program both captivating and alarming. The curious part was the ease with which the African American women openly admitted their culinary transformation. As each approached the mic to confess her culinary sins, she did so appearing confident that she was on the right track and thus would be celebrated for marching to the right beat. The alarming part was that they had done what society said was right and then were implicitly shamed for doing so. I do not doubt that these women's lives may have changed for the better, but there was something disappointing about seeing their confessions go uncelebrated. They had rejected their tastes and desires for what they perceived as the "right" way of eating, only to be told they were drastic in their decision-making. This seems to be the epitome of trying to right the crooked chair in the crooked room. No matter how much African American women try to situate their tilted chair by twisting themselves and even precariously balancing on only one or two legs (in this case, making and then testifying about their healthy food changes), they will never be able to get the chair balanced (that is, receive positive reinforcement or acknowledgment) because the playing field itself is unlevel.

In both the Schlosser Q and A and the luncheon at the museum, it was African American women who appeared to be deceived. Sharing their actions with others did not result in public praise but rather in lack of acknowledgment, dismissal, and, to some extent in the Schlosser event, rebuke. Nonetheless, in each case, these Black women created their alternative stories by carving out new culinary spaces for themselves, presumably where their health and well-being were improved. And this is not new. Black people—women in particular—have been creating alternative stories and abiding in crooked rooms all our lives, despite the shame and its accompanying guilt. Both of these emotions are exactly why the African American D.C. Metro employee discussed in the introduction admonished her ridiculer, "Worry about yourself."

Despite living in the crooked room, African Americans try to operate efficiently in uneven and unlevel environments that are laced with stereotypes, myths, and systemic barriers that often breed shame. Eurie Dahn refers to this state of being as a "visual dynamic." She says that in the early twentieth century, "shame [was] a force in shaping the content of public discourse concerning race." We see this visual dynamic most vividly in African American newspapers and literature of the period. On display was an internalized and externalized racial shame. Class-based instructions on proper behavior, etiquette, and comportment told African Americans how to be accepted in the eyes of white society. At the same time, white society continued to see African Americans as inferior. In his September 1933 essay "On Being Ashamed of Oneself: An Essay on Race Pride," W. E. B. Du Bois suggests "the Negro" is still overwhelmingly ashamed of him/herself because of differences in wealth, education, and social standing. He proposes that upper-class African Americans are ashamed of the "mass of untrained and uncultured colored folk and even of trained but ill-mannered people and groups of impoverished workers." The fear that all African Americans would be lumped together and judged accordingly was an unwanted burden. Du Bois goes on to suggest that "organized economic and social action" are two ways of overcoming this shame.[6] Through emphasis on racial uplift, sexual morality, and ethics, middle- and upper-class African Americans sought to control and police the bodies and actions of those they considered their "lesser" brothers and sisters. This practice of intraracial or internalized surveillance has not necessarily abated but instead has joined interracial (externalized) judgments that make many African Americans constant targets of bodily discipline.

The visual dynamic of shame is often set off by bodily surveillance of African Americans, a practice as old as our presence in the colonies.[7] Angela Hattery and Earl Smith argue that chattel slavery is the genesis for the "story of policing Black bodies" because watching and studying African cultures, lifeways, and movements aided enslavers in being able to capture them.[8] During the Middle Passage, many captured Africans experienced starvation—self-imposed as much as forced—vitamin deficiencies, and even death. Given these and other psychological, emotional, and physical traumas during the journey, many of those who survived the ordeal arrived malnourished.[9] Slave narratives, for example, provide useful details about life on the plantation. The young, in particular, were made to eat from troughs, often without spoons. Robert Shepherd, in recounting his experiences on a Georgia plantation, said that their crumbled cornbread and buttermilk was served in a trough that "would be a sight . . . 'cause us never stopped to wash our hands, and 'fore us had been eatin' more dan a minute or two what was in de trough would look lak de red mud what had come off of our hands."[10] There is no end to the ways in which white enslavers sought to establish control over African American people using everyday forms of physical, emotional, and psychological violence. Food became an excellent weapon, a ready tool with which to conduct this violence, but it was also used by African Americans to push back with fortitude.[11]

We find resilience and determination on visual display in the TV adaptation of *Roots*, based on Alex Haley's best-selling book. In January 1977, the miniseries played across America. Almost forty years later, in 2016, the History Channel aired a four-episode remake of the series. In the 2016 version, we find the main character, Kunta Kinte, on a Middle Passage ship, refusing to eat the gruel forced upon him by his captors. After Kinte spits out the food, another captured soul says, "Kunta Kinte, you will not live if you do not eat." Then another says, "Kunta, *live*. . . . See what comes!" After a while, the men start to identify themselves by name, village, and tribe. As they argue about which tribe is to blame for their current fate, a woman's voice cries out, "Do not fight, brothers. It won't help you." One or two of the men respond and a call-and-response takes place, revealing how some of the enslaved people take comfort in communicating through singing. At one point, someone sings, "It's good to hear a voice from home." Then another asks, "Do you know this ship? Can we take it from the white man?" The question is met with silence.

In the next scene we see young men being shoved on deck, where whips force them to move their bodies to the beat of a drum. As they assemble beside familiar faces and start to move their feet, we see they are also surveying their surroundings, noting the location of their captors' guns. They begin to sing again, encouraging one another to dance so that the white men do not notice their inspection of the deck and therefore do not feel threatened by them. As the singing continues, one of the older enslaved men, whom Kunta Kinte refers to as "Uncle," calls out to the Mandinka woman who sang to them when they were below deck: "My sister, I am looking for you!" The women, though also on deck, are out of view of the men, cooking and washing behind a wooden wall. One of the women calls out in response, "Oh my brothers, I will help you if I can." So as not to give away their communication, the women all join with the men in singing, "Oh my brothers, dance!" The self-designated African leader then asks, "Sister, do you think we can take this ship?" To which one of the women responds, "Only if you get behind the wall. Seize the big gun. Kill the captain. They close the door each time someone steps through." Shortly after this, the captured Africans are hustled back down below as Kunta's betrothed riles the men by trying to jump overboard and thereby escape what was intended to be a gang rape.

The producers took a fair amount of creative license with this version of *Roots*, because these elements were not present in the original miniseries. In doing so, they offer some often-overlooked aspects of the treacherous Middle Passage that, while presented here in fictionalized form, are historically accurate. Slave revolts happened aboard ships, but we seldom hear about the roles of women in helping to carry out these mutinies. In this fictional account, when the men decide they will fight to the death, they acknowledge needing the help of the women to pull it off. When the men return to the top deck on another day and begin their ritual of dancing and singing, they instruct one another, "You, brothers, will capture the white men to work these great sails." The women join the singing and bring to the captives a basket containing knives and other weapons hidden beneath clean clothes. As the drumming increases, the men and women attack their captors using the newly acquired weapons. Though the attack is unsuccessful, foiled by guns and cannons, the creative license of the producers and writers opens up avenues for thinking through the roles of women on the slave ships, who may well have used their domestic duties to conceal their participation in revolts.[12]

I detail this fictional incident to give more multisensory texture to how food and food roles may have functioned on slave ships. African women were never passive to a point where food, or the lack thereof, totally eclipsed the goal of freedom. And they used food and food contexts to do more than cook, serve, and clean. Through the lens of food, we get stories of horror but also of early Black acts of agency from which emerge two important variables: adaptation and creativity.[13] Slave ships were stocked with African foods and livestock and then restocked with other goods at ports along the way as the boats sailed to the Americas. In their study of African food and botanicals, Judith Carney and Richard Rosomoff explain in detail that African women were needed to prepare food and, in the words of one captain, "dress the victuals."[14] Carney and Rosomoff further detail what the 2016 version of *Roots* depicts when they discuss that women were partitioned from men above deck and confined to an area where they could cook and serve food to the crew and to small groups of enslaved men at a time. Accordingly, the wood-burning cookstove was placed above deck "to heighten security of the galley area in the event of a slave revolt." Moreover, the maintenance of food preparation was such a critical dimension of the journey that it influenced the design and basic outfitting of the slave ship.[15]

The majority of provisions used to keep Africans alive during the Middle Passage were brought on board from the continent. Milled and unmilled cereals, including sorghum and rice, were brought aboard. African women cleaned rice, pounded raw grains, and cooked corn, among other food tasks. In his travel log, Thomas Trotter, a physician working aboard the infamous slave ship *Brookes*, describes the conditions under which enslaved Africans contracted scurvy during the forced transport from Guinea to the West Indies. In his journal, he tells of the foods that they were fed, often forcibly and always under threat of punishment. Trotter also names and describes specific foods: "Their diet consisted of beans, rice, and Indian corn, alternately, boiled: to which was added a sufficiency of Guinea pepper, and a small proportion of palm oil and common salt."[16]

This discussion about the diets of enslaved Africans forced to travel the Middle Passage illustrates not only how the slave ship was an "agent of botanical dispersal" but also how food intricately connected those imprisoned with their captors.[17] Millet, tubers (yams), rice, and other foodstuffs became as much a part of the economic, political, and cultural fabric of slavery as the enslaved people themselves. Africa contributed other foods to these voyages as well, including okra, black-eyed peas, plantains and bananas, pigeon peas, watermelon, peanuts, sesame seeds, and melegueta peppers. They also brought with them knowledge of cooking techniques such as slow cooking (like stewing and cooking down), grilling, roasting (using cabbage instead of banana leaves to wrap meat), and deep-frying. They introduced plants and herbs such as tamarind, hibiscus flowers, and kola nuts to improve tastes and to fight diseases resulting from vitamin deficiency. And they had knowledge of spices, grasses, and herbs that were used for medicinal purposes as well as to disguise spoiled meats and to enhance flavors.[18] Sowande Mustakeem in *Slavery at Sea* mentions other foods like "stockfish, flour, bread, and beef" along with salted meat, "beef, pork, biscuit, flour oatmeal, pease [sic], butter . . . cheese," and alcohol as additional provisions that were brought aboard slave ships or bartered for and used as trade along the treacherous passage.[19] Manuals and accounts by slave merchants, captains, and doctors are instrumental for detailing food acquisition (including shoreline purchases and bartering), preparation, and distribution. These accounts are also useful for providing evidence of the first instances of food policing. These were not minor details. They are a part of the food stories that encompass African American culinary footprints, and they speak to some of the many reasons that culinary inventiveness was necessary. For African American men and women, foodways were a major vehicle for the expression of culture and identity in the ways in which foods were stretched, augmented, made tasteful and useful to fulfilling ritual and tradition.

Throughout enslavement, Africans had to adjust to new surroundings. It was undoubtedly difficult to get comfortable in any one place, seeing as how men, women, and children could be sold at will and without a moment's notice. So Africans were constantly becoming familiar with new geographies, new ingredients, new utensils to cook and eat with, and new ways of preparing food. In the colonial era, this meant that African traditions had to merge with those of Indigenous peoples as well as those of the white settlers who took Indian lands. These new amalgamated practices enabled Africans not only to survive but also to help colonists do the same. Despite this, Africans still found their foods to be highly regulated, carefully watched, and minimally dispersed, which spurred them to find new ways of acquiring enough food. For some, gardens were an option; others were able to trade and sell the foods they produced; still others foraged and scrounged.

Georgian ex-slave Ed McCree described the "eatments" on his plantation:

Bout dem eatments, Miss, it was lak dis, dere warn't no fancy victuals lak us thinks us got to have now, but what dere was, dere was plenty of.

Most times dere was poke sallet, turnip greens, old blue head collards, cabbages, peas, and taters by de wholesale for de slaves to eat and, onct a week, dey rationed us out wheat bread, syrup, brown sugar, and ginger cakes. What dey give chillun de most of was potlicker poured over corn-bread crumbs in a long trough. For fresh meat, outside of killin a shoat, a lamb, or a kid now and den, slaves was 'lowed to go huntin' a right smart and dey fotch in a good many turkles (turtles), 'possums, rabbits, and fish. Folks didn't know what iron cookstoves was dem days. Leastwise, our white folks didn't have none of 'em. All our cookin was done in open fireplaces in big old pots and pans. Dey had thick iron skillets wid heavy lids on dem, and dey could bake and fry too in dem skillets. De meats, cornbread, biscuits, and cakes what was cooked in dem old skillets was sho' mighty good.[20]

The recollections of Mr. McCree are somewhat atypical in that many enslaved people did not have as many options, or at least not in the sense that enslavers provided them with a number of choices. But Mr. McCree's account is instructive for how it describes that on this plantation the enslaved were allowed to go hunting. Some undoubtedly also set animal traps and/ or enlisted children to hunt and forage if they were not already relegated to the fields. In short, the many experiences of slavery fractured the culinary experiences of African people, so new ways of practicing food cultures had to be created. It was never as simple as merely cooking and consuming pork scraps. Instead, experiences such as Mr. McCree's bear witness to a culinary imprint and contributions that far exceed what we have been led to believe because of myths and stereotypes.

Slavery in the United States lasted over 300 years and mostly spanned the broad swath of land we define as the American South. While the "peculiar institution" persisted and became more and more vicious, its incarnations remained varied, with different characteristics depending upon where the plantation or farm—large or small—was located. While these facts are well established in scholarly circles, they still are not clear to most laypeople. For many, popular culture has served to cement a *Gone with the Wind* or *Django*-esque perception of enslavement.[21] In reality, there were several different kinds of plantations throughout the antebellum South that produced different primary crops; rice, cotton, tobacco, and indigo were among the most prevalent. And some specialized in human breeding because enslavement was deliberate. It was based on an economic and racial system of labor that differed depending on geographic location, crop production, weather cycles, and even skill set. And all of these dynamics heavily affected food production and consumption patterns.

When we consider the vast numbers of African-descended people who were taken from their homelands, we should expect to encounter disparate lifeways. According to the scholarly records and extent evidence, for example, there were a significant number of Muslims among the enslaved.[22] Khaled A. Beydoun observes that "46 percent of the slaves in the antebellum South were kidnapped from Africa's western regions, which boasted 'significant numbers of Muslims.' These enslaved Muslims, most of whom were men deported from Senegambia (Senegal, Gambia, Mali, and Guinea), strived to meet the demands of their faith, most notably Ramadan fasts, prayers, and community meals, in the face of comprehensive slave codes that linked religious activity to insubordination and rebellion."[23] The practice of Ramadan necessitated not only fasting but also avoiding certain foods. And while work cycles might have prevented complete observance of the practices, "reports of [Muslim] religious activities appear in court and police records, plantation logs, newspapers, books, and runaway notices. [The] portraits [of enslaved Muslim Africans] are captured in paintings, prints, daguerreotypes, and photographs; and they have left a few manuscripts written in Arabic."[24]

We also see examples of this in popular culture. The 1997 film *Amistad*, directed by Steven Spielberg, was loosely based on the events in July 1839 aboard the slave ship *La Amistad*, during which abducted Mende tribesmen and women from Sierra Leone, led by Joseph Cinque, overtook the ship near Cuba. Then there is the real-life story of Senegalese Ayuba Suleiman Ibrahima Diallo (whose name was later Anglicized to Job Ben Solomon), who would not eat meat unless it had been slaughtered by a Muslim.[25] Apparently, while in England he adhered so closely to the rituals of Ramadan that at one point he appeared sick and weakly. Some readers will be familiar with Charles Wilson Peale's famous painting of Yarrow Mamout, who continued to pray and abstain from pork and alcohol while in bondage to Colonel Samuel Beall Jr. of Montgomery County, Maryland, for over forty-four years, until he was freed in 1796. Perhaps best-known is Abdu-l-Rahman Ibrahim Ibn Sori, also known as Abdul-Rahman or "Prince," who gained notoriety for his knowledge of cotton production on a Natchez, Mississippi, plantation. He, too, was said to be among those Muslim men who maintained allegiance to his religious practices, including abstention from pork and alcohol.[26]

If some Muslims maintained practices that led them away from the traditional notion of "scraps"—the poorest cuts of pork, several quarts of dry cornmeal, and other low-subsistence ingredients and foods—what did they and some other enslaved people eat? When hungry and surrounded by woods, most people began to use the rich natural resources around them. If we accept this commonsensical fact, then we can believe that they most likely used their surroundings to their advantage. Archeological evidence, such as that offered by Mark Warner, reminds us of an "influencing factor in food choices that is occasionally overlooked": urban/rural food contrasts. Warner writes, "The presence of a number of species of wild animals is much more commonly part of a rural faunal assemblage than that identified in urban settings. Living in a rural setting, an individual has direct access to a variety of wild foodstuffs through hunting or trapping that a city-dweller typically cannot readily acquire."[27] On the East Coast and along coastal areas in general, Warner and others suggest, the enslaved looked for wild berries, plants, acorns, and chestnuts, and also for various kinds of birds, including chicken, turkey, and duck. Museum installations at such institutions as George Washington's Mount Vernon and Thomas Jefferson's Monticello illustrate that some enslaved people fished for bass, herring, perch, croaker, and so on. When possible, they also hunted for opossum, squirrel, snake, terrapin, and turtle. None of this leads to the conclusion that enslaved African Americans ate well. Rather, it illustrates enslaved people's resourcefulness and subsistence, which is also conveyed in the now-ample scholarship on African American foodways.

It is far more convenient and easier to reduce the whole of African American foodstuffs to that which is simple, neat, and compact, no matter how erroneous. This point of view reminds us of Chimamanda Ngozi Adichie's warning that we risk a critical cultural misunderstanding when we forget that everyone's lives and identities are composed of many overlapping stories. She says, "The single story creates stereotypes, and the problem with stereotypes is not that they are untrue, but that they are incomplete."[28] This limited understanding, while common, can easily serve a more harmful role. This way of thinking becomes normalized and rooted in the ways that we think about other people's cultures. So, to Adichie's assertion "Show people as one thing over and over again, and that's what they become," I would add that the even more harmful part is that it is what people become in their own minds, not to mention in the minds of others. This is what leads to policies, decisions, and ways of interacting with people that cast them as inferior and incapable. This way of thinking has certainly been the case for African Americans, and it is exacerbated for the poor and working classes.

A reliable novel, for me, for depicting early twentieth-century Black life is *Contending Forces*, by Pauline Hopkins. In it, Hopkins deals with a number of issues pertaining to the everyday lives of Black Bostonians at the time, including miscegenation and lynching. Most interesting to me are the ways in which Hopkins details the food served at small events and gatherings. Hopkins uses such features, at times, to designate class differences. For example, during a church fair where a raffle takes place, some of the congregation members compete for prizes ranging from a timepiece to a sideboard to a piano. One competitor has her friend from a southern state bring her an opossum, which she makes into a dinner to give away with her raffle tickets. Because of this clever maneuver, she is able to persuade a lot more people to buy her raffle tickets. As a result, she sells the most and therefore wins the top prize, which is a piano. In the introduction to her study *Dividing Lines: Class Anxiety and Postbellum Black Fiction*, Andrea Williams references this novel and a criticism levied against it by one of Hopkins's contemporaries, Boston clubwoman Addie Hamilton Jewell. Williams explains that Jewell's primary concern with Hopkins's historical romance was her "depiction of the contentious class relations among African Americans . . . between blacks on a 'lower scale' and other blacks 'on the so-called higher plane.'"[29] It was Jewell's belief that Black people needed to appear unified in their public images as they rallied for the causes of racial uplift and advancement. Williams makes it clear that Jewell was not altogether opposed to class hierarchies. Jewell claimed she wanted Hopkins to write a sequel where she showed that those on the "higher plane" "were always 'respectful' in their manner when dealing with those they consider[ed] their inferiors."[30]

Intense scrutiny of Black food and cultures from within the Black community did not abate with the ending of the slavery, so shaming and policing has not stopped.[31] Jennifer Jensen Wallach expands upon this phenomenon and its connection to respectability politics in her expansive historical study *Every Nation Has a Dish*. One of the examples Wallach uses early in the text comes from the HBO series *Boardwalk Empire*, which aired from 2010 to 2014. Set in Atlantic City during Prohibition, the drama focuses on the town's treasurer and local gangster, Enoch "Nucky" Thompson, and it features a rich display of African Americans who worked the underground economy to increase their wealth and opportunity. Among them is Albert "Chalky" White, one of the city's most notorious and shrewd African American business-men. He is a community leader who shares holiday gifts of food and money and performs favors for his people. Chalky hails from a working-class background. His father, a Texas carpenter, was hanged by a mob when Chalky was young. His wife Lenore, by contrast, was born into a wealthy family that was part of the educated elite. Lenore's family did not accept Chalky until he resolved a financial problem for his prospective father-in-law. The married couple has three children, and they live in one of the largest and most luxurious houses in Atlantic City.

Wallach discusses one scene as an example of how "the dinner table, which served as a site of physical and intellectual empowerment . . . could also become a place where antagonistic visions about racial, class, and national identities could come into conflict with one another."[32] While this is true, the ways that writer and producer Terence Winter builds the scene add as much to the process of food shaming as the food itself. In the episodes leading up to the dinner in question, Chalky is feeling an overwhelming loss of power and social status for several reasons: First, he is in jail for killing a white man. Second, Chalky knows that even though his white counterparts approve of the murder, his arrest jeopardizes his connections to these politicians, with whom he has enjoyed a unique position of good standing. Nucky Thompson even goes so far as to tell Chalky, "You can thank me by being a good boy." Third, while he's in jail Chalky's wife tells him that her daughter's suitor wants to come to dinner. She then hands him a copy of the book *David Copperfield*, which their son has sent for him to read while he's waiting to be released. Chalky has managed to keep hidden from his wife that he is basically illiterate, something he suspects his son has detected.

Chalky's probable illiteracy is critical to the episode and to Chalky's sense that he has lost the respect of his people and therefore his power in the community. When a fellow inmate and newcomer to the town, Dunn Purnsley, asks Chalky to tell him about the novel, Chalky responds incorrectly, revealing that he thinks he is reading *Tom Sawyer*. Purnsley apparently is able to read and realizes Chalky cannot, so he decides to make a spectacle out of him. Clearly unfamiliar with Chalky's prestige and standing in the community, Purnsley taunts Chalky for being "uppity," having a light-skinned "bitch" wife, fine clothes, and books before calling him just another "jigaboo in a jail cell." After he knocks the book out of Chalky's hand, Chalky calmly inquires about the well-being of several of his fellow inmates. All of them owe Chalky a favor or two, so they wordlessly defend his honor. After they give

Purnsley a brutal beating, one of them hands the now-slightly-bloodied book back to Chalky. His secret having been revealed but his honor vindicated, Chalky asks his fellow inmates who among them "know[s] [his] letters" and then gives the book to one of them to read aloud.

The next scene cuts to Chalky having breakfast with his family at home two months after he was released from jail. While enjoying his home-cooked meal, he asks his wife for more eggs. She responds with a rebuke: "You've had nearly a half a dozen already, Albert." At that moment, the youngest daughter asks Chalky to check her homework. Her brother Lester, an accomplished pianist who is bound for Morehouse College, responds, "You asking Daddy?" Ignoring his son, Chalky responds, "Let your mother do that for you. . . . Your brother know I'm too strict." He gives his son a side-eyed glance, reminding viewers that it was him who sent Chalky the *David Copperfield* novel in prison. Lester responds, "If you say so," prompting his mother to admonish the teen to "stop toying with your father." Swiping his hair in an only half-playful manner, Chalky ends the conversation with, "He know who bring home the bacon." At that moment, the eldest daughter, Maybelle, tells her father that her beau has been invited by her mother for dinner the following night so she can be courted in a "respectable manner." Looking at Lenore, Chalky says, "Did she now?" Maybelle says that her intended plans to study medicine, and Chalky remarks, "An educated buck." Then Chalky says, "I suppose it be alright . . . dinner with all the fixins. . . . I been cravin' hoppin' John since the moon was blue." This prompts an evasive "Umm . . . " from mother and daughter as they resume eating in silence.

Set against the backdrop of Prohibition, European immigration, and Jim Crow, *Boardwalk Empire* acknowledges the many African Americans who left the South in search of new freedoms and economic opportunities in the early twentieth century. Chalky White is an example of one such migrant who used the chance to reinvent himself and create a better life for himself and his family. On the show, white politicians see the African American community as a powerful voting bloc, and they look to Chalky to deliver those votes for them. Chalky's wife Lenore's priorities lie in the projects of racial uplift, Black respectability, and raising her children to be intellectually informed. But while she is kind and polite toward Chalky, she does not necessarily respect him or take him seriously.

The relationship between Chalky and Lenore reflects long-standing intraracial tensions within Black communities around physical markers of class and colorism. In her research on social class and Black communities, folklorist Audrey Kerr discusses this phenomenon and the belief that "blurring racial boundaries increases the social mobility of black people (within, but more important, beyond black communities)." In other words, the lighter in hue you were, the better you were believed to be. Kerr further argues that this "resulted in a rather sophisticated albeit unwritten series of social rules governing black social organizations."[33] This belief was in part the catalyst for Purnsley's assaulting Chalky by calling him "uppity" and "a jigaboo in a jail cell." Though Purnsley is lighter than Chalky, he appears to have none or few of the material accoutrements that would solidify his status in the community as a "boss." Thus, out of jealousy Purnsley seeks to bring Chalky down a peg or two. In refusing Chalky's basic requests for foods, such as more eggs or hoppin' John, Lenore is displaying a similar kind of disrespect for Chalky. Lenore at times seems to be telling Chalky that she sees him as not quite deserving of her, and she seems also to have passed on this sentiment to her children, who have no problem craftily disrespecting their father with material goods like books and food. For everyone but Chalky, hoppin' John is a clear symbol of lower-class leanings and thus should not be served to a would-be physician, and especially not to one who is courting the White family's eldest daughter.

Juxtaposed with the tensions he feels at home is the waning sense of comfort Chalky finds within the larger Black community, among the working-class people with whom he most identifies. After his son's remark during breakfast and the realization that he will be surrounded by Black intellectualism at the next evening's dinner, Chalky attends a church meeting where Black community members share their troubles with him. Having reestablished some measure of security in his identity as a fixer for and savior of the Black working-class community, Chalky prepares to leave, but not before inviting everyone to partake in the light repast he furnishes. But he cannot leave, because he is confronted by several Black women who press him about their husbands and sons who have died or otherwise been harmed through their connections to Chalky's illegal liquor business. After being accused by one of the women of putting himself in charge and walking around "taking a bit off of everyone else's plate" while giving "nothing back 'cept a summer clambake and a Christmas turkey," Chalky is left vulnerable and speechless. Like the white politicians and his nuclear family, who constantly remind him of his place both directly and indirectly, the very people whom he considers his true family do the same. The rebuke by these darker-skinned Black women with whom he greatly identifies is sharp and swift, cutting deeply to the core of his identity. Chalky is a ship without a sail—he is too Black to be loved at home and not Black enough for his community. With this background and its many tensions, the pump is primed for a "dinner gone awry."[34]

The dinner scene begins with a pan-in on the family busying themselves with putting food on the table. Amid the flurry of activity, we find a sullen, somewhat contemplative Chalky sitting in silence at the head of the table, swirling what looks to be a brown liquid in an old-fashioned glass. Wallach describes the scene this way:

> The setting denotes middle-class domesticity and includes a table covered in a white cloth and laden with china, crystal, and carefully arranged food: a roasted duck, homemade biscuits, and a bowl brimming with peas and carrots. To an impartial observer, nothing about the materiality of the dinner table scene would suggest that either the funds used to purchase the food, or the implements used to serve and consume it, were funded by proceeds from extralegal activities. Nor is it readily apparent that the Whites are members of a despised racial group only decades removed from the legalized debasement of slavery. The carefully groomed members of the family sit with perfect posture, offering up their bodies as evidence of their refinement, which is also evoked by the elegant domestic interior and the painstakingly prepared meal. It is clear that the bodies surrounding the table, the food destined to sustain them, and the dining accoutrements used to choreograph the meal are all carefully curated and chosen to serve as powerful signifiers of status and of a certain set of values.[35]

As they sit for dinner, Lenore invites the daughter's dinner guest, Samuel, to grace the table. In many Black families, gracing the table is an honor usually bestowed upon the eldest male. So when everyone joins hands and Chalky refuses to take Samuel's, it should not be surprising. Chalky instead continues to sip his liquor while studying the table. As Samuel begins to pray, Chalky interrupts by asking, "That a duck?" To this Lenore responds, "Yes, Albert, of course it is." Samuel starts to pray again, and Chalky again disrupts the prayer. "I thought I asked for hoppin' John." Stating the obvious, Lenore says, "There's duck, peas, carrots, fresh-baked biscuits," to which Maybelle adds, "I made chocolate pudding for dessert." The scene continues:

Chalky: I asked a question.
Lenore: Albert, please. [turning to Samuel] She made that pudding all
   by herself.

Samuel: It's very nice.

Chalky: [angrily interrupts] Where the damn hoppin' John?

Lenore: Albert, you know that's not proper food for a guest. Now let's allow Samuel to finish.

Chalky: [interrupts again with arms folded] Well, maybe our guest woulda like some.

Samuel: Well . . . I have always enjoyed that type of food, sir.

Chalky: What type of food?

Samuel: [nervously smiling] My grandma would make it.

Chalky: I say something funny, son?

Samuel: I beg your pardon?

Chalky: You laughin', what's the joke?

Lenore: Hoppin' John, Albert . . . you're being ridiculous.

Chalky: I been eatin' rice and beans all my life. Tell me it ain't good enough. [He says this last part as he derisively looks down his nose at Samuel.]

Lenore: You'll have to forgive my husband's country ways.

Samuel: I completely understand.

Chalky: It's my house! [slams hand on the table] And my country ways put the food on this goddamn table.

Lenore: Albert! You're drunk.

Samuel: Sir, I apologize. I'll leave.

Chalky: You stay right where you are, son. Right there! *Inside* the house. Pretty clear who the field nigger is.

With this exclamation, Chalky leaves the table. The episode later closes with sounds of the family being entertained by the son, Lester, playing the piano while Chalky sits outside in the shed, whittling a stick with a pocketknife. He glances with scorn toward the house, from which emanates sounds of laughter.

Wallach provides an apt summary to the "seemingly unexceptional act of sitting down for a family meal":

[Chalky] sees the public rejection of the beans and rice dish as a denunciation of more than his criminal activities; he interprets it as a personal indictment by family members who possess more cultural capital and as a betrayal of their shared racial heritage. He seems to sense that it is a particular version of blackness, not his illicit occupation, that his family regards as criminal. . . . By accepting or rejecting the roasted duck, they were sending messages about their understanding of their class and racial status. . . . Although the blandly American, middle-class dinner menu seemed designed to pave the way for assimilation as full-fledged members of the U.S. nation-state, Chalky's brooding presence and his hostile reminder that he "put the food on the table" reminded the family that both their patriarch's occupation and their racial heritage precluded them from full national belonging.[36]

While Wallach's assessment is spot-on, I suggest that the interaction also simply boils down to one word: power. I took pains to detail the events leading up to the fictionalized dinner in order to illustrate how our food lives are circumscribed by a host of factors. Here, Chalky White is in the crooked room, and he is trying to right himself by balancing precariously on two legs of the chair. He is part of a system that is not set up for him to succeed, yet he engages several avenues to try and do so. He marries "up," and he endears himself to the African American community both because they are "his people" and to align himself with white politicians for protection in operating his illegal activities. Yet none of it is enough "to belong," nor does any of it allow him the power to assert full control over himself. At a time when he perceives himself to be losing major influence, his home should be his sanctuary, as the edicts of the Black women's club movement dictate. Accordingly, the fictional Lenore, who is presented as a would-be member of this real-life historical movement, should be ensuring that the home is indeed an "ideal refuge" for Chalky from being thought of and referred to as "boy," from fearing he will be lynched for killing a white man, and from worrying that his illiteracy will be mocked.

The public version of home, in this instance the Black church and the interior Black community, should not be a place where Chalky's altruism is questioned, especially not by the church sisters. So when Chalky experiences similar rebuke there, he falls into a downward spiral. He asks for foods that would enable him to perhaps straighten himself upright, even if for a short while. Yet his wife's refusal to grant his food requests—both the eggs and the hoppin' John—are about more than her simply saying no. Because Lenore controls the house and the goings-on therein, her denial of the foods is her means of exercising domestic power and influence. Her rebuff of Chalky's food requests and her label of them as "country" and "ridiculous" is another means of shaming and policing his body, along with the shaming Chalky receives from everyone else leading up to the food event. Having lost this ability to control himself, he resorts to using a switchblade to carve and shape a stick while sounds of the piano—an instrument used to demonstrate respectability and decorum—float in the background amid the joyful noise of communal family laughter.

When a person is told they cannot eat the familiar foods that sustain and comfort them culturally and spiritually, especially in times of turmoil, it is almost as if someone has taken a wrecking ball to their identity. We cling to foods that give us comfort, especially if they also taste good and are satiating. Hoppin' John, for Chalky, is comfort. But, more than this, it is a touchstone of who he is—his struggles, his past, and his present. No wonder he responds to being refused the food with anger and disdain. Chalky sees himself as worthy of anything he requests because of his ability to work the underground economy. In his mind, it is this work that keeps the "plantation" moving. This is one reason, among many, why the distinction made between being the "house Negro" and the "field Negro" is so important. Even though those who were assigned to work in the Big House often were more forward-facing and visible, we know that the plantation would not have survived without the labor of those in the fields. In fact, the forced labor of those in the fields provided the economic means for those in the Big House to exist. Without the production of crops and other goods, there would be no income. Chalky's ability to define himself vis-à-vis the nation is critical, but equally important is his family's recognition of his contributions to the nation-building in their own home. But Lenore seems to have no interest in comforting him or recognizing his pleas. In fact, she seems to see him through the eyes of white society, and certainly through her own class consciousness in the same ways that some African Americans see one another, as inferior and in constant need of correction.

Though *Boardwalk Empire* is a fictional show, the scenario it presents with the White family is not far from reality. The roles of African American men and women who worked for the causes of justice after emancipation have been well documented, including middle-class Black women's self-help and reform activities. Through grassroots organizations, churches, and national institutions, Black women, individually and collectively, sought out ways to use food and other aid to assist African American communities in need. Though beset by racism, sexism, bodily violence, political disfranchisement, and limited resources, Black women instigated progressive social reforms for positive social change at every turn. This racial uplift was geared primarily toward the vast number of rural southerners who migrated out of the South. Joining with organizations like the National Urban League and the NAACP, reformers sought to convey and promote the virtues of thrift, industry, temperance, honesty, and piety. In accomplishing this, it was believed, African Americans would achieve not only a kind of racial trustworthiness but also acceptance among white society.

Newspapers and magazines such as the *Baltimore Afro-American*, the *Chicago Defender*, the *Cleveland Call and Post*, Washington, D.C.'s *People's Advocate*, and the *Colored American Magazine*, among others, offered instructions and guidance for migrants, hoping that the newest arrivals would behave in ways that enabled the race to be fully accepted. Columns like "The Change of Food" and "The Value of Oatmeal" (figure 1.1) admonish African Americans not to eat "cakes and pies" because they are poor in nutrients. Women and girls are particularly called out as being "starved" because "their food is poor," especially the "dainties" that are apparently consumed a lot. These small bites "spoi[l] the appetite for substantial food." The columnist in "Change of Food" encourages readers to instead eat a "proper and nourishing variety of food [that] is made up of fruits, vegetables, grain, and animal food, the latter consisting of healthy meat, eggs, or milk in its various forms."[37] Another column, "Until the Doctor Comes," written by Dr. U. G. Dailey for the *Chicago Defender*, provided information on "Proper Eating" to remind readers of the importance of a well-balanced diet.[38] Writing in 1943, Dr. Dailey also encouraged an expansive diet that incorporated different food groups. Nearly twenty years later, in 1961, in the *Chicago Defender*, we find experts indicating that "Americans" are generally "eating themselves to death." The article, contributed by the Tuskegee Institute, reports on concerns raised at the Sixteenth Annual Food and Nutrition Institute. The institute notes, "Obesity (excess weight) . . . is one of 12 diseases or conditions primarily of nutritional origin. . . . It is a disease in which Americans 'take great delight.'" The article goes on to say that heart disease is also a common issue but seldom for the "skinny female."[39] Many other articles of the first half of the twentieth century suggested that when given *equal access*, African Americans had the same health success as the rest of the nation. For example, writing in 1935, Dr. A. Wilberforce Williams said,

> Although the Negro constitutes about one-tenth of the total population in these United States of America . . . statistics show that under the same environments, the same locality, the same conditions as to hygiene, sanitation, housing, and working condition, the same medical care and hospitalization, the health of the Negro compares favorably with the health of other human unities living in similar environmental

conditions. Therefore, we do not believe that there is any real Negro health problem. . . . But he must become inured and learn the art of mastering and controlling his environmental conditions.[40]

Though Williams's concluding argument somewhat undercuts his assertion of equal access, he argues that all things being the same, African Americans (especially those in the same locality) make similar or the same food choices as others and thus reflect the health profiles of society overall. In 1967, an unknown author writing for the Washington, D.C., news desk of the *Chicago Defender* said, "In the slums of the big cities of the North and in the back-country hamlets of the South, poorer Americans are eating better because of an expanding food stamp program." The new program enabled recipients to move beyond selecting only "surplus foods" that were usually "dried beans, corn meal, peanut butter, canned meat, and flour."[41] With the new food program, recipients were able to choose from a select group of meats, vegetables, fruits and cheeses.

In her research on Chicago, historian Tracy Poe illustrates how the newspapers used food to perpetuate racial shame in their columns and writings.[42] As part of the racial uplift goals and the inward turn toward an intraracial class focus, food was a central tool. The numerous columns devoted to etiquette, proper diet, and the like were, as Eurie Dahn has observed, one way that "the newspaper and its readers produced and shaped a shared ethical community grounded in shame [and] the community forcefully combatted the national logic of racism though discussions of racial unity and equality [even as it] affirmed class differences."[43] In explaining the important work of Black periodicals in advancing the rhetoric of shame, Dahn further writes, "The periodical forum is one inward site that allowed African Americans who shared urban middle-class sensibilities to talk about shame and to demonstrate their difference from those who did not share these sensibilities."[44]

Christian and non-Christian houses of worship and religion were another venue where Black identities and food conjoined and this kind of politics was advanced (see figure 1.2). In their article on soul food and Sunni Muslims, Carolyn Rouse and Janet Hoskins explain that "debates over food taboos and eating rituals developed early in the Nation of Islam and occurred at about the same time that the black middle class was rejecting southern cuisine." Specifically citing Elijah Muhammad's column "How to Eat to Live," a regular feature in Nation of Islam official newspaper *Muhammad Speaks*, Rouse and Hoskins explain that Muhammad "made the rejection of traditional black southern cooking a practice of faith." Citing the period of the late 1970s

Fruit Juices.

There is often a decided objection to the use of our coarsest fruits, especially in sickness, or when the stomach or bowels may be in a sensitive state, on account of the irritation of the angular and sharp seeds, and peel or skin. Like the hull of the wheat—or hulls, as there are five different layers, which should be removed, in most if not all cases, from the flour—these seeds and rinds are often sources of irritation to the sensitive coats of the stomach, causing many forms of disease, particularly in the hot weather. It is exceedingly fortunate that these juices do not require digestion like the solids, but, like water, enter the system unchanged, there to be assimilated, of course affording nutrition, with no use of the digestive apparatus, or but slight effort, that of absorption. (If desirable, these juices may be prepared at this season, thoroughly scalded, canned like fruit, kept from the air and in a cool place, and used in the following spring, when such are exceedingly valuable, especially for those having debilitated digestion.)

It is very plain that if they demand no digestion, still containing all of the nourishment of the berry, securing rest for the stomach, the dyspeptic, etc., may well use this juice as a substitute for solids, for such a part of the time as will allow rest, time for the digestive organs to recuperate and become sufficiently strong to perform their usual amount of labor.

I will here remark that their use all the time, instead of at the last meal, or when the appetite may be particularly imperfect, would tend to debilitate the stomach, since, like all unused organs, the time would come when it would lose the power of action. As a general principle, the substitution of these for solids for one or two meals at most, using the simplest form of solids, as the raw egg, or boiled rice, would be as much as would be advisable, save in extreme cases, when such nourishment for a week or less would be a choice of evils.

Milk should not be regarded as of this class, since it is solidified before digestion. It is not a proper drink between meals, since it requires digestion like solids. When there is much feverishness, with some appetite, the more acid juices, like that of the strawberry or the currant, may prove of great value without sugar, for that is a "heater." These tend to reduce feverishness, though, if too acid, they may irritate the stomach, producing the canker.

The fresh juice of the apple—not fermented juice, or cider—is very appropriate and useful, the apple containing more nourishment than the potato. These juices may be used with great propriety when the appetite seems waning, or when but little food is indicated, for nourishment is obtained without labor.—*Golden Rule.*

Figure 1.1. Articles in African American newspapers often highlighted better nutrition. *People's Advocate* (Washington, D.C.), August 4, 1883.

Figure 1.2. Untitled photo, possibly related to this description from the Library of Congress: "Outdoor picnic during the noon intermission of an all-day ministers and deacons meeting. Near Yanceyville, Caswell County, North Carolina, [Oct.?] 1940." Photograph by Marion Post Wolcott. Courtesy of the Library of Congress.

or "the transition"—two years following the death of the Prophet—Rouse and Hoskins go on to maintain, "The movement [changes] in political, religious, and personal identification with Islam and America changed how food taboos were articulated. These changes demonstrate a historical dimension to ideas of purity that argues that relational metaphors of pure and impure are profoundly contextual and temporal."[45]

Despite these historically specific changes in meaning, foods like chicken and watermelon consistently and across time have been wielded as symbols of shame and therefore a means of controlling some social behaviors and consumption habits of African Americans.[46] As I have written elsewhere, there are countless African Americans who refuse to eat fried chicken in public for fear that they will be ridiculed. One person interviewed for a previous study shared that she thought eating chicken publicly, especially at work, was "ghetto." She was clear that the stereotype of African Americans as having a fondness for chicken was enough to steer her away from eating the bird publicly, a concern that has been well documented.[47] We saw this issue regarding African American stereotypes around chicken and watermelon play out further when Barack Obama was first elected president of the United States. Associations of President Obama with chicken were everywhere—on banners and awnings, in store windows. According to the *New York Daily News*, two fast-food restaurants, one in Brooklyn and another in Harlem, began calling themselves "Obama Fried Chicken." One restaurant began advertising the "Obama Chicken Lunch Special" for $6.99 alongside breakfasts that included eggs, grits, turkey bacon, and scrapple. From China to Germany, foods like "Obama-[Chicken]-Fingers"—one German ad read, "Fertig gebraten, mit curry dip" (Ready fried, with curry dip)—were suddenly available for purchase. At times these references seemed to have been made in homage to the nation's first African American president. Nonetheless, they caused a great deal of consternation and ire because they reflected a racial stereotype that is very much present, although many want to believe it is in the past. And these restaurants were not alone. Several businesses rebranded themselves in this way without regard for the negative connotations, in an effort to profit off the newly elected U.S. leader. While many of these establishments may have argued against the stereotype, they would have been hard-pressed to explain why this particular dish was named for the nation's first African American president.[48]

Initially writing for the blog *Very Smart Brothas*, cofounder Damon Young laid out his thoughts in an article titled "Perfectly Normal Things Black Men Just Know Not to Do Because America Is Racist as Fuck." The article lists about ten actions that African Americans are careful not to do for fear of reprisal, shame, or even death. Casual actions from "assisting random white women in public" to "jog[ging] at night" to "get[ting] angry at work" are included. Number eight on the list is: "Eat chicken and/or watermelon at office potlucks and/or BBQs—Which sucks because everyone loves watermelon. And there's nothing worse than loving watermelon but feeling a certain way about showing your love of watermelon because you know everyone assumes you love watermelon. Which sucks because EVERYONE LOVES WATER-MELON!!!"[49] As the ninety-plus comments indicate, almost all African Americans are aware that eating chicken and watermelon publicly might result in their being shamed. Though many are in disagreement with what their response should be to these acts of public shaming and accountability, we are aware that the acts occur. The association of African American people, and especially the president of the United States, with foods like chicken is so incendiary that a particularly potent visual was removed. Whether this had to do with *Very Smart Brothas* being sold to Univision or not, when I first accessed the article in 2015, it included a close-up picture of President Obama eating a fried chicken leg. Though the image was replaced and Young's initial caption is now included in the article itself, the statement read: "We're all aware of the potential criminality if caught driving while Black. And shopping while Black. And walking while Black. And walking with your hands in your pockets while Black. And waiting for a bus while Black. And sitting while Black. And eating while Black. And tipping while Black. And . . . well, you get the point."[50]

President Obama was also not spared from the racist stereotypes associating Black people with watermelon. One postcard that began circulating showed a well-trimmed lawn littered with watermelons. In the background were neatly planted red rosebushes, manicured hedges, a sprinkler, and the White House. Dean Grose, mayor of the small Southern California town Los Alamitos, left his post after calls for resignation abounded following his sending the postcard's image via email. Grose apologized, saying he "wasn't aware of the racial stereotype that blacks like watermelon."[51] It is appropriate to ask why Grose did not question the association of this president with this particular fruit at this particular time. Why not some other kind of fruit? It is equally interesting that while Grose says he was unaware of the connection, it appears that the postcard did not pique his curiosity enough that he googled "Obama and watermelons" before forwarding the email.

The August 9, 1937, issue of *Life* magazine featured a study on watermelon in the South. The article, which discusses the profitability of watermelons once they are shipped to the North, includes images primarily of African Americans harvesting and eating the fruit. The article goes on to note, "White or black, southerners know how a watermelon should be eaten," a point emphasized by the column title, "All Southerners Like Watermelon." On the magazine's cover, however, is the now-iconic image of an African American man sitting on the back of a wagon filled with watermelons. Writing for *HuffPost*, Nneka Okona describes the scene this way: "A bald, middle-aged Black man with broad shoulders sits on the back of that truck, shirtless and outfitted in worn pants held up with suspenders. His name is Roy E. Parrish, hailing from Adel, Georgia, and as he sits on the back of the truck, he peers out into sprawling acres of farmland on either side of a winding dirt road." Mr. Parrish was quite possibly a sharecropper, but maybe a farmer, and in his left back pocket was a brown paper bag twisted at the top. Maybe it held a bottle of something to swig from as he passed the time, or a refreshing drink for when it got too hot. As he looked out on the fields that most likely contained more watermelons, Mr. Parrish probably could not imagine that over seventy years later an African American man would be in the White House, or that even though most African Americans are no longer sharecroppers, we are also no longer farmers because of rampant discrimination. And if Mr. Parrish did imagine someone like Obama as president, he probably wouldn't have thought that over a half century after his picture was taken, Black people would still be perceived as mere watermelon pickers and eaters.[52]

As much as there has been a focus, historically, on middle-class Blacks who shunned southern foods as "backward," there are many indicators that African American diets are as varied as African American people. Moreover, as the *Life* magazine article maintains, "all southerners like watermelon," so Black southerners who eat the fruit are right in line with others from the region. While it is important to know how food shaming has taken place and continues to do so, it is equally if not more important to consider the ways that African Americans live their lives regardless of this criticism. The ways that African Americans and Black people generally exercise agency is key. And this is why finding and telling new and varied narratives of African American food cultures is especially useful. Because if there is one new story, perhaps there are others. Doing the work of uncovering new stories should encourage us to keep going until there is little danger of reinventing "a single story."

As I have suggested elsewhere, photographs from the Farm Security Administration / Office of War Information Collection at the Library of Congress provide an extensive pictorial record of American life. The images depict the living and social conditions of Americans in suburban, urban, and rural areas during the Depression and World War II.[53] Feggen Jones and his wife, along with their fourteen children, were captured on film by photographer Arthur Rothstein. In the 1940s, the Joneses lived on an eighty-six-acre farm in Zebulon, North Carolina, purchased through the FSA (Farm Security Administration).[54] Having gone from sharecropping to owning a farm, the Joneses had two cows, three mules, four hogs, and 200 chickens, along with more domestic animals. The family owned two vehicles—a Ford truck and an Oldsmobile sedan. Their cash crop was tobacco, but they also grew cotton (five acres), wheat (seven acres), corn (twelve acres), and other vegetables (two acres).

Additional probing would uncover a number of more intimate details of the Jones family's life, but for the purposes of this study, some basic background

Figure 1.3. *Zebulon, North Carolina. Feggen Jones and His Wife in the Smokehouse.* March 1942. Photograph by Arthur Rothstein. Courtesy of Library of Congress.

Figure 1.4. *Zebulon, North Carolina. Feggen Jones and Family at Dinner.* March 1942. Photograph by Arthur Rothstein. Courtesy of Library of Congress.

suffices as a complement to the visuals provided by Rothstein. Putting the Jones family's narrative in conversation with studies such as Monica White's *Freedom Farmers*, Natasha Bowens's *The Color of Food*, and Leah Penniman's *Farming While Black*, as well as oral histories and biographical narratives, we gain more than a story about feeding and growing, resiliency, and survival in the wake of widespread systemic exploitation and oppression: together, these stories unveil the ways African American people thrive and help others to live by sharing food.

During hard times and even during times of plenty, many subsistence farmers aided their neighbors by providing foodstuffs. Historian Kelsey Bates describes an incident in Gee's Bend, Alabama, that prompted residents to come together in support of one another following a catastrophic event. Part of what sustained the community was its food traditions. After the white merchant who had been lending Gee's Benders agricultural supplies passed away, African American residents had their agricultural equipment violently seized. According to Bates, the African American community survived by finding comfort in the familiar foods that had become a part of their tra-dition. Not only did they use the foods they had stored away, but they also shared what they had with one another. Their collective narrative "reinforces the idea that Gee's Bend food traditions developed out of a long history of adversity with whites, food sharing and frugality, and reliance on God."[55]

These stories—Feggen Jones and the residents of Gee's Bend—are not sin-gular, but they may be new to many because they are not the traditional stories we hear about African American food cultures. From stories such as these, we get glimpses of what Monica White describes as "collective agency," whereby African American people come together using food and agricul-tural knowledge to effect change and make a difference in their own lives and those of others in their community.[56] Furthermore, stories such as these enable us to peel back the layers, to understand Black Americans' farming politics and deep knowledge of agriculture and food systems as well as their love of the land.

I first came upon the story of the Howards, another African American family who had a snapshot of their life captured on film, when I worked at the Still Pictures Branch of the National Archives and Record Administration in College Park, Maryland. I was a graduate student, and the division had just received a major piece of new technology: a color copier. The researchers were asked to test out the quality of the copier by xeroxing various images from the record groups. It was an excellent opportunity to further my own research on African American foodways. In the process of exploring vari-ous record groups, I found caches of photos that showed African American coal-mining families in domestic situations. In addition to the domestic in-teriors in the photos, I was intrigued by the descriptions and the images of the photos that displayed family meals.

Mr. James Robert Howard worked for the Gilliam Coal and Coke Company as a miner in Gilliam, West Virginia. According to the data provided with the photographs, the Howards lived with their four children in a three-room unit of a two-family house. In 1946, they paid seven dollars a month for rent and about four dollars for electricity, which ran on a meter. The house itself was then about fifty years old with few amenities, but they did own an electric refrigerator, washing machine, iron, and radio. Mr. Howard had also installed running water in the family's kitchen. Handwashing was still "usually done at the front yard faucet," where trash collected and decayed and "seepage from privies collect[ed] in low spots." Mr. Howard worked the night shift at the mine, which started at 6:00 P.M., so the family ate supper around 4:30. Figure 1.5 shows the family preparing to eat a meal that consisted of green beans, corn on the cob, boiled beef, cucumbers, tomatoes, and biscuits. When looked at closely, figure 1.6 suggests that the family may have been gathered for a special occasion. There are coordinated plates, a tablecloth (made from the same cloth as the curtain partition in the background), an empty chair, and an extra place setting, at the head of the table. All of this hints that they may have a guest for this meal. Furthermore, the dinner may well be atypical because the description mentions the infrequent treat of a cookie for dessert.[57] Though brief, this overview provides an initial thread that can be pulled to learn more about African American coal miners, generally, and those living in West Virginia, specifically, because this is a yet-untapped area of research in food studies. Although it is the Howard family for whom we have many details, there are many more mining communities that employed and housed African American families, making the records from these communities a storehouse of knowledge waiting to be tapped.

Stories like those of the Jones and Howard families, as well as the Gee's Benders, illustrate just some of the many reasons why I was irritated that day at the museum while listening to the presentation on the history of African American foodways. The realities of these families' lives points to why stories that reduce African American food cultures to scraps are farcical and absurd. I did not expect the presenter to know all or even most of this information, but knowing even a fraction of this would have gone far toward dismantling the many mistruths that pervade common conceptions of African American life and culture.

But for whom is it useful to dismantle this misunderstanding? Not for everyone. As Ta-Nehisi Coates writes in "Letter to My Son," "In America, it is traditional to destroy the black body—it is heritage."[58] It is deeply ingrained

Figure 1.5. Mrs. James Robert Howard and her daughter at supper. August 13, 1946. Courtesy of the National Archives and Records Administration.

to view African Americans and their cultures as inferior, and the degree to which this view becomes corrosive depends on the number of people who believe the lies and continue to speak them. This is a perfect example of what Adichie means when she states that dispossession begins with telling people's stories in ways that render them as secondary or "less than." Adichie writes,

> Power is the ability not just to tell the story of another person, but to make it the definitive story of that person. The Palestinian poet Mourid Barghouti writes that if you want to dispossess people, the simplest way to do it is to tell their story, and to start with, "secondly." Start the story with the arrows of Native Americans, rather than the British, and you have an entirely different story. Start the story with the failure of the African state, instead of the colonial creation of the African state, and you have an entirely different story.[59]

If we start the story with what Africans were given to eat once they arrived on the shores of America, instead of what they ate before they were captured

Figure 1.6. The Howard family asks the blessing before eating supper. August 13, 1946. Courtesy of the National Archives and Records Administration.

or how they survived once they got to the Americas, then we will have a different story. Repeating a single culinary story, without knowing the dynamic histories of Black people in America, makes it easier for us to fall for a simple, monolingual narrative instead of recognizing the textured layers that inform and comprise the lives of the African American people. It is this falsely singular point of view that also renders African Americans grossly susceptible to food shaming and food policing, interracially and intraracially. Because it is this simple story that leads to the belief that African Americans are in need of policing and/or saving. And this may well be what fueled Natasha Tynes's belief that she had to call out the D.C. Metro employee who was eating on the train.[60]

We began this chapter at a museum, listening to a lecture on African American foodways. Perhaps it was not the intention of the speaker to reinscribe anti-Black racist ideas in her discussion. Nor was it necessarily the intention of the African American woman who complimented the meatless greens to buy into assimilationist rhetoric that gives rise to anti-Black racist ideas.[61]

But when the lecture attendee complained about her mother-in-law always using pork to cook her greens, she also implied that ignorance about "eating healthy" was at play. Moreover, this attendee accused her mother-in-law of being old-fashioned and unwilling to change, without considering that her mother-in-law has her own tastes and traditions that she clearly enjoys. Embedded in this attendee's rationale was shame and blame—her own shame in being associated with such practices and, out of embarrassment, blaming her absent mother-in-law. Writing for *The Undefeated*, Lonnae O'Neal captures an argument of Ibram Kendi's that speaks to this point: "'You can be someone who has no intention to be racist,' who believes in and fights for equality, 'but because you're conditioned in a world that is racist and a country that is structured in anti-black racism, you yourself can perpetuate those ideas.' . . . No matter what color you are."[62] The discussions in this chapter have teased out some of those perpetuating behaviors when it comes to food and African American communities.

The remaining chapters discuss some other ways in which food shaming reveals anti-Black racism. As I have repeatedly suggested, often these actions are unintentional. In fact, often these behaviors are exhibited within attempts to try to help others. But when we do not take into consideration or think deeply about how histories of racist conditioning might affect our actions, we often end up reinforcing and reinscribing the very white-supremacist beliefs we are attempting to demolish.

CHAPTER 2

In Her Mouth Was an Olive Leaf Pluck'd Off

Food Choice in Times of Dislocation

As a PK (preacher's kid), I grew up with knowledge of the Bible along with its many interpretations. In addition, my dad, trained in Black liberation theology, and my mom, trained in special education, made sure my sisters and I were exposed to many different facets and denominations of organized religion and forms of spirituality. We experienced different world faiths and beliefs and were left to decide for ourselves the spiritual paths and beliefs with which we wanted to engage. Both parents being educators, we were introduced early on to the usefulness of a Bible concordance—a comprehensive reference book that provides guides and words used in scriptures—and as a practicing Christian, I am familiar with the many great stories in the Bible. So when I was preparing to give a keynote address on food and displacement, dislocation, movement, and migration, the first thing that came to my mind was the story of Noah and the Great Flood.

The passage that I homed in on is taken from Genesis 8:6–12. After God sent the forty-day flood, Noah sent out a raven from the ark to see whether there was dry land. But the raven returned because all the trees and land were all very much underwater. Then Noah sent out a dove to see whether the water had receded, but the dove also returned. Seven days later, Noah sent out the dove again, and this time when it returned it had in its beak a freshly plucked olive leaf. After seven days Noah again sent out the dove, and this time it never returned.

I used this scriptural story in my talk for many reasons: First, it worked to frame a discussion about food choices (or the lack thereof), especially during times of calamity and chaos. Two, it illustrated the ways that movement—voluntary or involuntary—affects how and what we eat. Three, I used it to consider how centuries of misinformation and misinterpretation, often deliberate, undergird anti-Black racism. Finally, it led to a discussion of how ideology, cultural capital, and class status connect with race to open our understanding of how food shaming takes place in our everyday lives.

Movement and travel always have been a consistent trope in African American history and culture. In many instances, movement is positive and life-affirming, but in far too many cases, for people of the African Diaspora, movement—jogging and walking, going across town, traveling out of town, and especially migrating—is not an enjoyable experience.[1]

Most discussions about African Americans and movement center on the Great Migration, but contemporary conversations have begun to consider African American movement with regard to leisure and tourism nationally, internationally, and globally. My interest in this conversation is on more contemporary moments of African American movement, especially those that involve food.[2] Sometimes these conversations do involve leisure. Sometimes they are about business, such as when one leaves home to go to college, join the military, or follow other career aspirations. At times, though, the movement can be involuntary, such as when children are forced into foster care or during a natural disaster such as Hurricane Katrina. Any of these movements can, and in some cases sadly do, result in tragedy, reflecting the tensions and traumas of living Black in America. Using storytelling, fiction, and personal experience, in this chapter I continue to explore how, in times of movement, food compels and sometimes allows people to live in ways that sustain them, thus encouraging a discussion of cultural sustainability. The overall aim here is again to continue the argument for a broader expansion and redefinition of the food stories told about African Americans food experiences. But it is also to encourage readers to consider when they may be imposing their own food biases onto others, and to recognize when anti-Black racism may be the root cause for shaming others.

During travel, especially by car, food conversations are bound to come up because people often talk about where they will stop to eat, get gas, or use the restroom. I experienced an instance of this one year when I traveled to a work meeting with a classmate. It was close to the Thanksgiving holiday, so naturally our conversation ventured in the direction of food. We started off talking about how much we looked forward to having dinner with our families since we were away from them, attending graduate school. We talked about our dinner menus and what we each would make in contribution, what the holiday's activities usually looked like, and so on. When I asked what her family would be having for dinner, she answered, "Oh, you know, the usual." In my mind, this surely included turkey, but beyond that I was not certain what she meant by "the usual." In addition to dishes we might expect—turkey, stuffing/dressing—she also mentioned lasagna, turnips, a cheese display, and a smoked meat and fish charcuterie.

Though the conversation took place several decades ago, I recall being as surprised by her menu as she was by mine when I told her that only a few of those foods would be at my Thanksgiving table. I told her that I would have turkey, dressing, gravy, collard greens, and mac and cheese. I was driving, but I remember looking over at her when she said she was surprised to know that her meal did not sound "typical" to me. My colleague's shock was not necessarily unusual. A lot of people in the world are unaware of how cultural traditions vary among and between racial and ethnic groups. At the heart of much food shaming and attempts at regulating is a lack of awareness and understanding of cultural differences. For African Americans, popular culture serves as a primary vehicle for flattening this awareness about our culture. Movies, television shows, stand-up comedy, and some music regurgitate images of Black people eating stereotyped foods like fried chicken, collard greens, and mac and cheese. And while it is true that many African Americans enjoy these southern-derived foods, it is not true that this forms the majority of African American culinary experiences.

This fact became most apparent several years later when I visited an African American church in western Maryland where, following the morning service the week before the Thanksgiving holiday, we had dinner. Though I had been studying African American food cultures for some time by this point, I would have my own assumptions about food fully tested. At dinner, I looked for the collard greens but found none. Instead, cabbage and sauerkraut were on the table. Initially, I was surprised and a little disappointed, until I recalled where I was visiting regionally with regard to the rest of the state. This area of Maryland is about forty minutes northwest of Baltimore and approximately thirty-eight miles southwest of York, Pennsylvania. The first settlers in this area were predominantly Germans and the Scotch-Irish who moved there from southern Pennsylvania, so there would certainly be culinary admixing by word of mouth, folklore, recipes, and trial and error.[3] Life circumstances brought about by travel and movement prompt us to adapt accordingly. Maybe a few people will completely disregard the food cultures they are familiar with and take up new ones, but most will make modifications out of necessity, curiosity, or for other reasons.[4]

Food choices are complex, with there being a lot of variables that go into the decision-making process. This is especially the case when a person has moved from one location to another. Some of these variables include having access to familiar foods, knowing what foods to substitute when the familiar ones are not readily available, and having the proper utensils and equipment to prepare, present, and consume these foods. Then there are sensory preferences (such as texture, flavor, visual presentation, and aroma) as well as socioeconomic and monetary considerations that must be factored in. All of this feeds into the concept of food choices; even when the choices are not obvious, there are always decisions to be made. Tanis Furst et al. state, "Conceptualizing food choice is a complex process with a range of influences and values that are negotiated differently by diverse people in a variety of settings."[5] Taking this argument further, Jeffrey Sobal and Carole Bisogni argue convincingly that there are multiple "macro- and microlevel factors and processes involved in food choice."[6] Sobal and Bisogni asked interviewees to explain what food means to them and how it informs their concepts of self-identity. In explaining the results, the researchers write, "This food choice process model includes: (1) life-course events and experiences that establish a food choice trajectory through transitions, turning points, timing, and contexts; (2) influences on food choices that include cultural ideals, personal factors, resources, social factors, and present contexts; and (3) a personal system that develops food choice values, negotiates and balances values, classifies foods and situations, and forms/revises food choice strategies, scripts, and routines."[7]

Using Sobal and Bisogni's framework can help us understand the food choices African Americans make and when, how, and why they make them. It may also better help to inform our understanding of African American food behaviors. This approach should also encourage those who encounter African Americans—from physicians to dietitians, community activists to laypeople—to be more flexible in their hearing, seeing, and understanding of our performances with food. Often, in today's public conversations, we focus almost solely on food access: Who has access to "good" food? From where do they get it? Is the area affected by food apartheid? and so on. This aspect of food is certainly important, but it may come at the expense of ignoring other valuable aspects, including habits, ideals and ideologies, quality, convenience, social and emotional frameworks, health and nutrition, location and dislocation, commensality and socializing, among many other considerations.[8] Because, as Sobal and Bisogni remind us, food choices are "multifaceted, situational, dynamic, and complex," so there are several different reasons people do the things they do when it comes to food.[9]

Considering this alone, it should be difficult to reduce African American food consumption to only one type of cuisine. Yet this is the reductionist approach that is often taken, and African Americans find themselves in situations where their culinary practices are surveilled and shamed—from what is eaten, to how the food is prepared, even to when it is consumed. There are myriad ways in which African American people negotiate, acquiesce to, and reject assaults against their everyday lives, and often we do this using food. By considering a wider set of variables, broader contexts in which these variables occur, and the negotiation between the offender and the recipient, this discussion suggests we take a hard look at considering when anti-Black racism and/or cultural ignorance is at play. The conversations that follow also allow us to bear witness to the ways in which African American healing takes place, as communities employ culturally sustainable means of righting the unstable chair that is always already unsteady in the consistently crooked room.

Bearing witness by expanding African American food narratives is no different than recognizing that we have diverse ways of dressing, talking, or practicing spirituality. Though African Americans have a shared history of association because of enslavement, we are not a homogeneous group of people; we diverge in numerous ways, regardless of the number of parallels. Though the haunting of enslavement ensnares our very souls, how we live out these traumas in our everyday lives manifests in the ways we perform life. Avery Gordon, who is mentioned earlier in this book in saying "life is complicated," is a useful voice to return to here. Gordon asked her undergraduate students to think deeply about Toni Morrison's novel *The Bluest Eye* and to make a very detailed list of all the reasons Morrison gives for "why dreams die." The class identified a number of explanations, including "what Morrison sometimes just calls the *thing*, the sedimented conditions that constitute what is in place in the first place." Gordon concludes that their list was reflective of the ways in which we conceptualize and make sense of who we are, "the complicated workings of race, class, and gender, the names we give to the ensemble of social relations that create inequalities, situated interpretive codes, particular kinds of subjects, and the possible and impossible themselves." The heaviness of who we are as African Americans in a fundamentally racist society and the day-to-day means of having to negotiate that identity in the mundane, as well as extraordinary, events of our lives amounts to "mov[ing] analytically between that sad and sunken couch that sags in just that place where an unrememberable past and an unimaginable future force us to sit day after day . . . because everything of significance happens there among the inert furniture and the monumental social architecture."[10]

But here is where the biblical Noah's search for dry land meets this book's argument for expanding Black food narratives—in the continuous pursuit and exercise of self-agency. Gordon provides a space for Black liberation theology to meet food studies when she goes on to write, "But . . . even those who live in the most dire circumstances possess a complex and oftentimes contradictory humanity and subjectivity that is never adequately glimpsed by viewing them as victims or, on the other hand, as superhuman agents." Gordon's discussion of complex personhood explains why food choices can never boil down to eating this way or that way. The evidence of our culinary histories shows that we are shaped by multiple experiences ranging from tragedy to triumph and sometimes back to tragedy. The fact that we have to continuously show and tell this to society suggests that society is not listening to, hearing, or seeing us in our wholeness. This willful ignorance also reflects a blatant disregard for Black life. Gordon puts it this way, and it necessitates quoting in full:

> It has always baffled me why those most interested in understanding and changing the barbaric domination that characterizes our modernity often—not always—withhold from the very people they are most concerned with the right to complex personhood. Complex personhood is the second dimension of the theoretical statement that life is complicated. Complex personhood means that all people (albeit in specific forms whose specificity is sometimes everything) remember and forget, are beset by contradiction, and recognize and misrecognize themselves and others. Complex personhood means that people suffer graciously and selfishly too, get stuck in the symptoms of their troubles, and also transform themselves. Complex personhood means that even those called "Other" are never that. Complex personhood means that the stories people tell about themselves, about their troubles, about their social worlds, and about their society's problems are entangled and weave between what is immediately available as a story and what their imaginations are reaching toward. Complex personhood means that people get tired and some are just plain lazy. Complex personhood means that groups of people will act together, that they will vehemently disagree with and sometimes harm each other, and that they will do both at the same time and expect the rest of us to figure it out for ourselves, intervening and withdrawing as the situation requires. Complex personhood

means that even those who haunt our dominant institutions and their systems of value are haunted too by things they sometimes have names for and sometimes do not. At the very least, complex personhood is about conferring the respect on others that comes from presuming that life and people's lives are simultaneously straightforward and full of enormously subtle meaning.[11]

In sum, complex personhood means you should worry about yourself because Black people are doing just fine in all our many ways of performing and living our lives with food, including our similarities and contradictions. These presentations of the self with food are acted out naturally through our bodies in what French sociologist Pierre Bourdieu refers to as "bodily hexis," the stored and/or ingrained actions and knowledge that we embody.[12]

It is the way of knowing acted out in, on, and through the body; it is a haunting. In the foreword to Gordon's *Ghostly Matters*, literary theorist Janice Radway offers this observation, "Avery Gordon seeks a new way of knowing, then, a knowing that is more a listening than a seeing, a practice of being attuned to the echoes and murmurs of that which has been lost but which is still present among us in the form of intimations, hints, suggestions, and portents. She terms these echoes and murmurs 'ghostly matters' and suggests that they haunt us at every turn." Inasmuch as these hauntings move with us and are embodied by our tastes, preferences, and habits, it behooves us all to engage in "new way[s] of knowing." Doing more listening and watching, before we reach in "to help" and to uplift, might yield better results. Engaging in practices that are "attuned to the echoes and murmurs of that which has been lost but which is still present" may also help us not to overlook how people reflect their class status, which is very important in food engagements. Because we seldom change our food choices and preferences, it often succeeds in revealing one's class leanings.[13]

Several of these tensions can be found in a poignant example provided by season 4 of David Simon's HBO series *The Wire*. Episode 9, aptly titled "Know Your Place," masterfully shows the intersections of movement and travel, social class, listening and watching, taking culinary choices for granted, and new ways of knowing. A public middle school in Baltimore City, Maryland, was the main focus of season 4's episodes where former police officer turned community activist Bunny Colvin works in an experimental classroom. Many of the middle-schoolers who are placed there are considered unable to succeed. They have been left to fall through the educational cracks because they are considered "the corner kids"—very aware and street smart but not necessarily interested in the protocols of school. Following a win for completing a teamwork challenge, Colvin rewards three of the youth with dinner—at the upscale Ruth's Chris Steak House. The kids are excited about their excursion across town. The evening starts well, but the class differences are immediately apparent in that not only have the children never been to the part of town in which the restaurant is located but also they have no idea how to perform the social graces expected of them when participating in a fine dining experience. From the moment they arrive at the restaurant, the two young men and woman appear uneasy and unsure. The experience of quiet conversation, soft background music, and lots of elderly white faces is off-putting for these unknowing young people. So, when the hostess approaches and asks if she may take their coats, they immediately turn to their mentor for guidance. His instant smile, answer of "Sure," and a nod of his head eases only Zenobia's mind—and only for the moment. Both of the boys—Namond and Darnell—respond with "Nah, I'm good" along with facial expressions that read, "You must be trippin'; I'm not givin' up my coat."

As the camera follows the group to the signature white-linen-clad table adorned by red cloth napkins, we see the children nervously looking around at the other restaurant goers. When they reach their table and the hostess pulls out a chair for Zenobia she takes one that is not offered, leaving the slightly embarrassed hostess to say to Darnell "Sir?" indicating he should sit at the proffered space. He asks the hostess, "That's your chair, right?" Colvin tells the youth, "No, you sit there." The evening gets worse for the unknowing, uncomfortable, unfamiliar students. First, Colvin has to explain the differences between the role of a hostess and that of a waitress, after the former informs the group that the waitress would be arriving to give them the specials of the day. When the students get into a round-robin conversation about the rules of fine dining, Zenobia acts as the cultural transmitter by first explaining to Namond what is meant by "the specials." She tells them, "What is on special . . . ain't no K-mart blue light special, dumbass"; it does not mean that the food is on sale or is cheaper. Rather, she explains, it means "they cook something different." In response, Namond tries to display a bit of awareness by admonishing Zenobia, "Yo, what about you? Drinking without a straw, looking all ghetto and shit," she quickly retorts in exasperation, "You don't drink water with a straw." And without missing a beat, she turns to Darnell and says, "And, put that on your lap, fool. . . . You see anyone else up in here looking all Fred Flintstone and shit?" referring to the big red linen napkin he has tucked under his chin. The table gets uncomfortably quiet after Namond laughs loudly at Zenobia's chiding of Darnell; they realize how loud they are, after noticing the other diners are staring disapprovingly. Noticing, Darnell shushes his friend so as not to embarrass the group any further.

Finally, Pam the waitress appears and begins rapidly detailing the list of specials. Most children and even some uninitiated adults would have been daunted by the menu's offerings: king salmon with sweet corn, chanterelles, and basil aioli; sautéed free-range chicken and mashed potatoes; fresh Chesapeake Bay blue crab, roasted garlic, shallot cream, and hen-of-the-woods mushrooms; and wood-roasted quail with grilled sapling bread salad. By the end of her announcement, the students are clear that they are well out of place, so much so that when she asks for drink orders there is silence until Colvin jumps in and says they will all have Cokes. By the end of the scene the kids clearly appear demoralized. What started out as a good evening field trip turned out to be a glaring indictment of their current life conditions. Exiting the restaurant, they refuse to be in the group picture that they initially wanted to participate in when they first approached the restaurant. Darnell asks Colvin to take them to McDonald's, explaining, "The food wasn't right . . . I don't like fish." Zenobia asks, "Why'd you order it, then?" He doesn't reply but proceeds to bicker with her about random things. Namond, meanwhile, turns up the music and continues to do so, despite Colvin's protestations. Whatever was ordered and eaten did little to satiate their bodies, minds, or souls, and by returning to the familiar—McDonald's, loud trap music, bickering and jonin'—they restored their own sense of order. Writing for *Entertainment Weekly*, Michael Endelman explains,

> *The Wire* represented the canyon-size class differences that separate not just blacks from whites, but these neglected, isolated, and uneducated kids from someone like Bunny Colvin—also black, but a successful professional comfortable in any stratum of society. Without much dialogue—just the self-conscious looks of Namond and his classmates, their nervous smiles, and their refusal to take off their jackets—*The Wire* made it seem like a cultural, economic, and social divide that will never be bridged. If these kids glaze over and shut down when a waitress mentions hen-of-the-woods mushrooms, how can they ever expect to have a life beyond the corner?[14]

But the students are not as unaware as they might appear. When they return to school Colvin recaps the experience for one of the professors (Dr. Parenti) involved in the pilot education program. But Colvin does so in ways that suggest he knew he was setting up the students but wanted to see how they would react and whether or not they would acknowledge how they felt about where they are in the world. Rightly, Dr. Parenti notes that the students might not be as unaware as Colvin believes, and he is correct. As the educators enter the classroom Namond can be overheard telling his friends, "Y'all missed that meal for real, though," followed by Darnell saying, "It was hot, yo. 'Party of four, Mr. Colvin?'" Zenobia chimes in with, "May I take your coat, Mr. Brice?" They continue to laugh and dap each other up while Namond and Darnell admit, "That shit was tight." Darnell laughs and says he is still dreaming of the chocolate cake with its "fifty-six layers." They further admit that they tried to sneak a peek at the check before Colvin took it off the table. Clearly, the corner kids, though initially appearing like fish out of water, used their street-smart wisdom to take in far more than they let on about the trip across town to the steak house.

I discuss this *Wire* episode at length because it speaks directly to the power of food and food experiences to shame, but it also it illustrates how African Americans exercise social and cultural capital—for better or for worse—to resist the shame. Colvin knew the dinner experience would be a challenge for the students, and soon this was apparent to them. But quite possibly it would be so for many students that age, let alone those unfamiliar with eating at restaurants like Ruth's Chris. Fine dining can be overwhelming for anyone who has not been exposed to it—educated or otherwise. For example, in the introduction to *Living In, Living Out*, historian Elizabeth Clark-Lewis details an experience she had having lunch with her great aunt's Bible club. As the women deftly moved through the multicourse meal (apparently more than six different dishes) using various utensils and tableware, Clark-Lewis was at a loss, despite being very well educated and cultured in other matters. After multiple faux pas, her aunt was prompted to apologize to the group for her niece's "obvious lack of manners" due to her having never done "service work." The women "nodded politely, making it clear they were fully aware of [her] embarrassing conduct."[15] As I shared early on in the book, power is negotiable, especially when it comes to food. So, what is notable about the students going to Ruth's Chris is how they turn the experience into one where they have a leg up on their cohort. Regardless of their love or hate for the outing, the fact that they were able to go, and others were not, means they "are the shit!"

These are some of the ways in which shaming can occur between and among African Americans, but also between and among people in general.

We tend to forget the importance of regional differences in thinking through food events. We also tend to forget age differences. Those students most likely would have been just as satisfied with going to any fast-food eatery different from what they are used to, were it located in their community. Colvin could very well have asked the students what they might like and allowed them to choose from a range of options, thereby empowering them to have more participation in the process. But this was really an exchange of power that occurred between Colvin and the students. In some ways, he was pushing them to show to themselves and others that they could survive anywhere.

Then there are the variables of taste buds and palate. Food habits and customs are a part of our cultural identity, or our habitus—meaning the ways we move about the world and how our behaviors, choices, and decisions are informed by what we have learned in our communities and from our social and cultural institutions, our socioeconomic backgrounds, educational levels, work environments, and so on. Our habitus and cultural identities, like our languages, are among the markers of identity that are seldom relinquished because they help to transmit cultural values, traditions, and practices that are important to carrying on the legacies that help us thrive. In an interview with Judi Moore Smith (Latta), the late culinary historian Vertamae Grosvenor once remarked that every culture has their own "get-down foods"—that is, foods that are considered an everyday part of their cultural lexicon. But even with "get-down foods" and other vernacular food traditions, taste buds and palate are important.[16] Food and human nutrition scientist M. Yanina Pepino notes, "Taste is the most resilient of our senses, . . . and no two people taste things the same way."[17] Philosopher Carolyn Korsmeyer makes a related argument when she reminds us that not only is taste the most resilient, but also it is "one of the most evocative senses."[18]

Even though taste is often left out of our discussions of food, it is a critical element, and it operates on several levels. One the one hand, flavoring our food is about pleasing our taste buds. Food flavors play an important role in how we identify with one another, memories we hold, emotions, desires, and aversions we carry; they also are used to highlight social, cultural, religious, and other occasions. Certain seasonings tend to be associated with particular races and ethnicities (such as lemongrass, soy sauce, and sesame oil with various Asian American cultures). As culinary historians have noted, herbs and spices played a role in food preservation and seasoning during the Middle Passage. Africans would not have abandoned this practice once they arrived in the colonies. Rather, by finding new herbs and using available vegetation as substitutes, they were able to change and add flavors to any number of foods. There is some suggestion that enslaved Africans actually recognized "substantial parts of the American flora." This kind of foraging, and learning from American Indians, was key to African survival.[19]

An impromptu "survey" I took of Facebook contacts revealed that some, maybe many, African Americans still prefer a variety of seasonings. In 2013, I posted a general query for anyone interested to share what was on their Thanksgiving menu. My interest was in hearing and seeing the geographical and regional variations among African Americans, especially from those in midwestern and western states. These are areas in which we know relatively little of African American food traditions.[20] The answers to my inquiry indicated a lot of similarity among the dishes themselves, but with variations in seasoning and flavoring. Most East Coast African Americans had some kind of turkey, stuffing, gravy, mac and cheese, sweet potatoes, ham, collards or other greens, boiled eggs, chitlins, and assorted desserts. But there was also curry chicken, gumbo, and lamb as well as codfish cakes (from someone who described themselves as Bajan). What was most interesting was the degree to which people took the time to detail their flavoring. These ingredients included pineapple, jalapeno, sausage, chives, lots of rosemary and sage, wine (for braising), brown sugar, nutmeg, and cinnamon. One or two recipients emphasized that their vegetables were homegrown; a number of respondents indicated that they prefer packaged foods such as jellied cranberry sauce, Parker House rolls, and Stouffer's mac and cheese. And though I never mentioned the word, they all shared these preferences, according to them, "without shame."

These beautifully arrayed descriptions of culinary improvisation "force us to confront the variations of Blackness."[21] They also force us to contend with the ways in which a shared history of enslavement has left a deep-rooted culinary impact on America, but especially on African American people. It is one that we continue to modify, change, and refashion no matter how displaced we are, how much we migrate and move, and how much we "lay down roots" in other parts of the country. Food is a touchstone, a place of familiarity when we are lost or feel out of place. This is why the Ruth's Chris restaurant experience in the *Wire* episode was so disconcerting to the fictional Baltimore middle-schoolers. Like everyone else, Black folks have comfort foods—no, it is not always fried chicken, and seldom do I hear that consolation comes from watermelon. For some it may be mashed potatoes, for others it may be popcorn. For my daughter, it is fruit cups filled with mandarin oranges; for culinary theorist Jessica Walker, like several others, it is pumpkin. Walker would argue that knowing this list of various but similar Thanksgiving menus and ingredients as well as the difference in African American comfort foods is part of "interrogat[ing] the assumptions we make about Black people's food consumption even as we explore incidents like 'pumpkin pie gate.' This is the belief that all African Americans prefer the taste of sweet potato rather than pumpkin pie."[22] What happens when African American people consume foods outside the traditionally perceived culinary lexicon? Walker's example shows how sometimes it can involve food shaming.

Jessica Walker tells the story of being invited to Thanksgiving dinner at the home of African American friends whom she describes as being "upper-middle-class." She writes, they are "members of Black sororities and fraternities, attend a Baptist church, and are the epitome of southern hospitality." After joking with the couple about inviting her to a dinner celebration of "genocide and colonialism," Walker enthusiastically and graciously accepts the invitation. In recounting the incident, Walker writes that she said, "Yes, of course, and I'll bring pumpkin pie." She goes on to write, "Then, [after] a beat of silence from the wife, 'Pumpkin pie? That's White people food. White people eat that. We eat sweet potato pie.'"[23] Most African Americans are familiar with sweet potato pie for the holidays, hence the closing comment above from the Thanksgiving host. Though Walker recounts the story in a somewhat comical vein, here is where geographical and regional differences, as well as personal tastes, preferences, and habits, should be considered. The foods available to someone in North Carolina may be less available in Ohio or New Hampshire, for instance; because of this, what a person is accustomed to eating, what people have access to, and what they recognize will vary. And yet, we shame people for having different affinities toward food without realizing or often even intending to do so. Walker explains it this way:

> Discomfort turned to shame that my knowledge of Black tradition was deficient in the moment—I quickly changed my contribution to sweet potato pie—a safe choice? But safe for whom? Or rather, what is the risk in me presenting pumpkin pie? I really like pumpkin pie, sometimes more than sweet potato! In that moment, however, even my taste preferences—which is an embodied knowledge—were deemed incompatible with my racial, gendered, and classed performance. This is even more complicated when I note that the woman who said that

is Ghanaian-American, forcing us to consider how these moments of discomfort, tension, and what I call "nervous kitchen spaces" articulate how imagined and real Black food traditions, and their often-oversimplified representations, circulate in non-Black communities or have the potential to be appropriated by anybody.[24]

Walker's point about Black food traditions being "oversimplified" cannot be overamplified. As she states, our habits, tastes, and preferences are socially constructed and learned behaviors; this is what I mean when I say we all operate within our habitus. Regional locations will have an overwhelming effect, as well as an individual's preferences and taste buds. Even knowing what combinations of flavors to use are a part of our socialization. Some of us learned to cook from our parents, others have learned from reality TV cooking shows, and even more have learned from social media venues like TikTok or Instagram how to (or how not to) season one's food. This process is, as Walker maintains, "embodied knowledge"—that is, knowledge where the body simply knows how to act.

Both here and in the listing of various flavors and seasonings that were detailed by the Facebook informants, we see how objects are value markers. In the case of the Thanksgiving dinner respondents from Facebook, their knowledge of mixing certain ingredients and their ability to experiment— to take a dish in different directions that are far from ordinary—might suggest a particular kind of social and cultural knowledge. At the very least it suggests economic flexibility. In her book *Food in History*, British historian Reay Tannahill reminds us that "food flexibility (as a matter of choice) is usually a characteristic of affluent societies. The nearness of hunger breeds conservatism. Only the well-fed can afford to try something new, because only they can afford to leave it on the plate if they dislike it."[25] From this point of view, those with means—the upwardly mobile, middle-class, upper-class, and the elite—are believed to have more time and freedom to make a variety of choices.

But these are not the only factors that influence food experimentation. Often overlooked is the tremendous amount of knowledge and skill needed for the preparation of new foods. Unfamiliar foods and spaces can engulf the uninitiated and the unversed. I found this to be the case in the answers from my Thanksgiving responders. One informant said, "My family isn't big into food adventures, so I'm baking and cooking conservatively this year." Yet she indicated that she would be making her friend's "lemon icepick cake" and mentioned that for one holiday meal she made "sweet potato cupcakes with candied ginger icing." Another respondent mentioned Stouffer's mac and cheese but said it would be "dressed up with chives and sharp aged cheddar!!!" Perhaps the most diverse set of ingredients and food combinations was contributed by a responder who lived abroad for many years and who primarily calls the West Coast home. Her menu consisted of "wine braised turkey legs w/ rosemary, sage & roasted veggies, nitrate free brown sugar glazed spiral ham, jalapeño corn bread w/ red pepper jelly, maple whipped sweet potatoes, collard greens w/ smoked turkey, cornbread stuffing w/ pancetta, cranberry jelly (the roll straight out the can is a must—and yes NO SHAME!) and for dessert, pumpkin pots de crème w/ maple bourbon whipped cream."[26] Her insistence that she is not ashamed to serve cranberry sauce out of the can suggests she is aware that the commercially made jelly stood out among the assortment of ingredients that tilt the flavor away from classic ways of preparing the dishes. None of the foods mentioned by any of the respondents who shared their menus were necessarily new. Rather, the diversity of their meals speaks to particular sets of tastes that the informants are clearly comfortable experimenting with and eating.

But we have to be careful here as well, because it is in these kinds of performance with food that shaming can really take effect, as Pierre Bourdieu makes clear in his discussion of symbolic hierarchies. For example, sometimes people think that some foods with names derived from languages other than English have a greater social significance than others (for example, shiitake mushrooms, calamari, arugula). Scholars of consumption and consumerism Douglas E. Allen and Paul Anderson further break it down when they say that this symbolic hierarchy exists and is maintained "by the socially dominant in order to enforce their distance or distinction from other classes of society."[27] In this way, objects—foods and ingredients alike—can often be used to separate members of the African American community from one another. We considered an example of this in chapter 1: Chalky White, the character in *Boardwalk Empire*, wanted hoppin' John at a family meal that featured glazed duck and mixed vegetables. When White's wife referred to the dish as "common food," she made it clear she thought the food was not fit to be served to a soon-to-be physician (her daughter's dinner guest), let alone their very upwardly mobile, cultured family. We can read the *Boardwalk Empire* scene using insights from Allen and Anderson, who refer to Bourdieu's definition of taste being used as "a 'social weapon.' This weapon defines and marks off the high from the low, the sacred from the profane, and the 'legitimate' from the 'illegitimate' in matters ranging from food and drink, cosmetics, and newspapers on the one hand, to art, music, and literature on the other."[28]

And here I return to the lecture attendee at the museum, whom I also discussed in chapter 1. I was not troubled that she asked the soul food chef for instructions on how to prepare greens without pork. She was seeking what she considered a healthier alternative while also exercising her right to improvise in her kitchen. Rather, my curiosity was invoked because while she seemed to want room for her own culinary creativity, she did not want to allow that same space for her mother-in-law to continue exercising her ingenuity and tradition. Additionally, the way in which she responded seemed to be in the service of using her palette and preference as a "secret weapon" that "marks off the high from the low, the sacred from the profane, and the 'legitimate' from the 'illegitimate.'" In this context, she was separating herself from her mother-in-law, who reflected an "old-school" way of cooking, one that is less reflective of "progressive" Blackness. This perhaps unconscious but direct rebuke of putting pork in the pot of greens was a means of denouncing a particular kind of Blackness—the pork-eating kind.[29] And it seemed especially important to let this be known in the company of young, educated vegans and vegetarians, the majority of whom were white.[30]

The argument that people use objects to enforce their distance or to distinguish themselves from other classes in society reminds me of the well-anthologized short story "Everyday Use" by Alice Walker. Walker's narrative is relevant to this book's discussion because it is one of those situations where food is in the background but reveals a great deal about the ways in which people use the power of objects to get what they need. "Everyday Use" tells the story of mother-daughter relationships, African American women's identity, the beauty of heritage, food shaming, and cultural capital. The story takes place in rural Georgia. It opens with Mama and her daughter Maggie waiting for the elder daughter and sister, Dee, to come home for a visit from college in Augusta. Mama and others in the community had to fundraise to send Dee to college, following a fire that burned their home down and severely disfigured Maggie. The story is told from Mama's point of view, so we learn that when Dee arrives home, she is dressed in a gown "down to the ground" in the hot Georgia weather. Mama says of the dress: "[It was] so loud it hurts my eyes. There are yellows and oranges enough to throw back the light of the sun. . . . Earrings gold, too, hanging down to her shoulders. Bracelets dangling and making noises when she moves her arm up to shake the fold of the dress out of her armpits." Mama goes on to describe Dee's hair: "[It] stands straight up like the wool on a sheep. It is black as night and around the edges are two long pigtails that rope about like small lizards disappearing behind her ears."[31] Along with making new sartorial decisions, Dee brings a new boyfriend, Hakim-a-barber, who greets the mother and daughter duo with "Wa.su.zo.Tean.o!" and "Asalamalakim." To this, Maggie and Mama are unsure how to respond. Shortly after the awkward greeting, Dee tells her family she now prefers to be called "Wangero Leewaika Kemanjo" instead of being called after her namesake, Big Dee (or Aunt Dicie).

The family settles down to eat the meal Mama has prepared for the celebration: collards and pork, chit'lins, cornbread, and sweet potatoes. Though the boyfriend refuses the collards and pork because he says they are "unclean," Dee "[goes] on through the chit'lins and cornbread, the greens, and everything else." The rest of the story continues with Dee trying to take from the house various belongings that have been in her mother's family for decades. Most of them are homemade and used daily. For example, the bench they sit on while having dinner was made by Mama's deceased father because they could not afford to buy chairs. The benches were aged with "rump prints," reminding everyone that they were being used as intended. Dee continues to think of all the ways she can use these home goods to decorate her house away at college in order to show others she is "down for the cause" because she knows her African heritage. Dee falsely believes that showing off these things will make her more accepted by members of the Cultural Nationalism movement with which she identifies at the moment.

Dee's performance is oxymoronic, of course, because she seems not to realize that she is full of contradictions. Dee no longer wants to be called by her multigenerational name, because she "couldn't bear it any longer being named after the people who oppress [her]." And she definitely wants Grandma Dee's butter dish, churn top, and dasher, despite not knowing the true history of how they came to be. Dee believes the objects were made by her uncle Buddy. But since Maggie lives with the history daily, she corrects her sister and softly tells her it was Aunt Dee's first husband Henry, "but they called him Stash," who was the carpenter. Unfazed by this information, Dee prattles on, ignoring the facts of the history while trying to collect objects to represent the history. But Mama puts a stop to all the confusion about the material items when Dee tries to take the family quilts to hang as decoration. Though Maggie is capable of making more, Mama refuses Dee's request, saying that Maggie will actually *use* the quilts. Mama then firmly places the almost-pilfered coverings in Maggie's lap. The ironic short story comes to an end with an exchange between Mama (the narrator) and the newly renamed Dee:

> "You just don't understand," [Dee] said, as Maggie and I came out to the car.
> "What don't I understand?" I wanted to know.
> "Your heritage," she said. And then she turned to Maggie, kissed her, and said, "You ought to try to make something of yourself, too, Maggie. It's really a new day for us. But from the way you and Mama still live you'd never know it."[32]

The funny part here is that even though Dee has found a new sense of self in dress, name, and perhaps even accent, long before the other items are mentioned, it is the food that gives away her actual heritage. The traditional soul food dinner "delight[s] her" and directly ties her to the place that she is trying hard to forget.

This discussion of Walker's short story connects my thoughts about those who perform or accept particular kinds of Blackness, vis-à-vis food, taste, class and social capital, to Ibram Kendi's idea of anti-Black racism. Walker's short story takes place during a period of great cultural change and protest in American society by African Americans and other marginalized groups. During the late 1960s and early 1970s, African Americans throughout the United States were redefining what it meant to be Black by claiming a particular social, cultural, and political identity that directly invoked their collective African roots. Dashikis, revolutionary poetry and literature, afros, funk music, street festivals, and Kwanzaa, along with the mantras "to be young, gifted, and Black" and "say it loud, I'm Black and I'm proud."[33] It was also a time when strong Black ideologies were being espoused by many groups, but perhaps most visible were the Nation of Islam and the Black Panthers. Boycotts, marches, and other forms of nonviolent protest for workers' rights were common, including those led by the unionized United Farm Workers and the Prisoner's Rights Movement in an effort to get better living conditions and civil rights overall. I recall the time. I especially remember because my dad was at Attica Correctional Facility in upstate New York to visit his friend "Big Black." Shortly after, the incarcerated men of the maximum-security prison led a rebellion to protest inhumane prison conditions and a lack of medical care, religious freedom, and educational opportunities. The takeover ended in too many of the men, and the hostages, being killed and little to no reform.

But this revolt and others like it were the genesis for today's prison reform movement.

The fictional Dee and her boyfriend may have been a part of the burgeoning Black Arts Movement of the era that spoke of a new Black aesthetic, among other tenets. This may, in fact, be why even though Hakim-a-barber greets Mama and Dee with the salutation commonly used among Muslims (assalamu alaikum), he denies really being involved with the hardworking Muslims down the road, who led a lifestyle of self-sufficiency through homesteading. His dismissive response, "I accept some of their doctrines, but farming and raising cattle is not my style," might be indicative of the hodgepodge principles to which both he and Dee ascribe. Both of the young people have missed the forest for the trees, in that while they speak the rhetoric of Black consciousness, don new clothes, acquire new greetings, wear new jewelry and hairstyles, they have yet to learn how to live in the space of Black liberation, which seeks freedom from subjugation for all people, especially those who look like them.

Though a fictional example, Walker's story serves as an accurate document of the ways in which some African Americans use objects like food and other accoutrements to exert superiority over those they deem inferior or less worthy than themselves. Dee uses her education as "the secret weapon." She has allowed her newfound educational "consciousness" to obscure her understanding of the very history she is yet seeking. In fact, Dee seems to have forgotten that it was because of Mama's sacrifices that she is even able to move away for college. She also seems to have missed that the culture in her mother's home, which she has left, is the very culture she is trying to find—and, perhaps worse, have in her home almost solely for the purpose of showing off. Interestingly, while Maggie lacks Dee's book knowledge, she nonetheless is the carrier of history for the family. It is Maggie who knows the meaning of Dee's name and the family members who created each and every piece of the material history that Dee wants to display. Maggie not only knows the origins of each square in the quilt, but she also knows how to quilt and thus is able to keep herself sufficiently warm during the colder seasons.

Above all the other objects in "Everyday Use," it may be the food that carries the greatest meaning. Despite all her other new cultural performances, Dee has no problem eating the traditional foods cooked by her mom. Lingering here for just a moment, we will see that Dee's food choice is not surprising. It is the closest she comes to revealing her true identity, and on some level it is the closest she comes to appreciating her heritage. This is not because these foods are what all Black people ate during slavery. Rather, this was everyday food for many and is a reflection of what many people consider foods that help you "keep on keepin' on." As I have written elsewhere, these foods signified an identity. As Sam Moore states, the song "Soul Man" told an important story. So too did the phrase "soul food." Both were suggestive of a need to be able to claim a sense of identity at a time when it was constantly questioned and more often threatened. Whether soul referred to food, clothes, music, or other aspects of Black cultural expression, it signified that untiring ability to "get up and keep moving."[34] Jessica Harris says it more plainly: "Bottom line, it was dinner."[35] And that dinner had a lot of meaning because for Dee it tasted good and it was a home-cooked meal made by her mom. In this example, the shaming is both in the food and the food event, the space in which the food is being consumed.

Dee's boyfriend, Hakim, flat-out refuses Mama's hospitality, saying right away he doesn't eat collard greens with pork because it is "unclean." In addition to being rude herself, Dee seems unable to stop her friend from disrespecting her mother's cooking and, in turn, Mama's home and heritage. Historian Jennifer Wallach explains, "Many cultural nationalists offered more concrete dietary prescriptions than the mandate to consume 'African' food. They sometimes placed an even greater emphasis on foods that should be avoided rather than on those that should be consumed. For example, the black-eyed peas served at the first Kwanzaa Karamu would have been considered an anathema by Elijah Muhammad, leader of the Nation of Islam."[36] Perhaps. As literary scholar Doris Witt notes, "Within African American culture, one readily encounters a multiplicity of competing discourses about what had come, by the early 1960s, to be called 'soul food.' These discourses span historically far-ranging social and political positions that have been obscured because discussions of 'soul food' tend to rely on simplistic, often insufficiently historicized dichotomies of master versus slave, white versus black, and especially black bourgeoisie versus ghettoite."[37]

To be sure, that is another element of food's functionality: it is capable of highlighting complexities of power but also contradictions involving gender, race, class, sexuality, and in this case family dynamics. This food event is a fleeting moment in the short story, not at all the central focus, but it tells us that the food is what really stops Dee in her Black aesthetic tracks. In this scene, Alice Walker is also exposing how Black women's aesthetic work is often criticized, belittled, and rejected. Here, it is under the guise of foods considered traditionally southern or soul. Mama went to a lot of trouble to cook what might be one of Dee's favorite meals. Having it rejected outright was hurtful. Dee, knowing both her mother and her boyfriend, might have helped them both avoid some embarrassment by telling her mom that Hakim did not eat pork. While Walker illustrates some of the contradictions that can arise within Black cultural nationalism's definitions of what constitutes Blackness, we also see how some aspects of Black masculinist discourse, especially when operating under the rubric of cultural expression, was actually an assault on Black women's creativity.

Stifling Black women's creativity with food is not reserved for fiction, and it certainly has not been reserved for cultural nationalists. In 2013, I delivered a lecture at a two-day symposium held at a small private college in the Midwest. The next day, as we milled around and waited for our follow-up panel to begin, I was told that a student had informed her advisor it had been a long time, four years to be exact, since she had eaten chicken. The Asian American student mentioned to my colleague that my lecture made her feel like she had "permission" to eat chicken again. She further explained during the conversation that on campus she "felt ashamed" because she is "not supposed to eat chicken," even though a lot of her cultural dishes had the meat as a main ingredient. Though she never specifically indicated who it was that told her she was not supposed to eat chicken, she suggested eating chicken simply was not done on their campus. While we were talking, the Asian American woman's sister joined the group conversation along with several other students. One of these women was African American. Hearing the impromptu discussion, she said something to the effect of when she first got to the college from the South, she was really craving foods from home. She said, "You know, [where we are from] we eat a lot of rice. But when I came here, I learned that everyone eats a 'microbiotic' diet. That's brown rice. I don't like brown rice." One other student contributed that her sister is growing up believing that Chipotle is "real" Mexican food. She chuckled and said, "Can you believe that? She tells me I should eat Chipotle because it's healthier than the food our mama makes."[38]

Considered individually, these unsolicited comments are simply part of random conversation. But taken together, they sparked a good deal of curiosity. When I thought about these statements as part of a whole, my emotions ran the gamut, from elation and pride that I was able to persuade students they no longer needed to feel ashamed about what they ate, to frustration and anger that this message even had to be conveyed. The more I thought about the shared confession, the more my thoughts grew troubled. What kind of social capital must a group possess to make an individual feel like they have to neglect a major part of their food traditions?[39] These women appeared to be traditional-age students, so they were eighteen or nineteen, and very impressionable. And as they moved along through their college years, these students had been told or made to believe all kinds of ideas about what was good and not good in their food lives. They had come into a community of higher learning to gain a better understanding of the world, and what they encountered from the outset were arbiters of what is "good" and "bad" food telling them to give up an incredibly important aspect of their identities. A point made by literary scholar Rafia Zafar is relevant here: "Food and dining within a racially mixed context signals transgression and danger for minority group members."[40] This was the case for the fictional middle-schoolers from the TV series *The Wire* who went to Ruth's Chris, and for these students here. Once these students decide they will rebuff the norm and return to eating from their own cultural foodways, they will be considered "transgressors." The most likely "danger" in this case is social ostracism, which for some can be isolating and very lonely, especially when away from home. I did not have the time to probe these students because the panel began a short time later. At the end of the event, students scurried off to class and I, admittedly, turned my attention to other aspects of my itinerary. But in the quietness of the plane ride home, I recalled the conversations and tried to figure out how to communicate what seemed to be their pain and my annoyance.

Later, as I prepared for another scholarly talk, I realized that I had been hearing variations of the same story for several years. The experiences of these young ladies, where food was used to divorce them from their culture, happen far more than we probably know or want to know. From one end of the country to another, men and women were telling me stories of how they were being told that their food choices were unhealthy, unclean, and even harmful. Many of these stories were told by African Americans from all walks of life. Experiences like those of the students at the midwestern college and Dee's in "Everyday Use" let us know how often these incidents are normalized. Dee's act of shaming her family using her education and newfound social network was counterintuitive because her tastes in food revealed her true connections to her people. These events do happen, and over time they can create a kind of psychic and cultural trauma that weighs on one's mind. In *Cultural Trauma and Collective Identity*, sociologist Jeffrey Alexander states, "Cultural trauma occurs when members of a collectivity feel they have been subjected to a horrendous event that leaves indelible marks upon their group consciousness, marking their memories forever and changing their future identity in fundamental and irrevocable ways."[41] For most African Americans, daily offenses of shaming and policing in our lives—from food to other aspects of their existence—cause us to relive awful experiences over and over again, every day. Food, then, becomes another layer of added stress and strain. Alexander goes on to assert, "By denying the reality of others' suffering, people not only diffuse their own responsibility for the suffering but often project the responsibility for their own suffering on these others."[42]

This projection of responsibility often plays out in situations of movement and travel. In an article for the *Oxford American*, I wrote about being a weary traveler in a familiar land since for most African Americans the intersections of food, travel, and movement are always tainted by a level of fear and discomfort. Similarly, as discussed throughout this book, travel and movement are not free for Black people. Black folk get tired of always being surveilled and watched, from enslavement to the contemporary moment. Feminist cultural critic bell hooks recalled how she once attended a conference on cultural studies, confident that she would be in the company of "likeminded, progressively 'aware' intellectuals." She says,

> Instead, I was disturbed when the usual arrangements of white supremacist hierarchy were mirrored, both in terms of who was speaking, of how bodies were arranged on the stage, of who was in the audience, of what voices were deemed worthy to speak and be heard. As the conference progressed I began to feel afraid. If progressive people, most of whom were white, could so blindly reproduce a version of the status quo and not "see" it, the thought of how racial politics would be played out "outside" this arena was horrifying. Without even considering whether the audience was able to shift from the prevailing standpoint and hear another perspective, I talked openly about that sense of terror. Later, I heard stories of white women joking about how ludicrous it was for me (in their eyes I suppose I represent the "bad" tough black woman) to say I felt terrorized. Their inability to conceive that my terror . . . is a response to the legacy of white domination and the contemporary expressions of white supremacy is an indication of how little this culture really understands the profound psychological impact of white racist domination.[43]

This kind of obliviousness is convenient and reinforces Alexander's point about projecting the responsibility of healing one's suffering onto the sufferer themselves. Even when Black people try to take responsibility, in ways that simultaneously aid in healing, more often than not, our actions are policed, and when food is involved, our ingredients are shamed. Naa Oyo Kwate, a social scientist of Black experience and health, reminded me of this with regard to transnational migrants when she shared an experience of her parents. In personal correspondence, she wrote, "The fact that you mentioned migrants who are defined as Black made me think about the tropical fats injunction in the 1980s. That policing came from industry—don't eat coconut oil, palm oil, etc., they have saturated fat. Eat margarine instead. And then everyone's cardiovascular health is trashed from trans-fats. This actually happened with my parents, who had been eating palm oil their whole lives, along with their family before them. American processed foods was their undoing."[44] In our follow-up conversation, Kwate elaborated by explaining that in African American contexts, telling Black people not to eat pork in their collard greens though it may alter the taste of the dish, is similar to telling an immigrant they cannot have a particular food like fufu, a culinary staple for many West and Central Africans.[45] How do you tell someone who has eaten this type of food for more than eighty years that they can no longer have it, especially when the food sustains their social and cultural lives? This seems to be a form of cultural violence. As the conversation with Kwate continued, we discussed how it is not only unfeasible to create a vegan version of every food dish but also that altering the taste so substantially disregards the cultural legacies of memories, emotions, and other intangible elements that help people to thrive.

Through this conversation, I was reminded of my visit to a women's aid center to discuss a possible grant project. In talking with the residential nutritionist, she shared the difficulties that are often encountered in working with their transnational clients, who comprise the majority of their visitors. The foods that are most sustainable, obtainable, and palatable for these women are not easily substituted by American food. It becomes so cumbersome that it is often very difficult to advise a pregnant woman because the caloric comparisons are either unavailable due to a lack of understanding or simply too difficult to make in substitution. This means that when an immigrant comes to America at a time when she is most vulnerable, she may not be able to enjoy foods that provide her with comfort, sustenance, and nutrition. When these women do not follow the "recommended guidelines," they are then deemed "bad mothers" or "unfit" because they are potentially harming their unborn child.

But the real harm here is in not allowing these migrant women to fulfill their basic human needs in ways that empower them and future generations. Food is instrumental to the processes of self-identification and place-making. This was true historically for African Americans during periods of migration throughout the United States; it is true for college students; and it is true for transnational migrants today. When going to or arriving at a new place, it can be difficult to acclimate to new surroundings, so relying upon familiar foods, food outlets, and tastes and smells can soothe the anxiety of settlement. It is essential to be able to rely upon the cultural practices that help to organize one's life, allow individuals to thrive, and communities to sustain their identities. Jon Hawkes reminds us that the cultural aspects of life are as "essential to a healthy and sustainable society as social equity, environmental responsibility and economic viability."[46] Food helps us to express "what it means to be human." So, the ability to practice the traditions and customs that give meaning to our lives are vital to helping humans flourish and successfully interact with one another.

Ethnic food markets can provide an option for food shopping that traditional grocery stores do not. They are not only hubs for food acquisition but also for clothing, housewares, remittances, and networking. Anthropologist Elisha Renne emphasizes how West Africans in the United States use food "to maintain social relations with their particular families, hometown associations, and religious groups, while also constituting national, regional, and global connections through the reinvention of food traditions."[47] So, attention to cultural demand should be central to discussions of sustainability because accessing recognizable foods can be challenging for immigrants in the United States. By not focusing on cultural preservation, we miss the importance of the transnational migrants' cultural rituals and practices. This limited focus leads us to assume that what is good for some is good for everyone. And this lack of broader thinking and concern for regions beyond America leads to a great deal of food shaming, especially when we set out to implement food campaigns that reduce everyone's food cultures to what is locally grown and produced.

The experiences of immigration often force participants to create culinary identities different from the ones to which they are accustomed, so reinventing food traditions is a key part of adapting and acclimating. This process of re-creation is rarely about discarding, but rather it involves making food substitutions. At one point in my Ghanaian–African American family, we would sometimes substitute cream of wheat for fufu, kenkey, or other starches when the local market was out of the primary ingredients or when we wanted a different taste. One of the several Ghanaians I interviewed for another project, Sarah, an educator at a western U.S. college, indicated that shopping for the foods of her home is much easier now than it once was. This is because of the opening of local markets or stores within a one-hour driving distance that specialize in foods familiar to those from Africa, Latin America, and the Caribbean. When asked how she accesses Ghanaian foods, Sarah said, "We use similar products, so we go to the ethnic stores, like those run by the Chinese and Japanese." Having located a store that will enable her to reconnect with the smells, tastes, and sights of home, she said, "It feels different. You feel rejuvenated."[48] And is this not what we all want? To move about the world feeling invigorated. Some find it in a macrobiotic way of eating that combines food and positive ways of seeing the world. Others find it eating foods from home that reinforce their cultural connections.

Food embodies and transmits cultural, social, and political connections. For those who have traversed continents, countries, states, and miles, the smell of familiar foods can instantly evoke a series of emotions and desires because food and food customs are carriers of identity, memory, and tradition. But while Sarah appreciated having access to foods that revitalize and refresh her, a more insidious side of food cultures comes to light that is hardly ever lost on those on the receiving end. In an interview with culinary expert Fran Osseo-Asare, Ghanaian chef Dinah Ameley Ayensu remarks on the irony of the ways "Brazilian or West Indian foods" are celebrated without recognition of the African cultural influences in those cuisines. She emphasizes the irony inherent in people appreciating a food when it is attributed to any other culture but an African one, even when it may look the same. Ayensu says,

> So why don't they give us Africans credit for the recipes that they are familiar with? They always push it aside. Now, groundnut soup has become international—everybody loves it, and palaver sauce, spinach, and even fufu. It took a long time before they would taste it, but now, they love it. Both kenkey and fried fish are the same. We fry fish the same way the Japanese and the Chinese fry fish—whole, with the head. However, if an African puts a whole fish with the head on a plate, they say "yuk. I don't want it." When a Japanese person does it, it's okay. I don't understand it. It's very confusing.[49]

TikTok content producer and Cameroonian chef Keith Atowo writes that he has seen people spitting out and scraping his country's food off their tongues.

Foods like fufu and other African cuisines that have a different texture or taste than the foods a person is accustomed to get not only this kind of physical response but also horribly unenlightened verbal reactions. Atowo says, "You know, that's not only demeaning, but that's disrespectful to a culture. . . . It's OK not to like food, but there's a difference between not liking food and disrespecting it."[50] This point holds true in many contexts, especially in marriages, where gender and food are tightly connected.

From a gendered point of view, shaming and policing of food work can be stressful, particularly in households containing more than one food culture. Whenever two or more people come together there will be a combination of different food cultures. The questions become, Do you mix together the foodways cultures? Do you keep them separate and apart? Or do you live together harmoniously in some other fashion? Everything, from how to boil the water for the proper amount of time to how to season particular foods to whether or not certain ingredients are used, can be sites of shame, embarrassment, and even harassment and violence. There are many situations where the primary food provider insists on learning to cook the foods that pay homage to their partner's culture. Sometimes they will go to lengths to try to do so "properly" because they enjoy the process and/or they see it as a sign of love and care.[51] Some women perform this task with affection, but others reject it. Consider, for example, these lines from Marge Piercy's 1976 poem, "What's That Smell in the Kitchen?" She writes, "All over America women are burning dinners / [. . .] it's steak in Chicago; tofu delight in Big Sur; red rice and beans in Dallas."[52]

Piercy claims that wives "all over America" are burning their husbands' dinners out of resentment and dissatisfaction with their roles as housewives. While Piercy's position sounds pervasive, this was not necessarily the case. The generalized circumstances of which Piercy writes did not apply to "all" women. A substantial number of women during the time period that the poem was written were not confined to their own domestic realm; they were confined to the homes of others to make a living for themselves. Piercy's predominantly white feminist agenda ignored the fact that many women were not simply housewives but had been working all their lives to help support their families. In particular, African American women were already working women, but not always out of choice and not necessarily as a matter of personal fulfillment. As a counterpoint, I offer up the work of African American feminist poet Nikki Giovanni, who offers another point of view regarding African American food and family in her 1972 poem "My House." "I mean it's my house / and I want to fry pork chops [. . .] and call it revolution."[53]

Here, Giovanni anticipates and counters Piercy when she celebrates love through her labor in her own home. Throughout Giovanni's poem, this "love language" is manifested by remnants of vernacular cultural expression—quilting (the result of spending "all winter" in carpet stores), frying pork chops, baking sweet potatoes (which some call yams), and making fudge.[54] While the poem draws readers in by presenting images of love that are relatable across race and gender, Giovanni is most likely addressing African American women and men since the poem was published in the early 1970s, at the height of the Black Power movement. Giovanni also speaks to foods that tend to be associated with the South and that in certain combinations are known as soul food, and she speaks of revolution.

Moving from poetry to ethnography, we can consider the essay "Why Migrant Women Feed Their Husbands Tamales: Foodways as a Basis for a Revisionist View of Tejano Family Life," in which anthropologist Brett Williams reveals her surprise at learning that many of her informants desired to cook for their husbands. Williams writes, "For middle-class women, [immersion] in household affairs is generally taken as a measure of a woman's oppression. We often tend to equate power and influence in the family with freedom from routines tasks." Williams explains that many women outside of Mexican culture would find the labor-intensive task of making tamales for their husbands to be an undesirable chore. But, rather than embrace stereotypes of migrant women as merely submissive to their husbands in this and other ways, Williams urges us to consider that sometimes for "the poor, public and private domains are blurred in confusing ways, family affairs may be closely tied to economics and women's work at gathering and obligating or *binding* relatives is neither trivial nor merely a matter of sentiment."[55]

Feminist scholar Arlene Avakian, in her work with Armenian women, also found foodwork to be Janus-faced in that it could be both oppressive and liberating because it allowed for an alternative (to men, to the public sphere) of power. Avakian notes that while cooking can be "compulsory" and "has signified and constructed [the] oppression" of Armenian women, many of these women assert that over generations the women in their family "created authority and control in their kitchens, which often became a space where they bonded with other women."[56] Food not only provides an opportunity for us to locate ourselves—our biases and our privileges—but also it suggests that we revise our notions of family life and realize that for some women domestic roles bring families together. Similarly, in the article "Female Identity, Food, and Power in Contemporary Florence," anthropologist Carole Counihan discusses how her research among other Italian women revealed that feeding others is a major component of female identity. As a result, it is here that women have the most influence over others and enjoy the most social and cultural capital within their families.[57] Literary scholars Peter Naccarato and Katherine LeBesco consider this to be what they call "culinary capital" and maintain that for transnational migrant women, doing food work can be burdensome but simultaneously confers a great deal of cultural status.[58]

But for all of the goodwill conjured up by food situations, intercultural relationships can also reveal a great deal of shaming. All relationships are cross-cultural in some way. When living with others, especially in a marriage that crosses race and ethnicity, whether same or differently gendered, it is necessary to figure out meals—who cooks, who cleans, what foods will be cooked, who will do the grocery shopping, what compromises will be made, and so on. Food differences invite conflict, and marriage is the breeding ground for such tensions. In her book *Intercultural Marriage: Promises and Pitfalls*, Dugan Romano states that food is often cited as the primary cultural source of difference between partners. However, she insists that the importance of knowing this goes beyond digestion. She says there need to be "house rules" that work for both people in the relationship.[59] Of equal importance is food choice and understanding the contexts of people's lives. Scholars Andrea D'Sylva and Brenda Beagan reiterate this point when talking about the role of food in ethnic- and gender-identity construction. They conclude their article by saying, "Gendered roles in foodwork may have multiple, complex and even contradictory meanings in non-privileged groups. For racially marginalized, transnational and diasporic groups . . . foodwork may carry other equally important meanings."[60] Many of these meanings come from sources that were unanticipated, including food shaming. Once, when my home was actively Ghanaian–African American, I prepared a seafood meal. Though it was the only prepared meal in the house, it seemed I was the only one to eat it. Shortly after, my family drove across town to visit Ghanaian friends, who immediately and customarily invited us to have dinner. My partner's response to the invitation was, "Now this is *real* food." Here, again, it is abundantly clear that preference and taste were at play. But more than this, the combination of smells, sight, taste, touch, and maybe even the sound of foods frying and bubbling on the stove, along with being in the company of friends from home, represented and evoked a number of emotions.[61]

On the one hand, the smell of foods from my then partner's home country evoked "an entire semiotic system of political, cultural, and social significations."[62] Among these meanings are the positive impact it has on transnational migrants. Lin et al. say, "The behavior of eating home/ethnic foods not only provides immigrants with necessary nutrition; the tastes of home/ethnic foods can also further release and decrease the emotions of nostalgia. In this regard, immigrants refer to foods derived from their home country as 'comfort foods' . . . since these foods provide positive psychological effects and further improve people's wellbeing."[63] As already discussed, these foods can help migrants adjust to some of the difficulties of life in a new country. But the same foods that bring comfort to one member of the family can be shaming to another member because of different cultural contexts, cuisines, taste preferences, and food systems. All of this makes meal planning very cumbersome and difficult, whether the primary food provider is an immigrant or not. This is especially the case when blending or building a new household. It is understandable that food registers differently for migrants, who are "distanced geographically and temporally from [their] childhood home [so that] food becomes both intellectual and emotional anchor. Psychically [transported] . . . [to be given] a sense of rootedness."[64] But it should not come at the expense of shaming the non-migrant spouse's attempt to make "home" exist in a new location. One emotion cannot and should not be validated at the expense of the other. But it can and does occur.

Understandably, it can be daunting to learn new foodscapes. But here is where Romano's point, about communicating what will work in the new household, has purchase. This is also where the social and cultural capital of being the primary food provider in the home comes into play. Though I study food cultures and understand the politics of food as locating and marking identity, on a personal level, the familial incident recounted above affected me as a wife and as a woman. Shaming, whether through food or otherwise, has this effect. But, as I have previously noted, "the beautiful and dangerous power of food is that it gives full voice to the differences that separate us as well as the ties that bind."[65] Dismissing the crab cakes was as much an affirmation of my partner's ties to his homeland as it was a statement of his culinary preferences. To be sure, it was a traditional way of connecting to home and more so, it signaled to other Ghanaians that "even though he was marrying an African American woman he would always maintain certain cultural practices that located him first as a Ghanaian or a member of the in-group." So then while he was "enjoying his kinfolk and reveling in the familiar smells and tastes with which he was accustomed, he was also working out the various social and cultural boundaries that inevitably accommodate marriage." Consequently, cooking and eating between people from very different cultures, whether migrants or not, can render home a place of (dis)location. As anthropologist Carole Boyce Davies explains, in another context, "The mystified notions of home and family are removed from their romantic, idealized moorings, to speak of pain, movement, difficulty learning, and love in complex ways. Thus, the complicated notion of home mirrors the problematizing of community/nation/identity that one finds in Black women's writing from a variety of communities."[66] We certainly saw this play out between Chalky White and his wife Lenore on *Boardwalk Empire*, even if the reasons were different.

To keep our food choices and preferences from becoming a marital battleground, I used my social and cultural capital in the family and my status as primary food provider to engage other women to cook for my husband by creating a culinary collective. In short, it was necessary to employ "flexible gender relations, co-mothering, and kinship networks" to help us make food work in our house; not only did we have relatively different tastes, but the collective helped to reduce culinary tensions. This is hardly new. In the 1970s when the Daniel Moynihan Report and other studies were released that sought to demonize the diversity of Black family structures, anthropologists like Carol Stack and Harriette Pipes McAdoo, among others, argued for the ways in which poor Black urban families relied upon extensive women-centered networks for assistance. Relationships of fictive kin were essential to fostering and maintaining a sense of well-being for all involved.[67] Engaging our kin, real and fictive, was essential because I was completing my doctoral thesis at the time. This meant that I had very little time to learn an entirely new cuisine, let alone adjust to marital life, other aspects of being a newlywed, and working full-time as an emerging scholar, all while commuting. So I agreed to a group effort in which my sisters-in-law, certain family mothers, and the Waakye lady, along with my husband and myself (occasionally), all made the food thing happen in a way that was compatible for our household. Here is how I recall it:

Like seasoning without measuring, it was decided that my home, literally and figuratively, would be open to a certain amount of outside influence—culinary influence. So much went into that pact of gastronomy as we stood among jars of shito (a homemade hot pepper sauce), cans of Titus sardines, Maggi cubes, jewelry, and Kente cloth. As spices and smells of foreign and home lands intermingled, we crisscrossed

continents and once again married not just families but also food traditions. Consenting to the food arrangement proffered by the sisters made
it clear that I was willing to engage in an act of culinary plurality.[68]

Families create such arrangements all the time, whether systematically,
haphazardly intentionally, or unintentionally. This is one of many reasons
that food shaming is ridiculous. No one has any idea what is really going on
in anyone else's home. To insist or even suggest that people should play out
food decisions in one way or another is to deny people the opportunity to
work through the complex dynamics of their individual and collective family
personhood.

The discussions in this chapter have reiterated that food choices are indeed
intricate and multidimensional. As shown, food decisions are influenced by
so many different variables, ranging from personal to cultural, social, to environmental. The aim has been to present how shaming happens on micro
and macro levels by using a variety of realms of movement and travel. This
can range from going to a local eatery across town to visiting an upscale dinner establishment. It can happen when a person goes away to college or when
they migrate to another country. There are no definitive answers to the quan-
daries that we can find ourselves in regarding food shaming because culinary
choices are overlayed with so many issues. And while cultural sustainability
and cultural preservation should trump "eating right," a lot of times it does
not. More importantly, sustainable cultural practices seem to get lost in the
project of telling others what they should and should not eat. Sometimes it is
because of anti-Black racism, sometimes it is due to interracial and interclass
disharmony, sometimes it is from marital negotiations, and sometimes it is
due to personal and collective trauma related to relocation and dislocation.
This last issue helps me to continue advocating for redefining African American food stories by considering what people have in their arsenal when it
comes to food choices. When issues of dislocation and displacement give
rise to personal and collective trauma as well as loss, all of these issues come
rushing to the forefront.

CHAPTER 3

What's This in My Salad?

Food Shaming, the Real Unhealthy Ingredient

Sacralization is when you find a way to support what you want
by tying it into scripture so you can then justify it as the will of God.
—Rev. Dr. Howard-John Wesley, Alfred Street Baptist Church

It is easy to blur the truth with a simple linguistic trick:
start your story from "Secondly."
—Mourid Barghouti, *I Saw Ramallah*

Katrina has always been with us. . . . It has a bunch of different names.
—Blink (Shameik Moore), *Cut Throat City*

The phone ringing pierced the already hot and humid, sticky summer air. It was August 29, 2005, and one of my girlfriends was calling with the horrible news that the levees in New Orleans, Louisiana, had broken. Though I could not understand it all because she was emotionally overwrought, I could gather that something horrible had happened and my friend's family was in danger. For the next several hours, we were riveted to the television as we watched Black people endure heat, thirst, mosquitos, destruction, and pain, amid putrid waters. It was a catastrophe of epic proportions on multiple levels.[1]

Writing for the *Washington Post*, staff writers David Von Drehle and Jacqueline Salmon called it "the largest displacement of Americans since the Civil War . . . as more than half a million people uprooted by Hurricane Katrina sought shelter, sustenance, and the semblance of new lives."[2] The calamitous devastation wrought by nature, years of systemic race and class disparities, and human error forced people to flee their homes—some willing and able, others unwilling and/or unable—to seek shelter in whatever space was available or that others were capable of providing. By Friday, September 2, 2005, the Red Cross had reported that "every shelter in a seven-state region was already full—76,000 people in Alabama, Mississippi, Florida, Georgia, Texas, Arkansas, and Louisiana. Hundreds of miles from New Orleans, hotels were jammed or quickly filling,"[3] and homes, arenas, stadiums, and more were bulging from offering shelter to those who were young and old, rich and poor, able and infirm, with and without medication. It was the beginning of nothing less than a saga of human tragedy that grew progressively worse as we watched an inept U.S. federal administration mishandle the crisis. As we mobilized into action at every level—local, state, national— I could not help but think, What about the food?

Weeks later, though my ideas were not fully formed, I participated on a panel at the University of Maryland sponsored by the Consortium on Race, Gender, and Ethnicity, where I asked, "Where's the Food in the Conversations of Hurricane Katrina?" Necessary conversations were taking place about poverty, racism, gender, representation, structural inequalities, power and more, but I had heard nothing much about how people were eating, what they were eating, or where they were obtaining food. And when these issues were being discussed they were primarily reduced to describing Black people as looters and thieves as opposed to survivalists. Given that so many people were being displaced and dislocated, I wanted to know how cultural continuity would be realized, since it would be one of the key tenets of surviving the trauma of this forced displacement and dislocation. The conversations in this chapter continue to pull at the thread of food shaming but in the context of dislocation and displacement along with social, emotional, and cultural trauma—issues germane to Black experiences in America, but understudied in food contexts. The discussions here will again draw our attention to how humans make food choices in the midst of turbulent times like massive hurricanes and wildfires, but also while enduring everyday traumas and distresses, including losses of loved ones through death, break-ups, and so on. With this, I continue pushing for an expansion of our food stories, and I highlight why food shaming reveals more about those who are doing the action rather than those who end up being embarrassed or humiliated.

Trauma is an interesting concept. Cultural and collective traumas, as I discuss in chapter 1, can be defined for African Americans through the horrific expanse of enslavement. But repeated traumas for African Americans occur daily, stemming from these horrors, and are maintained and continued through popular culture, social media, news media, individual beliefs, ideologies, and behaviors. They are even perpetuated through interpretations of the Bible. Chapter 2 began with the biblical story of Noah, the ark, and the

Great Flood, found in Genesis 8. The primary emphasis in that chapter was on food choices in the midst of movement and travel. This chapter continues the discussion by focusing on food and dislocation but also more intentionally on race and gender. Ideologically, it picks up with what happens after the lone dove that Noah sends out in search of dry land never returns. Genesis 9 goes on to tell how Noah, "a lover of wine," has planted several vineyards. On one occasion, he gets excessively drunk and lies uncovered in his tent. When his son Ham happens upon his father and sees his nakedness, he tells his brothers, Shem and Japheth. They, in turn, walk backward with a covering to lay across their father's body. When Noah awakes from his wine-induced sleep and learns what has happened, he is furious and condemns the behavior of his youngest son, Ham, ultimately saying, "Cursed be Canaan; the lowest of slaves will he be to his brothers" (Gen. 9:25 NIV).

There is a lot to be gleaned from this story that is relevant to this book's discussions. Among the important issues are dislocation, trauma, shame, and race. But where is the food?, you may be asking. For the moment, the food is background fodder; but it will shortly become a central part of the narrative. In the third part of his sermon series "All in the Family," titled "The Curse Is Broken," the Rev. Dr. Howard-John Wesley, pastor of Alfred Street Baptist Church in Alexandria, Virginia, discusses this story as a "genealogy that has been misread and misappropriated for much of history."[4] Though Wesley is not the only one to speak on this theme, his discussion is most suitable for my purposes. One need only google the story of Ham, race, and slavery to find a number of results that discuss the ways in which Genesis 9 has been used since time immemorial to justify racial hierarchies. In an article for the International Missionary Board titled "The Curse of Ham: How Bad Scripture Interpretation Inspired Genocide," writer Eliza Thomas explains, "The use of Genesis 9 to justify slavery and racial hierarchy grew from a particular strain of European anthropology, not from sound exegesis of the biblical text. Those who wanted to establish a biblical basis for racial superiority suggested that God had sanctioned the curse of Ham and, by extension, all those descended from him, relegating them to be slaves." But as several biblical scholars have maintained, God is actually silent in this text. He does not actually curse Canaan, Ham's son; it is Noah who places the curse. Thomas goes on to add more clarity, "It's important to remember that Noah, too, was a guilty party in this story, set in motion by his own drunkenness. While it's not clear that the curse of Ham was part of God's design, it is obvious that all three sons came from the same father—they were not different races. . . . Rather than act as a foundation for racial superiority, this story serves to foreshadow the conflict that would later develop between Israel and Canaan."[5] Thomas's explanation is insightful, but so are Pastor Wesley's conclusions that, through the use of dubious and inaccurate theological arguments, Black people have been led to believe we are living under a curse from God and thus are naturally inferior to white people. The reality is that this is a historically repeated lie designed to buttress the ideas and goals of white superiority. In other words, African American people have been repeatedly subjected to a heinous single story.

But there is more. Citing biblical scholar Cain Hope Felder, Rev. Wesley defines sacralization as an act whereby a group of people "with a vested interest take an ideology, or historical phenomenon, and recast it as biblical truth to give it theological justification." Wesley continues, "Because if you can sacralize something, if you can attach it to scripture, if you can convince yourself that it is the will of God, you can absolve yourself from any guilt no matter how evil your actions are, because you have persuaded yourself that it's the will of God—that if I can just prove to you and to me it is the will of God, I can do it no matter how evil it is." This act of sacralization has been repeated throughout history to justify any number of atrocities, from the most monstrous to the least. Wesley elaborates,

> So, with sacralization you can kill a million Jews in the Holocaust and say it's the will of God, because the Jews killed Jesus. Through sacralization you can convince yourself that it is all right to eradicate Native Americans and their tribes and put them in reservations while you steal their land and call it Manifest Destiny, because you liken yourself to Israel and America is your Promised Land. Through sacralization you can oppress LGBTQIA+ because you got a distorted understanding of the word "abomination." And through sacralization you can endorse the enslavement, the torture, the lynching and the killing of African people and support the apartheid system because you believe in the curse of Ham.[6]

Black people have been living under the alleged curse of Ham since enslavement. Somewhere in the history of invocations of this passage from Genesis, Canaan—the one who was actually cursed—disappeared, and Ham became his stand-in as a representative of Black people. Hence, Black people have been living under this misguided interpretation for centuries, and this scripture has been used to justify punishing us for any and every ill in society.

Living while Black can be traumatic. And anyone who has experienced a form of trauma knows that it can leave you "[scanning] the surrounding world anxiously for signs of danger, breaking into explosive rages and reacting with a start to ordinary sights and sounds," according to sociologist Kai Erikson. Simultaneously, living traumatized leaves you nervous and numb against a background of "depression, feelings of hopelessness, and a general closing off of the spirit as the mind tries to insulate itself from further harm."[7] And lest we believe that trauma is always monumental in occurrence, it is not. Erikson points out that trauma can come from sustained exposure to conflict and confrontation as well as from major calamities. It can emerge "from a continuing pattern of abuse as well as from a single searing assault, from a period of severe attenuation and erosion as well as from a sudden flash of fear. The effects are the same."[8] Amid this level of pain and anguish that replays over and over because the "traumatized mind holds on to that moment," it is difficult to fathom that food has any resonance in such a scenario. But as previously discussed, food is a touchstone, a marker of home, comfort, and community. In the moment of living and reliving traumas, food may be all that a person has to help them cope. In Erikson's estimation, "something alien breaks in on you, smashing through whatever barriers your mind has set up as a line of defense. It invades you, possesses you, takes you over, becomes a dominating feature of your interior landscape, and in the process threatens to drain you and leave you empty. . . . Above all, trauma involves a continual reliving of some wounding experience in daydreams and nightmares, flashbacks and hallucinations, and is a compulsive seeking out of similar circumstances."[9] Taken together, the trauma of living through the "wounding experiences" of a horrific event like enslavement, genocide, or even a natural disaster, coupled with dealing daily with negative societal beliefs, means most Black people are living in bodies of pain born from repeated distress.

The damage of Hurricane Katrina extended well beyond the physical landscape and those who were directly affected. It included extended family members, friends, and even those of us watching with no direct connections at all. In the immediate days that followed the moment of the breaking levees, we were told via the news, but also from communities of friends, that people were trying to get out of New Orleans. My friend was a part of an organized network of people from NOLA (New Orleans, Louisiana) who organized assistance across the DMV (D.C.-Maryland-Virginia area). Through this group and many others, we learned of specific families who wanted

provisions in anticipation of soon-to-arrive family, friends, and even strangers. I recall driving late at night into one of the suburban areas of Prince
George's County, Maryland, to a well-apportioned single-family home. As
we brought the materials inside, I noticed a sense of discomfort from the
hosting family. They were grateful but also seemed to be uncomfortable. Of
course, we were strangers. As volunteers we saw ourselves as pitching in,
like we did for survivors of September 11. But for those who had family and
friends who were surviving the storm, emotions were high, even overflow-
ing. These were real people, and they were overwhelmed, resentful, and even
ashamed. Years later, I spoke with my friend about my suspicions, and she
confirmed as much. She said,

> So, yes, to some degree, there was a little shame because these are
> middle-class professionals and they are not used to this. . . . People were
> bringing furniture—sofas and chairs, I brought some chairs, blankets,
> sheets. . . . Some of it I didn't want to part with . . . but they needed it
> more than me. And remember, we put the word out with Fox 5, and they
> covered it, so they were overwhelmed by that. So, yeah, bringing them
> a lot of food at that time was probably a lot because they were thinking
> about their families and all that was going on.[10]

The shock and distress of this experience added to the many daily stressors
already being experienced as part of the assemblage of life experiences that
informed this particular happening. All of this, on top of the already per-
sistent condition of being Black in America, was overwhelming. In 2005,
Facebook was just a thought and it would be another decade before they
deployed the mechanism of a "safety check-in." Even more than fifteen years
later, talking about this time with my friend resulted in her voice breaking
and at times her gasping while she recalled the sheer magnitude of that time
of living hell. She remembered,

> We put the call out and there were lots of decisions about how and where
> the stuff was going. We decided this one couple would take it because
> they had a basement. They were overwhelmed by how much stuff was
> shared. It filled up two eighteen-wheeler trucks. . . . You remember this?
> Because I rode with one of them back down there to take the stuff. For
> the people who are receiving . . . it was overwhelming. We wanted to
> have stuff for people to descend upon our homes, but we weren't pre-
> pared for the number of people. . . . We just wanted to figure out how to

make the family members who were expecting people [to be] comfortable. Then it turned to people who are going to be renting rooms, how can we help so they don't have to buy stuff whole? Then it was how can we get stuff back home for people who couldn't leave but have nothing? Then it was how do we take care of people whose kids are in school. . . . [voice breaks] But then we started a scholarship fund. . . . I'm sorry, I didn't know it was still . . . you know, that's what we do with the Mardi Gras Ball.[11]

I have quoted my friend's recollections at length to impress upon readers how food is never just about the physical products we put in our mouths. As this discussion illustrates, foods are laden with layers upon layers of experiences and contexts. In this instance, the food that was to be shared was somewhat immaterial to the circumstances surrounding how the food arrived on their plate and how they came to be eating it. During this time, dinner was hardly just another everyday affair. Not only do you have the consumer, the newly arrived New Orleans citizen who evacuated or was evacuated, but also you have the one who cooked the food—relative, friend, stranger—who came by the goods in any number of ways. The mixture of emotions on that plate, represented by the rice, beans, seafood, beef, or pork, is enough to both choke and soothe, depending upon how and when the food is received.

There were many different people who fled or were evacuated from the city. Some had the financial, physical, and emotional (that is, relatives and friends) means and wherewithal; they were able to leave when the order was urged by mayor Ray Nagin. Some had no means to leave, because they were surviving at or below poverty level. Some had never traveled out of the state, flown on a plane, or even owned a car. Some relied on city transportation—buses and taxis—so they had no driver's license. Many women, undoubtedly, stayed behind, caring for the young, the elderly, the sick, the disabled, the mentally and emotionally distressed. From what we did see on television and in the media, several residents required medical attention. Still others were stranded in NOLA because they were trapped and incarcerated by a system that considers them too irredeemable to be let out of harm's way. This being the pre-iPhone era, and thus no Waze, Google Maps, or other GPS, even those with ample transportation may have opted to stay because they did not have the funds to rent an out-of-town hotel or did not know where to go or what direction to take even if they were to leave the city. Lastly, among the many other reasons people stayed was their belief that history would be on their side, since they had survived many other hurricanes and natural disasters.

People vacated to every state with the majority being taken to the Astrodome in Houston, Texas. But many others went to California, Colorado, and Michigan, while some came east to places like Washington, D.C., Virginia, and Maryland.[12] According to newspaper accounts throughout the nation, for some the disaster offered the chance for a new life and a fresh start. For others the return home was longed for and much anticipated. Some NOLA residents were not comfortable in unfamiliar surroundings; so they had many different kinds of difficulties navigating the new landscapes. Finding new jobs and childcare in unfamiliar territories whether skilled or unskilled was a challenge. And then there was the food.

Whether I was deliberately searching or not, news articles during this time would often contain tidbits about food and survival. Most often, these observations were not the main focus of the story; then again at times they were. In one article, for example, a resident who had evacuated to Houston, Texas, had this to say about the city's attempt to create New Orleans–style food: "They didn't have no crawfish. No sausage. No jambalaya. . . . Their food just didn't taste the same."[13] Writing for the *New Orleans Tribune*, Wilmarine B. Hurst, who herself was displaced from her home by the hurricane, captures a number of food experiences from fellow city residents. In her article "A Lil' Taste of Home: On the Sixth Anniversary of Hurricane Katrina New Orleans Cuisine Reigns Supreme," she showcases how many of those who found themselves "scattered near and far" continued to cook the cuisines of New Orleans. She quotes one such resident, Clara "Sky" Jackson, as saying, "People have always come from all over the world to taste our good cooking. Living in Lafayette after Katrina, it has been a little difficult finding the things that make our finest cuisine. I still make my own roux from scratch. But here they buy it [in] a bottle—never even knew that existed until I moved here. I find myself coming back home shopping for the things that they don't sell here. I miss home." Rhonda Miller, another New Orleans resident, ended up in Carrollton, Texas, after the hurricane. She said, "Whenever we were in Louisiana (primarily Baton Rouge), we always brought back what we could not find or what was too expensive [at stores in Texas]."[14] Re-creating tastes during their displacement was an important element of restoring some aspects of home and the dignity that comes with helping themselves and others to feel at peace. Equally important was the reestablishment of culinary practices and traditions. Everyone in New Orleans and even many beyond the city know of the Louisiana Creole practice of eating red beans and rice on Mondays. For Amanda Coleman, who also went to Texas, the centuries-old tradition of having red beans and rice on Monday was incomplete without pickled pigtails:

> Pickled pigtails are an issue for me. There's nothing to compare to what they do for the red beans. I haven't been able to use anything to duplicate the flavor. I so look forward to visiting New Orleans and eating red beans and returning home with a couple of pounds of pigtails in my carry-on luggage. I do get the hot sausage and smoke sausage occasionally from Fiesta store, but I can't find the N.O. French bread. I truly miss the Po-Boy loaves, (oysters, shrimp, and hot sausage). That makes my mouth water just mentioning it. When I visit New Orleans, getting a taste of its food is one thing I look forward to doing.[15]

Crawfish. Po-boys. Jambalaya. Double D (or D&D) hot sausage. Gumbo. Stuffed peppers. Mirliton (also known as chayote; a pear-shaped vegetable that tastes like squash). Leidenheimer's French bread. Cream cheese pie. All of these are ingredients and dishes are particular to the city of New Orleans and the region in general. For example, referring to celery, onion, and bell pepper as the "Holy Trinity" and green peppers as "bell peppers" are cooking terms you learn if you are in the kitchen with someone from New Orleans. I recall once committing the offense of using a box of my roommate's Zatarain's dirty rice. This was long before Hurricane Katrina and well before it was distributed outside of New Orleans. Not knowing the significance of the rice mix and that it was like grains of "gold," I used a box and told her I would replace it. I felt like I had broken into Fort Knox. Given that we would often share foods and that she had several boxes in the cabinet, I did not think much about using one. It was not until she told me how difficult it was to get the boxed rice that I realized the culinary violation and felt appropriately ashamed. My ability to be able to regularly access collard greens, my family food of familiarity, when she could not access hers, made me feel really bad for not having sought permission beforehand.

Strong feelings elicited about food can easily turn into shaming others, as I discussed in chapter 2 when my then partner preferred Ghanaian food to the crab cake. And it is not always about any one particular kind of food but may involve personal food habits and ways of cooking. According to one *Washington Post* article, Bruce Norwood relocated to a DMV suburb, where he found work at the deli counter of a local supermarket. When one customer came, Norwood said it took him a while to locate what the customer wanted in the meat case: Livingston Farm brown-sugar ham. Once a coworker helped him locate the lunchmeat, he began carving, but apparently he was carving it too thickly:

> "A little thinner than that," the customer said.
> He sliced it again. "How's that?"
> "Can it get any thinner?"
> "It'll be almost shaved," Norwood said.

According to Norwood, he had only been on the deli counter job six days and was still trying to figure it all out. As the *Washington Post* indicates, Norwood said, "There're 40 kinds of cheeses. All I knew at home was two: American and Swiss."[16]

For certain, New Orleans had more than two kinds of cheese, but they were unknown to Norwood, a new transplant to Maryland who had the good fortune of finding a job and a place to live. Mr. Norwood might not have realized that he'd landed in a county where the social, cultural, and intellectual capital leaned toward the affluent. And while Mr. Norwood might have suspected some of this, he might not have known that at that time, the area could boast of highly educated professionals in the medical fields, government contracting, higher education, management, information technology, medical research, and other key economic sectors. A quarter of the county's residents over the age of twenty-five held graduate or professional degrees, which, when combined with a median household income of $100,000, made it among the most affluent large jurisdictions in the nation and certainly in the state.[17] No doubt Mr. Norwood recognized some elements of these class dynamics. And if not, then he most likely soon became aware, especially since the area is known for its particularly expensive cost of living. Even longtime local residents can feel the stress and discomfort of the costs of living in the county. So it is not insignificant that the deli worker had limited knowledge of the meat and cheese products in the case. This combination of workplace shame and anxiety while trying to adjust to a completely new living environment could be a source of even more distress.

Like the transnational migrants in chapter 2 of this book, new residents who ended up in areas unfamiliar to them had a lot to contend with. And here is the problem with shaming: most of the time, we do not know one another's business and personal circumstances, so when we make these judgments and/or act on assumptions, we are operating from a position of unawareness.

And sometimes we are ignorant and mean. We make assumptions all the time about people's financial circumstances, knowledge, and claims to goods and services, especially when people are in need of assistance. Just because the deli worker does not know a variety of cheeses does not mean he cannot afford them. It simply means he is unfamiliar with them. How many customers at that meat counter knew that, at forty-eight years old, Mr. Bruce Norwood was starting his life over again in a foreign place and space? And how many of them asked where he was from or listened long enough to know he was fleeing Hurricane Katrina and that previously he had done a different kind of work? And how many cared why his knowledge of some kinds of foods was limited? How many considered that he might not want to know those things because he was comfortable in his routine consumption of the foods that gave him fulfillment and satiation?

Most likely, the answer to most or all of these questions is, "Very few." Most of the customers saw Norwood as a worker who was at the deli to cut their meat, slice their cheese, and get other foods for them. And yet some of these same folks would have been among the first to declare, "We need to help those people displaced by Hurricane Katrina." But unless Mr. Norwood engaged them in an extensive conversation, they could not have known that he was part of that very group. They also could not have known that his food knowledge or language was very different from theirs. For example, they didn't know that where he was from, they had their own terms for preparing a deli sandwich. If Norwood had asked if they wanted their sandwich fully-loaded and, following their affirmative response, added ketchup, it might have engendered looks of confusion and even disgust. But for some New Orleans residents a "dressed" sandwich means "with shredded lettuce, very thinly sliced tomatoes, mayonnaise, pickles, and (sometimes) ketchup."[18]

Judgments rendered in smirks, looks of disgust, murmurs, and outright rudeness are not few and far between when it comes to food. Most often, the only witnesses to such events are those involved and maybe a few bystanders. Sometimes it is in the company of friends where "crackin but factin'" takes place. This happened one day when my friend Tee from New Orleans invited me and two others to her house for a cookout; we were repeatedly bragged to about a brand of Louisiana hot sausage that we absolutely had to try. Though we have been friends since graduate school it was almost fifteen years into our relationship before I had ever heard of this particular food from my friend. But now that she is married, with a house, and other trappings of middle-class African American life, including an enclosed back porch and a stainless steel Weber grill, she wanted to open up the interiors of her life to us a bit more.

My friend loves Patton's hot sausage, which is one reason she said she was "SUPER excited to share this with [us], hoping [we] would love it as much as [they] do." In recounting the story, she said, "I was so excited to share such a huge part of our culture with y'all." On the day of the cookout, we reminded our hosts, even as the grill was being prepped, that at least two of us would not be able to try the delicacy because we do not eat pork. Finally, the hour had arrived. Because the third member of our group eats pork, we looked to him to be the taste-tester and judge. It seemed appropriate, since this friend self-identifies as a gourmand with an ever-expanding and diverse palate. After a couple of bites, he shrugged and, as I recall it, he said, "It tastes like kielbasa." Our host recalls that he said, "It tastes like breakfast sausage." Not unproblematically, my pork-abstaining sister girlfriend and I fell out laughing uncontrollably while our host was shocked at his reaction. She dismissed his insolence by saying something like "You so silly." But, when I later asked my friend about how she felt that day, she replied,

My dad even froze it and sent us some in advance in preparation for the party. When [he] said it tasted like breakfast sausage, I was totally deflated! LOL . . . How could you not love it as much as we all—everyone I know from home—do? People from NOLA will call me to ask if I have any Patton's in my freezer and vice versa. It is SO very popular at home for hot sausage Po-Boys. So much so, I am not even sure that anybody who sells them would use any other brand of hot sausage. It's never been anything else when you go to get a hot sausage Po-Boy . . . no matter where in the city you go.[19]

Sausage seems to be a central part of the culture, indeed. Another brand of sausage, D&D (Double D Meat Company), was often mentioned by displaced residents in reference to missing tastes from home. Tasha Thomas-Naquin, for example, stated,

Early after Hurricane Katrina, getting that taste of New Orleans required a little ingenuity and driving. . . . When I was in Charlotte, N.C., Patton's sausage was one of the things I missed most, and the DD smoke sausage [sic]—especially when I wanted to make gumbo. . . . I would take the ten-hour ride back home with my cooler in the back of my van and stock up on all of my favorite New Orleans foods I couldn't get in

North Carolina—blue crabs, DD smoke sausage, Patton's hot sausage, alligator sausage, and Louisiana seafood. If it wasn't for a lil' taste of home during those times I think I would have lost my mind. The food brought me comfort.[20]

For years after the event, we continued to laugh and joke about that dinner party. But since learning how deeply proud my friend is of this cultural tradition, I have repeatedly reconsidered our responses. I appreciate her desire to share this aspect of her culture and have long since apologized for laughing during this disappointing (and clearly hurtful) moment for her. We have been friends for years and remain so. But it is very easy to forget that we all have complex personhood and that even those of us who strive to live our lives appreciating the cultures of others may well fall short. We, too, may forget that those close to us also have contexts and histories that will show up in relationships. I use the example of my NOLA friend's cookout to illustrate how none of us is immune to food shaming, either inflicting or receiving it, and that when we laugh at each other's food cultures it can easily cause further harm.

Seldom is shaming one-sided. Those who migrate, whether voluntarily or by force, also have their thoughts about the food cultures in their new locales. For most of our adult lives, my friends and I have celebrated major holidays together. So it is common for us to talk about these events and the things that have happened over the years as a result of our combined gatherings. During one of our many conversations, my friend shared this story:

Most folks that I know at home try to recreate the Thanksgiving they had when they were growing up with all the same items on the table that their parents/grandparents/families prepared. So when folks started moving to MD after Katrina, they would have a visceral reaction to a table that did not have the food they were used to. [I] would have [to cook] an entirely separate meal at home for our house after we came from having dinner with y'all, so that [my husband] could have the dinner he was familiar with as a child . . . which was slightly different from the food I had growing up, so it required me to adapt my cooking/ tradition. They always had dirty rice (with chicken livers/gizzards and shrimp) as their dressing. Meanwhile, my family always had dressing with bread, breadcrumbs, ground beef, shrimp, and crabmeat. So [there were] major differences between uptown (my family) and downtown (his family) tables. Perhaps part of his grieving process [over Katrina] was why he didn't leave the house for holiday meals; but I did not realize this until much later.[21]

My friend's reflections again speak to the complicated nature of people and food, within racial groups, within regions, within marriages, across class differences and during experiences of migration. My friend has lived in Maryland for decades, while her partner came to the area because of Hurricane Katrina. And even though everyone is asked to contribute to the dinner, this discussion suggests that some holiday traditions and differences are just too varied to be satisfied outside the home. For those who pride themselves on being generous hosts, finding out that your hospitality is not well received can be its own form of shaming and disappointment. Perhaps this is how our vegan cookout host felt when she saw plates of discarded tofu lying around (see the introduction), a point not lost on me. This then confirms and reinforces that when food is involved, it is always a good idea to be aware of the dynamics in the room.

Understanding the myriad issues that pervade our day-to-day relationships and conversations about food reinforces how much we cannot take them for granted, even when they involve close friends and family. Because we often do take food for granted, seeing every food situation as one of comfort, we seldom temper our opinions and thoughts about what is being acquired and consumed, and by whom. We may be remiss in not "reading the room" or in not being aware of other people's experiences. Rarely do we stop to consider the difference between what we intend to happen and the impact of those good intentions or the ways in which the situation actually turns out. This tends to happen across the board, from comments we make to friends to posts sent in group chats or on social media, from random conversations with store cashiers to in-depth admissions to caseworkers and academics. We all make unsolicited and often derogatory comments about the food experiences of others, even when we intend for our interventions to have a different impact. The intention/impact dilemma can even present itself in an exposé on young people.

In May 2008, the *Washington Post* joined the conversation about obesity in American society by publishing an in-depth, five-part exposé titled "Young Lives at Risk: Our Overweight Children."[22] As one interested in the intersections of food and society, I noticed many of the articles in the series. Along with an overview of childhood obesity, the series included such topics as "10 Facts You Should Know [about Childhood Obesity]," "How to Choose

Healthy Favorites without Making Your Taste Buds Suffer," and "What's Your Nutrition IQ?" In addition to the print version of the story, there was an online version that highlighted stories about children throughout the DMV, from counties considered well-off to those where poverty levels soar. A full-page spread showed an illustration of the outline of an obese white boy, his organs accompanied by various snippets explaining the effects of obesity on these bodily tissues, from the heart to the lungs. Other discussion pieces covered hormonal changes and various diseases that are complicated by excessive fat in the body, such as asthma, Blount's disease, and metabolic syndrome. The study was well-sourced with experts ranging from academics to pediatric gastroenterologists, pediatric diabetes specialists to cardiologists, representatives from the CDC to the National Institutes of Health. From all appearances, the subject was well covered.

Several years later, when I was invited by the University of Maryland (UMD) Counseling Center to participate in their Research and Development enrichment seminar for faculty and staff, I immediately thought about this *Washington Post* series. My topic for the discussion was titled "You Don't Have to Give Up the Corn Pudding: Black Women, Food, and the Quandary of Self-Identity." The description for my presentation at the meeting read,

> Creating healthy bodies requires a redefinition of the food stories that define our cultures. If we accept that this is true, then humanities scholars can intervene in questions of nutrition and food policy by discouraging people from demonizing and degrading the foods that help to create and sustain our communities. Rather than urging people to change what they eat, a more effective approach may be to help communities incorporate healthier preparation techniques and ingredients into foods already rich in cultural meaning. This discussion is designed to weigh issues like abandoning culturally specific foods like corn pudding in favor of the "naturally fresh" salad. It encourages us to consider an "and/or" rather than a paper vs. plastic mentality.

My angle for the UMD conversation was focused on the particular narrative of Latrisha Avery, who was a part of the overall story—in print and online—of young people living with obesity. The results of my discussion that day form the basis for this portion of the chapter's discussion but is not a perspective that argues against or defends the science around obesity; that body of literature is vast.[23] Instead, this discussion is about how the *Washington Post*'s entire exposé seemed not to involve much of a cultural or humanistic

point of view. Consequently, this resulted in as much shaming as it did en-
lightenment of readers about the horrors of obesity.

I start this conversation with a panel that I participated in during the
Association for the Study of Food and Society's annual conference in June
2008 in Albuquerque, New Mexico. My colleagues and I shared what we have
learned from our experiences into what we call "the frontiers of food studies,"
the space where science-based, measurable thinking tends to dominate. Five
of us, all trained in American studies, primarily focused on what we knew
to be the histories of American food practices. As we shared our experiences
working with scientists, consulting with policy think tanks, and working
with those whose focus is mostly numerical data, we offered how we thought
their research could be strengthened by cultural points of view.[24] One of the
many important insights that emerged from this collaboration is Charlotte
Biltekoff's observation about the extent to which ideas about food "that are
grounded in science and justified in terms of their impact on 'health' has
grown considerably not just in the last few decades, but over the course of
the last century." She goes on to note, though we increasingly continue to
think "about dietary ideals as 'objective,' we fail to recognize their ideological
content." In short, though there are many arguments out there for "eating
right" that are grounded in "scientific and medical epistemologies," almost
all of them fail to taken into consideration how history and culture inform
these conversations. We ignore them at our peril. Biltekoff wonders what
would happen if we allowed our food and health conversations to be based
on "our most common-sense ideas about health [and] good diets." She rightly
reminds us that "good eaters are shaped by culture, values, and ideologies."
We are, of course, aware that "to some extent, science-oriented studies on
food and health already 'include' the idea of culture." But simply acknowledging "that biomedical matters take place within culture" and recognizing
that "'culture' can sometimes get in the way of healthy eating," leaves "the
scientific hegemony over the concept of dietary health untouched." In other
words, nothing actually changes by simply recognizing this. What we need
from the scientific world is what is needed from society at large: new narratives and new discourses. As Biltekoff admonishes,

> If we are going to bother with this at all, we may as well start to imagine
> a new way of thinking that starts from the premise that dietary health
> cannot be considered from a purely scientific or medical perspective.
> Dietary health cannot, of course, [also] be considered from a purely cul-

tural perspective either. So, talking about food is going to require some very radical, productively unsettling conversation, collaboration, and cross-fertilization across social, disciplinary, and professional divides.[25]

The rest of this chapter builds off Biltekoff's argument that any approach that focuses solely on the medical perspective or on the cultural perspective does not go far enough in its analysis. I demonstrate what can happen when cultural perspectives are considered primarily as an afterthought, or worse, not at all. Furthermore, this conversation encourages food enthusiasts, practitioners, service providers, and journalists who too often work from a "one-size fits all model" to be more intentional about recognizing thinking along the lines of the status quo. Doing anything less is neither effective nor ethical.

Tucked in between the *Washington Post*'s online interactive invitations to learn how to "Buy Better Groceries," join the "Lean Plate Club Discussion Group," and test your "Nutrition IQ," I found the photo story of Latrisha Avery. It may have been the lone thumbnail of a dark-skinned, heavyset face, with tears rolling down her cheek, that captured my attention. As I scrolled through the approximately forty-five images of Latrisha at school, at home, and in the community, I was struck by the direction of the story and how this very young African American girl was being put under a great deal of pressure—if not in life, certainly by the way in which her story was being told.

The photo story begins with a picture that has three captions. The one in the upper-left corner reads, "Different Worlds, One Problem." On the opposite side of the photograph is another that says, "Young Lives at Risk, Special Report." And in the lower right-hand corner of the picture, the caption reads, "The Voice of Latrisha Avery, 12," suggesting that the entire set of images to come will share Latrisha's thoughts and feelings in words and images. The picture in this first panel shows a group of girls standing in a single-file line, some facing the camera and others facing to the left, wearing what looks like a school uniform: white polo shirts and dark pants or skirts. Though we are shown the girls' bodies only from the neck and shoulders down, the caption makes it clear which of these girls is Latrisha when it states, "When Latrisha Avery, 12 . . . graduates from elementary [school] . . . she hopes to leave behind her nickname, 'King Kong.' At 5-foot-7 and 220 pounds, Latrisha stands out from most of her friends." Right at the outset, we are shown the difference in size between Latrisha and her classmates. In the first photo, she is one of four girls at the end of the line. Judging by their waistlines and where their polo shirt is tucked in, the three girls in front of her are the same height.

Latrisha's waist is in line with where another girl's arms are folded across her chest, suggesting that she is much taller than her classmates. But this is not altogether correct. When we look at the entire line of girls, not just the three in front of Latrisha, it becomes apparent that they are of varying height and weight. At least one girl's full body almost can be seen, even though the photographer tried not to capture the girls' faces. Unlike the other girls in line, whose shoulders are at the top of the photograph, we can see this young lady's nose, mouth, and chin. And some of the other girls in the picture are just slightly shorter than Latrisha, but one would have to look carefully to see this because they are facing ahead in line while Latrisha, the shorter girl, and a few others are directly facing the camera.

The next four images show Latrisha outside on the playground with some of the same girls, who may be her friends. In one of the pictures, a schoolmate is hanging from metal playground rings while Latrisha looks on. In another picture, a different girl is climbing a fence; again, Latrisha looks on. One of the four images is taken from a distance, through the rings of the trapeze equipment on the playground, and it shows Latrisha and her friends walking off the playground holding hands. The captions for these photos read as follows:

Caption no. 1: Latrisha is working hard to lose weight. At a Boys and Girls Club in Southeast Washington, she spends four hours a week at a free fitness and nutrition program sponsored by the District's Project Health Initiative. She has lost 15 pounds since the beginning [of] the program last fall.

Caption no. 2: Forces greater than Latrisha's own willpower—like her neighborhood—present a difficult challenge. With dangerous playgrounds, an abundance of fast food, and celebrations around food, Latrisha faces many obstacles.

Caption no. 3: A recent Carnegie Mellon study found that the closer children are to outdoor recreation and the farther they are from junk food, the slimmer they will be.

Caption no. 4: The District is awakening to the idea that neighborhoods like Latrisha's can make kids fat. A range of government, community, and nonprofit organizations are working to reduce urban barriers to weight loss.[26]

Taken together, the captions and images present a particular kind of narrative about Latrisha Avery. First, to emphasize the deleterious effects of obesity on the mental and emotional health of our young people, the news story immediately tells us that Latrisha is teased in school because of her weight, height, and skin tone and that some of the kids viciously call her "King Kong." By placing Latrisha beside some of the children who are smaller, the photos accentuate these differences and heavily contrast Latrisha's body with those of her friends. Second, when the girls are outside, at least twice we are shown full-body images of Latrisha standing around while her friends are playing. Having two pictures where we see girls being active on the playground while Latrisha looks on seems to emphasize that exercise is key to weight control, and the captions reinforce this point. At least one implication is that while her friends play on monkey bars and other equipment that requires them to lift their own weight, Latrisha is unable to do the same.

Along with the photographs, the captions help inform the overall narrative of the article. The information in the captions is correct in saying cities and towns need to do a much better job of providing safe neighborhoods for all children. More importantly, municipalities everywhere should ensure that playgrounds and recreational facilities are available to all young children. And, yes, they should be safe as well. Even before the authors of the article define what they mean by "safety," it is clear from words like "urban" and "inner city" that gun violence is the primary problem and the main reason the children cannot play outside. Left unsaid, however, is that gun violence plagues rural as well as urban areas, and that shootings take place both in and out of schools, a point we tend to overlook. This is not just the case in southeast D.C., where Latrisha lives and goes to school. The fear of gun violence surrounds us all. Caption number four says, "The District is awakening to the idea that neighborhoods like Latrisha's can make kids fat," reflecting some of the literature on urban planning, transportation, and public health that highlights the failure of city planners to be accountable to Black communities. Wen et al. argue, "Features of neighborhood design such as walkability, access to various activity-promoting resources (e.g., recreational facilities, open space, public parks), aesthetics and green spaces, and land-use patterns are important contributors to physical activity and healthy weight of adults and children." Though spatial inequality exists in built environments, they say, it is "not well understood. National-level analyses are particularly lacking for how neighborhood income patterns and racial-ethnic compositions are linked to built environmental attributes."[27]

In their article "In D.C., Where Kids Live Sets the Tone for Weight Loss Success," *Washington Post* staff writers Steve Hendrix and Hamil Harris explain there is no playground near Latrisha's house on Brandywine Avenue SE. They also emphasize that because of "drug dealing and gunfire," Latrisha's mother "would let her play outside only when she could keep watch. Sixty percent of the residents live within two blocks of a public park, the Urban League study showed, but 56 percent of parents would not allow their children to play outdoors, mostly because of safety concerns." Undoubtedly because there is not enough space in this kind of photo spread for additional details, the article does not explain how the city is addressing this problem. However, the writers do state that "a range of government, community and nonprofit organizations are working to reduce urban barriers to weight loss, from a U.S. Transportation Department's 'Safe Routes to School' project to licensing food carts that sell hummus and salads. The department will soon test a free 'borrow-a-bike' project based on a popular program in Paris."[28] All of these are interesting concepts, but they are very unlikely to benefit the people who most need assistance because other factors also have to be addressed. *Washington Post* writers Hendrix and Harris speak to some of these other factors that contribute to Latrisha being full-figured, namely being surrounded by fast food eateries and other "bad [places]." Their article states, "Almost all the food choices in Latrisha's neighborhood are bad ones, with corner stores and takeout joints serving fatty calories through bullet-proof glass windows." To complement this narrative, photos show Latrisha walking along a roadway with a Popeyes restaurant as well as a liquor store in the background. According to the pictures, Latrisha's caregiver's house is surrounded by all the community "ills"—fast-food restaurants, Chinese carry-outs, liquor stores, convenience stores—and has no playgrounds. In fact, Hendrix and Harris write, "a 2007 study by the National Urban League found that 81 percent of the food vendors in Ward 8 were either convenience stores or fast-food outlets. Until a new Giant opened in December as the only full-service grocery in a ward of 70,000 residents, Latrisha's sole source of fresh produce was a bus ride away."

If fresh food is out of reach, it seems that exercise is, too. In the images where Latrisha stands watching her friends, it is clear that the girls are very different in size, but the photos also make it appear that the other girls are more fit. The children who are smaller and thinner are shown actively climbing, while their friend, who is larger, appears simply to be watching them play. But how true to life is this portrayal, really? Although the pictures shows Latrisha looking up at her friends while they climb and hang on the bars, we do not know if Latrisha has herself just gotten off the equipment or is waiting for her turn. We are led to believe that she is simply standing by, inactive and wishful.

We are also reminded in various ways that Latrisha attends an after-school program called FitNut, which is operated in conjunction with Children's National Medical Center. The aim of the program is to educate children like Latrisha on nutrition and fitness. At FitNut, Latrisha plays "running games and learns about healthy food," including how to make and eat a salad. The girls in the program, who range in age from six to sixteen, learn how to select healthy options even when they go to fast-food restaurants. Hendrix and Harris explain, "At a recent session, after a primer on the least-bad menu items at McDonald's (plain hamburger), KFC (grilled chicken breast) and Wendy's (ultimate chicken sandwich), Latrisha and her classmates sat down to snacks that might have been from another planet: baked veggie puffs, carrots, celery and organic natural peanut butter. Some of the girls looked dubious, but Latrisha's plate was clean in minutes. 'That peanut butter was good,' she said." And we as a society want Latrisha to make these kinds of choices and enjoy the foods she selects. But enjoying these new food options may not extend to the salad they put in front of her.

In the photo essay there is one picture of Latrisha and another girl (who phenotypically looks to be Latina) sitting at a lunch table, laughing and appearing to have a good time. Before them sits an empty plastic container—the kind that might hold a takeout sandwich or salad—a small box of orange juice, and another of chocolate milk. Another photo shows Latrisha sitting with a salad in a plastic container in front of her. It has lettuce, tomatoes, cucumbers, a slice of red bell pepper, broccoli crowns, and a scoop of tuna fish salad. Beside the salad are two small round containers with an orange label that reads "Naturally fresh lite ranch salad dressing." For me, the most significant part of the photo is Latrisha's fingers picking out the small crowns of raw broccoli. The caption reads: "Latrisha is making an effort to implement her nutrition education and chooses a salad for lunch over a hot dog. Still, she removes the broccoli from the mix."

Several other photos round out the "Different Worlds, One Problem" photo essay featuring Latrisha Avery. They range from Latrisha and her aunt attending church service and cooking to Latrisha sitting at a dining room table, preparing to eat Easter dinner, with a closeup of her very full dinner plate. The photo essay concludes with Latrisha, having finished the FitNut program, jumping with glee at her success. And we are again happy for the young child. In all, we have been presented with a snapshot of a young African American girl's journey from "obesity to health" because she has taken personal responsibility for her weight.

But herein lies some of the problem, doesn't it? This "pull yourself up by your bootstraps" portrayal omits some very important details and shows a young girl who is forced to be accountable for eating healthy and exercising daily in ways even some adults cannot be. To further guide the rest of this discussion about Latrisha, I refer back to Charlotte Biltekoff's observations that we need to employ common sense when we talk about health and good diets. Furthermore, we need to consider cultural values and ideologies and not just science when we have these conversations. Using a Black womanist liberation perspective that centers the lives and health of women and young girls, I work through the ways that this story about Latrisha could have been broadened, using a combination of biomedical and cultural perspectives, compassion, and awareness, to communicate its larger points without food- and body-shaming. But first I want to say a word about Black womanist liberation and its application to food studies.

Black womanist liberation perspective is a methodological approach that centers the experiences and perspectives of Black women. Alice Walker popularized the terms "womanism" and "womanist" in her 1983 collection of essays *In Search of Our Mothers' Gardens*, where one of the definitions she provides is "appreciat[ing] and prefer[ring] women's culture, women's emotional flexibility (values tears as natural counterbalance of laughter)," and she emphasizes many of the things Black women love, including music, dance, and even the moon. Walker concludes this portion of the definition by saying that a womanist "loves the Spirit. Loves love and food and roundness. Loves struggle. Loves the Folk. Loves herself. Regardless."[29]

In addition to womanism, my approach is also based on liberation, which is grounded in Black theology. As such, it is a "theology of 'blackness.' It is the affirmation of black humanity that emancipates black people from white racism, thus providing authentic freedom for both white and black people. It affirms the humanity of white people in that it says 'no' to the encroachment of white oppression."[30] Similar to biblical scholar Cain Hope Felder and Rev. Dr. Howard-John Wesley of Alfred Street Baptist Church, both of whom I discussed at the beginning of this chapter and both of whom reject false theological arguments about Black people being cursed by God, Noah, or anyone else (sacralization), so too do I reject narratives that tell Black people we have to forsake our cultural lifeways in order to lose a few pounds. Stay with me here. A Black womanist liberation perspective finds ways to affirm the humanity of Black people, including the love of food and roundness (if that is the choice), even as it strongly advocates for overall health and well-being.

Since 2008, when the photo essay and article on her were published, I have been rereading the print and digital versions of Latrisha Avery's story. From then until now, my training as an American studies scholar working at the intersection of race, gender, and food has prompted me to recognize the ramifications of knowing that Latrisha is not eating the way she does in a vacuum. More to the point, it has led me to consider how good intentions can sometimes have an unwanted impact. For certain, many readers (myself included) are proud of the progress made by Latrisha. But it seems that if the article had provided more context, it could have avoided the instances of shaming in documenting the young girl's path to success.

Latrisha's story, as it is presented by the newspaper, is an illustration of how apparent good intentions can land on us in ways that are just as shame-inducing—if not more so—even when we do not realize it. It is also an illustration of how we can use people and situations to justify any perspective about Black and poor people if we reiterate well-worn refrains— that Black, Brown, and poor children in inner-city neighborhoods are bound to be obese because they have little access to affordable and healthy fruits and vegetables; that they are unable to adequately exercise because of violence in their neighborhoods and little or no access to parks and other recreational facilities; that they are most often surrounded by fast-food restaurants, liquor stores, and other stores that provide few options for healthy living. None of this is necessarily inaccurate or untrue. But recall the words of Nigerian writer Chimimanda Ngozi Adichie, whom I discussed earlier. In her TED Talk titled "The Danger of the Single Story," Adichie says, "Power is the ability not just to tell the story of another person but to make it the definitive story of that person. The Palestinian poet Mourid Barghouti writes that if you want to dispossess people, the simplest way to do it is to tell their story and to start with, 'secondly.'"[31]

What is Latrisha's "secondly" story? That she is obese, tall, and dark, worthy only of being teased and bullied, never desirable. But her story is actually much, much more than that. The article and photo essay are illustrations of how complex personhood can get reduced to a single story by a powerful, white-controlled corporation whose primary aim is to increase its own wealth. So here we have a very complex story, told in forty-five or more photographs along with lots of writing, and the message we are supposed to walk away with is that children like Latrisha need to take personal responsibility for their weight by eating right and exercising, no matter the obstacles. After all, there are others in her neighborhood who are small and thin. Latrisha can be, too, if she works hard enough. This important story about a young, underprivileged Black girl living in Washington, D.C., is so deeply mired in a political angle that feeds a frenzy about obesity, that readers can easily lose sight of the fact that there is a lot about Latrisha's life that they do not know. At issue here is how we frame stories—the parts we choose to tell and the parts that we choose to omit. Also at issue is how those with power try to control the complex narratives of Black lives by turning them into simple, single stories of personal accountability, or the lack thereof. These simple stories not only affect how others understand us and how we understand ourselves; they are told at the expense of our community's most vulnerable asset—our children.

Secondly. The *Washington Post* article begins with the focus on Latrisha's desire to lose weight to stave off her family history of diabetes and to keep from being bullied. Hendrix and Harris write, "Latrisha Avery knows losing weight could head off the diabetes that runs in her family. But the fifth-grader has a more immediate reason for her goal of losing 20 pounds before she starts middle school next year: So kids will stop calling her 'King Kong.'" They go on to indicate that while Latrisha is among several children in her neighborhood who are overweight, "Latrisha knows she stands out" because her height and weight "mak[e] her taller than most of her classmates and heavier than any."[32] Note that they refer to her height and her weight combined. But since she cannot control her height or her rate of growth, they must focus on her weight. And because the article is part of a series about obesity, it glosses over the many aspects of Avery's life that fall under the umbrella of American studies scholar Becky Thompson's notion of "hunger and hurting," along with "cultural trauma" and culinary dislocation. Let me explain further.

Even though the photos show Latrisha with other girls around her, the article indicates that the young teen feels isolated and alone in school. In the opening paragraphs, along with mentioning her concern about diabetes and her feeling that she is bigger and taller than her classmates, the writers say Latrisha wants to lose weight because other kids bully her about her weight. "'They pick on me all the time,' she said in a quiet voice. 'I let it go, but I do not need a bigger crowd of people talking about me. I do not need to be the heaviest girl in middle school.'"[33] Bullying among school-aged children, we know, has long been a problem, and nowadays, with social media, these vicious attacks have gotten worse. For girls in late elementary school—and certainly in middle school, when menarche often occurs—these issues can be exacerbated. Anxiety about bullying leaves young people feeling vulnerable and constantly seeking comfort from whatever and whomever they can. Sometimes that comfort comes from food. In her study on women's eating problems, Becky Thompson writes, "What girls grow up thinking is acceptable—how they can move, who they can play with, who they can touch, what they can eat and wear, and who they can trust—is determined as much by their femaleness as by their race, class, and sexuality. Understanding this offers essential clues about why many girls grow up distrusting their bodies and their appetites and why, when their bodies are belittled and manipulated, food often becomes their drug of choice."[34] In the chapter from which this passage is taken, "Hungry and Hurting," Thompson cites several reasons why young girls grow up to be women with these immensely burdensome feelings: emotional and physical abuse, heterosexism (that is, denying one's identification with lesbianism), poverty, immigration and acculturation, psychic violence, and physical violation. Some of these issues may pertain to Latrisha, as I believe she lives with a lot of cultural and psychic trauma.

By starting their newspaper article with the quotes that they chose, quotes that reveal very vulnerable feelings shared by this twelve-year old, the writers start Latrisha's story with "secondly." For one, they make it appear that the desire to lose weight is all on the shoulders of this child—alone. These are her goals and desires, and thus she is going to take responsibility. It is not that society is pressuring her to lose weight; she wants to do it for herself. This emphasis is framed by the statement, "But the fifth-grader has a more immediate reason for her goal of losing 20 pounds before she starts middle school next year." In 2008, Latrisha was in elementary school. Yet she felt immense pressure to lose weight so that she did not get teased. Adults go to excessive lengths to lose five, ten, fifteen pounds, or more; so why was society putting this kind of weight-loss pressure on a child? Moreover, where were the people to whom Latrisha can report bullying? Understandably, in the age of "snitches get stitches," she most likely would not have sought help; but was this option even made available to her? If this child so willingly shared her pain with strangers from the *Washington Post*, how likely is it that she also mentioned her anguish to some of the other adults mentioned in the exposé? The photographs included with her story showed grown-ups from at least three parts of her life—her aunt (who also may have been referred to as her godmother or maybe even her mother; it is not clear), a substitute teacher she was close to, and the volunteers at FitNut. Did all of these adults buy into the narrative that the foods she ate and the amounts she ate were all Latrisha's fault?

In the introduction to this book, I recalled how, after one of my presentations, my daughter publicly shared her own experience of being bullied by her health teacher because of her shapeliness. Having heard my public presentation on the *Washington Post* feature many times, she recalled the pain of her experiences to offer a perspective on the news article:

> [By] starting with this quote, and with this focus, [they] completely take away the innocence of this young girl and place all the blame and shame on her. If we are going to target the problem, let's target all of them. Did anyone ask what was going on at home? Where were the teachers when this bullying was going on? Is she anxious? How is her body changing? The fact that the first response to her being bullied means that *she* needs to change might follow her through life, so she believes that whenever anybody has a problem with her, she feels she needs to change. That's what trauma will do to you, and that's all it is at the end of the day—trauma. I know this story too well. . . . Having to weigh yourself in front of the whole class is horrible. . . . Even as a junior [in high school] having to get on the scale in front of everyone is crazy. . . . And for what, so everyone can see how much I weigh?[35]

This revealing testimony is echoed by Becky Thompson, who writes, "In fact, women's changed eating patterns more often begin as solutions to problems than as problems themselves."[36] Latrisha's wanting and needing to change her eating patterns is taken as a necessary solution, but nowhere is there a discussion of what is prompting her to consume so much food ("Is she anxious?"), nor is there any indication that culturally speaking, Latrisha may not buy into the American ideal of slimness. There is absolutely no mention in the article of anyone telling Latrisha that she may not have to change what she eats, that instead she may have to adjust how much she consumes in one sitting. Ultimately, the focus not only is on Latrisha losing weight but also is on eliminating the kinds of food she eats—soul food.

Until now, we have been considering Latrisha's story from the position of "secondly," a term Adichie borrows from Palestinian poet and author Mourid Barghouti, who in his memoir writes,

> It is easy to blur the truth with a simple linguistic trick: start your story from "Secondly." [Neglect] to speak of what happened first. Start your story with "Secondly," and the world will be turned upside-down. Start your story with "Secondly," and the arrows of the Red Indians are the original criminals and the guns of the white men are entirely the victims. It is enough to start with "Secondly" for the anger of the black man against the white to be barbarous.[37]

Barghouti explains how those with power can convince you that they are the actual victims and you are the perpetrator. This is one of the many ways that power is invisible but deadly to your psyche. When those with power say a thing and do a thing toward you repeatedly, you may end up believing that you are at fault and that they are the perennial victims. All the while your suffering goes ignored. This is how the cry "Black lives matter" becomes "All lives matter." It is also how Black lives only matter when we reinforce stereotypes about thugs, or violence, or drug dealing and other acts of criminality while the reasons that we sometimes get involved in many of these activities—our centuries of disenfranchisement, our anger, frustrations, and despair—are rendered unimportant or, worse, criticized and turned back on us. It is also how, by altering the order of things, the *Post* article made Latrisha responsible for the violence inflicted on her body by "bad" food, teasing, and bullying. And when it is written in a major newspaper and backed by so much science, who will question this perspective? I contend that unless we talk about the traumas and dislocations in Latrisha's life, then we are always starting her story with "Secondly." Now let us move away from this point of view for a moment and start anew.

Firstly. In both the *Washington Post* print article and its online counterpart, passing mention is made of the fact that Latrisha has been living with Veronica Gray (whom she sometimes refers to as her godmother and sometimes as her aunt) for at least a year. So we know she is not living with her biological mother or father, though we do not know why this is the case. The fact that she refers to Ms. Gray as her godmother or aunt might even suggest that they are not related at all. How might the absence of young Latrisha's blood relatives be affecting her overall disposition? For what reason is she separated from her actual kin? Where are her grandparents? Does Latrisha have siblings? If so, where are they? Does she ever see them? Might she be grieving their absence and her loss(es)? What happened in the last year that caused her to move away from where she was? When did Latrisha first begin eating a great deal of food and putting on weight? Is her consumption affected by a traumatic event or set of events? According to the news story, when Latrisha sees food, she eats, even if she is not hungry. She says it is "a habit." Is it a habit stemming from years of hunger, current nervousness, or just seeing food and always wanting it? Is her need to eat a coping mechanism to ward off loneliness, anxiety, or depression? Is her mental health causing her to eat more? Is it the reason she moved?

Let's go further. There are additional questions related to Latrisha's physical location. The journalists identify her community as one suffering from blight and lacking a grocery store but filled with liquor stores and fast food. Fair enough. But Latrisha has been living in this community for only a year. Is Ms. Gray's house a foster home? Where was Latrisha living before she moved to this location? Are there other children there? Did Latrisha have to leave friends or other children she had known since kindergarten? Was she forced to leave her home due to neglect, or physical, emotional, or sexual abuse, or even eviction? And what about her clothes and her other belongings, things to which she is attached? We know that she has a school uniform because we see it in the photos. At first glance it appears that Latrisha is dressed similarly to her classmates, but if you look closely, you can see that instead of the polo shirt that many kids wear as a required part of their uniform, she actually has on a pale-blue short-sleeved T-shirt. And we know from seeing her in several different pictures that she does everything in that shirt, including exercise. This leads me to ask, How many of these shirts does she have? Are they frequently washed? Does she have proper toiletries? Living with Ms. Gray, presumably the answer is yes. But in the pictures where Latrisha faces the camera, we are able to see that under her blue T-shirt her breasts are well developed and her stomach slightly protrudes, showing that she still has a lot of "baby fat" throughout her body. On closer examination it looks like she is not wearing proper undergarments as her growing breasts are spilling out of her bra, leaving me to wonder if she can afford better underclothes to fit her ever-growing body. The list of questions is potentially endless, but they need to be asked and considered in the constellation of conversations that surround this young child before I am convinced that losing weight will solve her problems. It may help in the short run, but what about in her future?

Given what I have asked about Latrisha's life up to this point, of paramount importance is whether she is receiving any kind of mental health counsel-ing. There can be a direct connection between mental trauma and food con-sumption. Again, I turn to Becky Thompson, who suggests, "Psychic abuse is sometimes more difficult to identify than physical assault, yet the effects can be devastating to one's sense of self. It is easy for women to deny or to minimize the damage done by psychic abuse—or by physical assaults that leave marks. . . . Both separating and ranking psychic and physical violence trivialize the consequences of trauma."[38] By focusing only on the kinds of food Latrisha eats, how often she eats and exercises, and her excess weight, the *Post* article minimizes the reality that Latrisha is a twelve-year-old girl who needs people to protect and care for her. Traumas can last a lifetime. As Kai Erikson explains, "Human beings are surrounded by layers of trust, radiating out in concentric circles like the ripples in a pond. The experience of trauma, at its worst, can mean not only a loss of confidence in the self but a loss of confidence in the scaffolding of family and community, in the structures of human government, in the larger logics by which humankind lives, and in the ways of nature itself."[39]

Latrisha's mental state is of critical importance to maintaining her dietary and lifestyle changes. Focusing on these possibly rapid life changes without addressing her entire being can lead to a lifetime of eating disorders or the worst form of self-hate. Margaret K. Bass points this out in her essay "On Being a Fat Black Girl." Bass explains that her parents raised her to be aware of what it meant to grow up in the Jim Crow South and to be confident in her Black identity and her overall racial self. What they did not do was em-brace her physical body or teach her to accept her shapeliness. Bass lived with her chubbiness in shame. And yet it was part of her physical identity, maybe even her genetic makeup—throughout most of her life, Bass's mother also struggled with maintaining a healthy weight. The result for Bass and her mother was a negative self-image that they each carried with them from childhood to adulthood. Bass grew up believing she was undesirable, that she was a "deviation from the norm," even disgusting. This is a "collective cultural attitude" that was reinforced by the man who should have protected her—her father. Instead, she watched him tease her mother incessantly by calling her "Two-Ton Tony" until she cried.[40] Watching this kind of emotional abuse over time wears on a person. Yet it is incidents such as this, which occur in and out of the home, that undergird the necessary question asked by Black feminist cultural critic Brittany Cooper: "Are Black girls ever worth fighting for?" Cooper admits that while she "still secretly hopes for a man who will fight for her honor," her reality more aligns with what many fat and full-figured Black women feel:

> As a fat feminist [I have] been in one too many rooms where brothers have gone on the attack, misreading my large body as unduly aggressive, often resorting to using their own bodies as physical intimidation, only to have other men in the room do and say nothing. It has never been fully clear to me whether I was left on my own out of resentment, passivity, or some twisted belief that it would be sexist to stand up for a feminist, especially a physically large one who seems infinitely capable of defending myself. I have learned to defend myself because I've never been able to rely on a man to do it for me.[41]

Bearing witness to this kind of incredible cruelty left an indelible mark on Bass, as it did on Cooper, as it can on any young girl or adult woman. As Cooper indicates, fatness and full-figuredness, especially when it comes to Black women, lead people to believe we are capable of taking care of ourselves and do not need any protection. But this kind of assumption also silences some women because they do not want to draw attention to themselves. They may even "live small" inside themselves. As Bass writes, "Fat silences. Fat makes you alone and lonely even when you're nine or ten. The truth of it shames you: you do not tell when people hurt you. You are ashamed to admit that you are fat—ashamed to be fat—so you do not tell unless you find someone who cares and understands."[42]

As a youngster, Bass found an African American teacher in whom she confided, believing she was a kindred spirit because the teacher was kind to her. In confidence, Bass wrote a letter to the teacher and poured out her heart, but the teacher grossly betrayed her confidence by sharing her letter with the class, referring to her as "this silly Margaret Bass." Though the *Washington Post* team may not have betrayed Latrisha's confidence by publicly discussing her weight, in some ways the journalists betrayed Latrisha in how they represented her. They told the world her story without mentioning the fuller context that surrounds and informs her habits and behaviors. No doubt, as a child, it was probably exciting for Latrisha to have her story covered by the newspaper. But as the young girl gets older, she will have to live with knowing she was considered a "problem"—a young person at risk because of her body size.

In this exposé, the *Washington Post* makes Latrisha do a lot of heavy lifting because, as I have reiterated, the journalists place the burden of her weight on

Figure 3.1. "Soul Food Sundays" banner seen at a restaurant in Birmingham, Alabama, 2012. Photo by the author.

the young girl's food consumption and a finite set of environmental factors. And all of these issues seem to be divorced from the larger systems of race and oppression that give rise to these kinds of scenarios. As briefly mentioned earlier in this discussion, one of the images in the photo gallery shows Latrisha sitting with a salad containing lettuce, slices of tomato, cucumber, red bell pepper, and tuna fish. Along with the light ranch dressing and the discarded mini crowns of broccoli, there is a cup of cut-up pineapple. Even for the most health-conscious of us, the jury may still be out on how appetizing, let alone tasty, such a lunch is when you are first starting to adjust your eating habits. For the uninitiated, not only can raw broccoli be distasteful, but it can produce a lot of flatulence or gassiness. Steaming or broiling might make it more palatable. Remembering that Latrisha is a child, we should not be surprised that she is uninterested in eating the array of fresh vegetables. When we compare this meal to one of the others we see Latrisha getting ready to eat—fried chicken wings, sliced beef, collard greens, corn pudding, potato salad, macaroni salad, sweet potato, and iced tea—few of us should be surprised by the meal she chooses. And why do her choices have to be so dramatic? So black and white, so to speak? Why can't Latrisha be allowed to eat the foods that affirm her culturally as well as eat the salad? Why must it be an either-or option?

Eating the foods that belong to the "soul food" lexicon in many Black

communities is part of a cultural tradition that is directly tied to our collective histories. So when medical advice is being sought or given, it is imperative that cultural experiences also inform and shape these conversations, so
that our whole health, including what we eat, is taken into consideration. We
know this is seldom done. Lack of affordable health care, lack of culturally
aware (even if well-intentioned) medical and nutritional professionals, and
a host of other factors constantly remind us that the system is not set up for
us to thrive. Even when we find those who will support and encourage us,
there is always something or someone that wants to convince us, albeit erro-
neously, that we are the cursed children of Ham.

In the *Post*'s narrative, Latrisha's caretaker, Veronica Gray, is referred to as
"one of Latrisha's strongest health advocates." Gray maintains that the child
has two challenges ahead of her: one is "willpower and discipline"; the other
is that the family enjoys a monthly "Soul Food Sunday." At twelve years old,
Latrisha is being asked to exercise "willpower and discipline" to reach her
fitness and dieting goals. Again, given that many adults spend a lifetime trying to put a check in this box, how likely is it that Latrisha will be successful
over time, let alone in the short run? She is already primed to fail according
to the benchmarks that she is expected to meet. For one, changing your eating habits, especially when cultural traditions are at play, is not necessarily
about discipline, nor is it just about changing what you eat, as Kimberly Nettles-Barcelon argues in her article "'Saving' Soul Food." She writes,

> If . . . the food itself is the culprit, then the answer is simply to stop
> consuming it. Yet the threat of disease and death fails to quell the urge
> to prepare and consume foods that are part of a cultural tradition, that
> are valued as a positive part of our communal life. . . . The plethora of
> "light" soul food cookbooks attempt to "save" soul food by encouraging
> the retelling of narratives that honor family, love, and community while
> simultaneously advocating personal responsibility and restraint. Even
> so, they do not go far enough. . . . These books pay very little attention to
> the problems endemic to our contemporary food system that contribute
> to disease and environmental degradation.[43]

As Nettles-Barcelon insists, focusing almost solely on foodstuffs means over-
looking other issues that contribute to disease—racism (environmental and
daily microaggressions), sexism, systemic inequalities, and the like. As social
epidemiologist Nancy Krieger reminds us, socioeconomic considerations are

very important, and "poor people living in poor neighborhoods are likely to have poorer health than equally poor people living in more affluent neighborhoods." These observations, Krieger explains, offer challenges to "aetiologic explanations and policy interventions." The data in social epidemiology has long since revealed that "racial discrimination at any economic level can harm health among African Americans, above and beyond—and also compounding—socioeconomic deprivation brought about by such discrimination." Krieger further suggests that we are best served by recognizing who "deliberately or inadvertently benefits from these inequalities, so as to inform efforts to secure social equity in health. Staying grounded in history can help us both avoid notions of a technocratic 'quick fix.'"[44]

Thus, if we focus on food in conjunction with these other variables, we will find a combination of issues that affect the health and well-being of Black people. This is not to suggest that eating large amounts of fatty foods rich in butter, sugar, and other ingredients often heralded by the pages of *Southern Living* will not ultimately cause concern, especially if we do not also exercise. The literature on obesity is plentiful in every direction, from agreeing to disagreeing about this. I am concerned, however, that our prescriptions seem to have no middle ground. I am further concerned about the lack of history and culture in these sweeping recommendations, which grandly lead to food shaming and culinary policing.

In the *Post* article, Ms. Gray points out that the other "challenge" for Latrisha is that the family enjoys a monthly "Soul Food Sunday." But why should this be viewed as a challenge and not a wonderful benefit to the twelve-year old? For all the rhetoric about slow food and home cooking, here we have a caretaker who cooks, and it is being read as a problem. Latrisha's guardian teaches her to cook, and even more important, they both "enjoy their power cooking sessions." Why are we not celebrating both this powerful transmission of culture and female bonding between caretaker and child? In any racial or ethnic group, maintaining and passing down cultural traditions is often done through food. There is a power in celebrating food traditions, and cooking together can be a major act of familial bonding, even if it is between fictive kin. Fictive kin can still be kin. But here, we are not told of the many creative and beautiful ways that the two generations of women bond in the kitchen. The world over, we know that kitchens are everything. It is where people gather, no matter how young or old. It is where important conversations take place and major decisions are made. It is where some households maintain strict religious practices or traditions that involve not just one but two refrigerators as part of the cultural heritage. It is where some people were born and some have died. It is where marriages are signed and sealed and divorces are delivered, and so on, and so on. Why, then, are Black kitchens being made out to be an exception to this well-established fact? Let me relieve you of any ways you have been misinformed about Black kitchens.

In addition to being a site of celebration, culinary historian Michael Twitty reminds us, the kitchen was also a site of violence during enslavement. More than any other space in the house, perhaps, it was a "site of rape after rape, sexual violations that led to one of the more unique aspects of African American identity—our almost inextricable blood connection to white Southerners. . . . These were not neutral spaces; these were places of power against the enslaved in the most dehumanizing way possible."[45] Long after enslavement, kitchens continued to be places of violence, as several historians have reminded us when discussing African American women who did live-in or days work in other folks' kitchens.[46] In the 1980s, Barbara Smith and Audre Lorde told us the kitchen was "the center of the home, the place where women in particular work and communicate with each other." In founding Kitchen Table: Women of Color Press, these two and many others "wanted to convey the fact that we are a kitchen table, grassroots operation, begun and kept alive by women who cannot rely on inheritances or other benefits of class privilege to do the work we need to do."[47] Photographer Carrie Mae Weems showed us this vision in black-and-white with her *Kitchen Table* photography series. In it we see everything from heterosexual Black love to a Black woman lovingly doing another Black woman's hair, from a baby girl learning about makeup to a Black woman sitting alone in quiet contemplation or maybe consternation. We see sister-friends laughing and crying with one another, and we feel the strained silence between a man and a woman, whether lovers, partners, siblings, or friends, we do not know. These black-and-white photographs are taken in a room, around a table, under a single low-hanging light bulb. They reflect joy, sadness, anxiety, despair, anger, and a range of other emotions. They are arresting for the ways in which they appear to imply simplicity and yet bear witness to human complexities.[48]

While many communities revere their kitchens for good food and conversation, Black folks celebrate the kitchen not just for the food that is cooked but also for the hair that is pressed (and burned), the drinks that are poured, the makeup that is applied, the laughter that is heard, and the tears that are cried. It is why today we readily recognize the intent when Jada Pinkett Smith, her daughter, Willow, and her mother, Adrienne, invite us to pull up a chair on *Red Table Talk* for candid conversations about life, no matter how ready we are. Because we know, as Twitty writes, the kitchen is "a place of worry, argument, and resolution,"[49] and it is also a place to live in your truth, whether gay, straight, queer, trans, or +. Jessica Walker also lets us know that so much happens in and around the "nervous landscape" of the kitchen, from issues of sexuality to those of raciality and cultural shaming, so that the space is a "central site of instability."[50]

In Latrisha's case, the kitchen also is a classroom, and it may also be one of her few places of refuge as she and her guardian work through some issues that might emerge during intimate conversations. Some of the questions I asked earlier about Latrisha might engender feelings of fear, disappointment, or intense sadness, or even trigger a mental health episode. Bringing up these issues while they are cooking might go far toward stimulating thoughts of healing rather than those that can cause young people to try (sometimes successfully) to end their own lives. When we think about all of this and the reasons why this young teen is living with Ms. Gray, as well as the amount of nurturing, emotional and physical care work that Gray must do to help Latrisha feel safe, perhaps we can understand the importance of cooking as holding critical space for doing important cultural work. Using cooking to introduce and instill African American culture in their home helps Latrisha be grounded and establishes a sense of belonging, a much-needed embodied process in the wake of unbelonging and trauma.[51] In her work on race, place, and taste, scholar Emily Walmsley explains,

> As with all the senses, taste and smell must be understood as culturally defined experiences that are physical, embodied processes. A particular taste or smell may invoke revulsion in one person but bring enormous pleasure to another. . . . Sensory knowledge is ingrained in people through their socialization in particular cultural settings. This early embedding of sensory associations leads to visceral responses to tastes and smells throughout a person's life, which identifies him or her with the cultural environment in which he or she was raised. . . . Sensory experience, therefore, draws attention to the processual nature of cultural identities: tastes and smells can be powerful markers of difference or belonging, but they are not fixed as one or the other. Their meanings are shifting, contingent, multiple and diverse.[52]

But in the *Washington Post* article, all of this critical cultural history is rendered subordinate to the argument that obesity kills young people. So despite our excitement that young Latrisha is thriving in the kitchen with her kin, we are told by a photo's caption that "the monthly ritual [of power cooking] often leads to unhealthy portions." Another caption tells us that dinner most often includes fried chicken, macaroni and cheese, roasted potatoes, mashed potatoes, and yams. Yet another reports that Gray "tries to lighten their Sunday feasts, occasionally serving turkey ham and leaving the fatback out of the greens. She also presses Latrisha to serve herself sensible portions, or 'lady plates' instead of 'truck driver plates.'"[53] With all of this going on in the photo gallery and news article, we can hardly really blame Gray for such an obviously sexist comment. And what else is Gray supposed to say if she is lacking any perspective but the one that blames Latrisha for not having enough willpower and simultaneously tries to make her fit into a narrow box of societal standards of beauty that never, ever applied to Black women—not even to this day, ever?

In this instance, Gray becomes like some of the other Black women previously discussed throughout this book sitting in a crooked chair in a crooked room who try to align themselves vertically. Gray is doing what she has to do and may not realize that she is in a no-win situation with these journalists and this story. No matter the praise she gives herself or the joy her family finds in Soul Food Sundays and the conviviality that comes with this event, the point of the essay is to vilify the food, culinary lifestyles, to some extent Ms. Gray, and certainly Latrisha. Because no matter how much background about Latrisha is presented or how much the young girl tries to tell people she is struggling to survive, the article's goal remains to emphasize that Latrisha is obese and that she, the people and environment around her, not to mention the food, are the primary blame.

If you think this is not the case, then consider what else we learn from the story, some of which we can infer from what is omitted. We are not told, for example, what the family eats the rest of the month, but the mention of Soul Food Sunday suggests that this type of food is reserved for that day and that day only. So it seems we are to believe that Latrisha's weight is the result of this once-a-month "transgression." But, far from being unhealthy, this monthly ritual might be helping Latrisha thrive. Spending time cooking with her caretaker may be calming for her because in the kitchen she learns creativity, she learns what seasonings go together, what cooking temperature is required for different foods, how to chop and clean greens so you do not bite down on grit or dirt—even when they are precut and bagged. She learns how to fry chicken, and season ham, and make cakes and macaroni and cheese from scratch. All of this is powerful emotional labor being done by Ms. Gray, and it is being poured into a child who appears not to get this kind of loving attention elsewhere. Gray is passing down recipes and knowledge about cooking that will be remembered, modified, and adjusted as they are needed, when they are needed—an excellent skill to have when one enters adulthood and has to fend for one's culinary self. And though we do not know if Latrisha cooks often, the article lets us know that Latrisha finds some of her joy in cooking. One photo, for example, shows Latrisha happy, smiling, and laughing when she finds out she will be attending a culinary school over the summer. Ms. Gray also enjoys cooking and lets the journalists know this when she shares, "We're not big drinkers or big smokers, but we have *food*," drawing out the word for emphasis. 'That's the joy; that's the good feeling. Food is comforting.'"

But, sadly, the reporters chose not to conclude their piece on Latrisha with this joyful note celebrating the cultural foodways of this Black family. Nor does it end by suggesting that, while practicing such traditions, Latrisha and her family could engage in a combination of strategies that would not only reinforce their traditions but also allow Latrisha to consume some foods that are lower in calories. Instead, the story ends with a comment from Ms. Gray voicing condemnation and demonization: "But in the long run, [the food] is only hurting us." Ending the story in this way, with this negative portrayal of Gray's and Avery's cultural mores, takes the focus off the array of issues that are most likely plaguing this family and especially this young girl. And it is here that the admonitions of both Nettles-Barcelon and Krieger have purchase. As African Americans, we need to redefine the food stories that are told about our culture and stop allowing others to tell us our food and foodways are bad for our health, our lives, our very being. Every culture has foods that are not good for them, especially when prepared with excessively fatty or sugary ingredients—oil, butter, cheese, sugar, and even honey. Yet these ingredients are consistently heralded in magazines highlighting "good" food, on social media platforms as food porn, and on reality TV shows as hallmarks of haute cuisine. Though there may be an occasional comment about high cholesterol or other health issues, everyone wants to know the recipe, or the kinds of implements used in the cooking process, or, humorously, when they will be invited over for dinner. Yet African Americans and the foods we consume are constantly deemed overly unhealthy and toxic.

One way we can intervene in these discussions—about policy or other topics—is by not buying into the rhetoric of demonization and degradation of the foods that help to create and sustain our communities without interrogating the origins and motivations of that rhetoric. What kinds of value judgments are made when African American men, women, and children are being told not to eat various foods? Why is one kind of eating privileged over another? Let me be very clear: this is not an argument for eating unhealthily—however an individual defines this term for themselves. We, as African Americans, need to be transparent about how we feel after eating certain foods: sluggish, satisfied, satiated, happy, cranky, and so on. In concert with health professionals, if necessary, we should decide how foods feel in our bodies. What feelings—physical, social, emotional, communal—are engendered by our eating certain foods? We also need to ask why our food consumption seems to garner so much attention. What is it about Black people in the act of eating that drives some people absolutely nuts? Why can we not decide how we want to live our culinary lives, just like everyone else? For example, why does the Food Network's celebrity host, restaurateur Guy Fieri, get to transgress when it comes to food, eating any and everything he chooses—as well as the many other white men before him and those who will follow—but the average Black person cannot do so without being criticized? Why are Black people the subject of everyone's gaze and everyone, including random strangers, feels empowered to comment on our food practices? What is it about Black people that makes everyone believe they have the right to comment on our personal food habits and behaviors? These are the questions we need to be asking.

This point reminds me of a study by sociologist Nicolas Larchet, who conducted an ethnography in Washington, D.C., at a corner market. He rightly argues that consumers are not "passive recipients" or "powerless victims" of the market and its forces. So food choices—what we eat, when, why, and how—and the many variations, selections, and decisions concerning them are wide-ranging and are made for a number of reasons. For example, one of Larchet's informants, James, "an obese, unemployed man," often goes into the corner market and buys a chicken platter with fries, which he tends to salt heavily. When Neshia, the African American cook for the market, sees him doing this, she "screams," "Oh! That's too much salt! Do you want a blood pressure test? You're gonna die!" To this, James replies, "That's how I want to leave!"[54]

The status of African American food culture is in a catch-22, like many other aspects of African American expressive culture. We bring so much to American society, but so little of it is appreciated. African American expressive culture is borrowed and stolen unrelentingly, most often without attribution. And when it is recognized, it is primarily so that it can be regulated and critiqued. This is the way surveillance, policing, and shaming work, and it is partially what cultural critic Greg Tate means by "everything but the burden." In his book of the same name, Tate expounds on the thin line between whites and other races of people loving Black culture and co-opting it for their own pleasure, without actually wanting to be Black or to carry the "burden" of what it means to be Black in America.[55]

Non–African Americans will eat what we call soul food and travel miles to do so, try to cook these foods, and even speak with reverence about these foods, while simultaneously chastising Black people for doing the same thing. Recognizing these contradictions, we must also stop allowing others to criticize and demean our foods, because when we do so, we permit people to erase major aspects of African American family, history, and culture. Our foods have been used to liberate and to wage protests; to secure homes, businesses, and places of worship; to feed the hungry and clothe the naked. The commensality and communalism associated with food cultures have sustained weary African American travelers in times of fear, relocation, and dislocation. From working in other people's kitchens to owning our own commercial kitchens through entrepreneurship, African Americans have used food "[to sustain] Black strategies for self-reliance and dignity, the preservation of historical memory, and civil rights and social mobility."[56] African American foodways have been a major part of the culinary, social, emotional, psychological, and economic fabric of America. So no one should be allowed to discount all of this rich and powerful history, whether it is in a book or sitting on a dinner plate, and especially when and if this history is celebrated only once or twice a month. In short, Latrisha should not have to give up corn pudding in favor of a raw salad that she may not even like. Helping her instead grapple with the harder issues with which she has to contend may ultimately lead to the lifestyle changes our society is so desperate for her to make.

But disparagement is the work of anti-Black racism and colonization. It seeps into our souls with the intent of making one feel ashamed of their life in ways that keeps them defeated and unmoored. It begins with scripts that include the deliberate and subtle, and not so subtle, devaluation of a culture by shaming what is cooked, how it is cooked, and when, how, and where it is cooked and consumed. This power to define what is correct, proper, and legible is exercised at the expense of honoring and crediting African American people. It is incumbent upon African Africans to work on decolonizing our minds so that praise and celebration replace shame and embarrassment. Decolonizing is a part of recognizing that food is complicit in the racial project of the "afterlife" of slavery, as described by Ashanté Reese and Hanna Garth. Building off the work of theorist Saidiya Hartman, who describes how slavery's racialized violence and horror persist today in "skewed life chances, limited access to health and education, premature death, incarceration, and impoverishment," Reese and Garth argue that "it is not enough to simply examine race in the food system. We must also consider how the food system is part of the larger structures that, by design, were never created for Black survival."[57]

And this is particularly what we mean when we say "Black lives matter." On a daily basis, debates surge around whose lives matter most, all the while missing the point that Black lives, lifeways, and existences are important because society does so much to tell us that they are not. Having emerged in the aftermath of the continuing racial unrests occurring in the United States, the slogan #BlackLivesMatter came to define the protests in Orlando, Florida, and Ferguson, Missouri—following the murders of Trayvon Martin and Michael Brown, respectively—where unarmed African American teenagers and men were killed by police. When I began work on this book, Trayvon Martin, Michael Brown, and Tamir Rice were among those most recently shot and killed by white people. In the years since, as I continued my work on this book, Eric Garner, Alton Sterling, Philando Castile, Botham Jean, Freddie Gray, George Floyd, and Ahmaud Arbery—not to mention the many others whose names we do not know or who have not made national news—were killed with impunity by white state violence. This includes the numerous Black women and girls who have been assaulted and killed.

Secondly. And herein lies another problem with the framing of Latrisha's story—the erasure of her identity as a young Black girl. In 2012, twenty-two-year-old Rekia Boyd was killed by an off-duty Chicago police detective. In 2015, twenty-eight-year-old Sandra Bland was found hanging in a jail cell in Waller County, Texas, three days after being arrested during a traffic stop. Atatiana Jefferson and Breonna Taylor both were shot inside their homes by white male law enforcement officers. Black trans woman Roxanne Moore was shot by police in 2020. Police handcuffed unclothed Anjanette Young during a botched raid conducted soon after she came home from work. These are all African American women. But countless African American girls have gone missing, and we know nothing about their whereabouts. Video recordings reveal too many instances of white male law enforcement body-slamming young Black girls to the ground, sometimes knocking them unconscious in the process. In their news article "'I Am a Child!': Pepper Spray Reflects Policing of Black Kids," correspondents Deepti Hajela and Lindsay Whitehurst write about the 2021 incident in Rochester, New York, where a nine-year-old African American girl who was in the midst of a mental health episode was handcuffed and placed in the back seat of a police cruiser. According to police body-camera footage, while she was waiting the scared and anxious girl cried out repeatedly for her father to protect her. According to news reports, as the police tried to wrestle the young child into the vehicle, they grew impatient with her. At some point, the child wailed, "Officer, please don't do this to me." The officer responded, "You did it to yourself, hon." After issuing another warning, "This is your last chance," the police officer threatened, "Pepper spray is going in your eyeballs." Critical to this exchange was the officer's admonition to the child, "You're acting like a child!" to which the girl replies, "I am a child!"[58]

Throughout this discussion of Latrisha, I have repeatedly and deliberately referred to her age of twelve years, because I intended to remind the readers that she is, indeed, a child, not even a teen. My goal was to point out that she is being treated like an adult, having to assume a great deal of responsibility related to her food habits and behaviors. But she is not an adult, and this is part of the "adultification" of young African American children in American society. By taking pictures of Latrisha from floor level, the report attempts to magnify her size vis-à-vis the other children. And by taking pictures of Latrisha alongside her friends, they provide more visual evidence to further amplify the girls' body dissimilarities, none of which should be judged as deviant. In the Associated Press news story mentioned above, Hajela and Whitehurst write, "Research shows Black children are often viewed as being older than they are, with greater chances to be seen as threatening or dangerous. Advocates tell us how police treat them in ways they wouldn't dare treat white children. In some cases, it has led to fatalities like the killing of Tamir Rice, a Black 12-year-old shot by a white police officer in Cleveland in 2014," along with so many others.[59]

Aside from an image of her on a playground, the *Washington Post*'s coverage of Latrisha strips away her innocence. Nowhere is she allowed to simply be a kid—a kid who loves to eat, as many kids do. She is not praised for walking home from school every day, also a form of exercise, or for being a relatively good seamstress, though we are told she wanted to wear her "self-sewn blouse" to church on Easter Sunday morning. Instead, one of the online photo captions indicates, "She couldn't finish the alterations in time. The blouse's pattern needed 6 more inches to accommodate Latrisha's frame." Journalist Stacy Patton describes it this way: "America does not extend the fundamental elements of childhood to black boys and girls. Black childhood is considered innately inferior, dangerous and indistinguishable from black adulthood. Black children are not afforded the same presumption of innocence as white children, especially in life-or-death situations."[60] Blackness is the key determinant for the lack of protection; not even with regard to an everyday item like food can we be free.

One might argue that other children of various races were also spotlighted by the *Washington Post*. This is true. But by trying to emphasize the universality of obesity by including children of all races and classes, the editors in effect denied the significance of race. This seemingly racially colorblind project represented race as inconsequential. Very little in society is race-neutral, including food. So, in operating from this premise, the *Post*'s editors set Latrisha up to take the fall, because they never acknowledge the myriad structural issues surrounding her that significantly affect how she lives her life. Even from the cursory reading provided here, it appears that there are many issues that this young girl has to deal with. The article acts as if she were not hampered by race, class, and gender inequalities put into place by decades of structures and systems that are not designed to benefit someone like her. Instead, the overall portrayal of Latrisha is one that suggests that her progress is impeded by her own lack of willpower—even her caretaker thinks this is the case. But this is the point of power: when it is conveyed through eloquent writing or a well-spoken tongue, it can blur the truth, omit facts, and leave out major parts of the story, and it can simply neglect to speak of what happened first, and focus instead on *secondly*. This kind of misinformation dissemination is what gives rise to notions that link heavier bodies only to "bad" eating and laziness. This unproductive and uncreative way of thinking about people and their lives occludes the host of other reasons why a person might be full figured. To be sure, it can be from overeating, but it could also be that Latrisha takes medications that can rapidly add many pounds to her young body. Or it could be that she has undiagnosed or undetected medical and health concerns, or it could be that a host of other stressors in her life caused the child's weight gain, many of which are on full display to anyone who reads her story with a compassionate and careful eye. And herein lies an important point—she is a child, so the conversations and recommendations for her life should take this reality into account. But sadly, the article, at times, does not. In not emphasizing the lack of control Latrisha has over her life, we can forget she is only twelve years old. Hajela and Whitehurst quote Kristin Henning, law professor and director of the Juvenile Justice Clinic and Initiative at Georgetown Law: "Black children have really been seen as older, more culpable, less amenable to rehabilitation and less worthy of the Western notions of innocence and the Western notions of childhood."[61] And being "less worthy" of innocence also means that they are less deserving of the care and protection other children receive. So, from this assessment, full-figured African American girls like Latrisha should be able to exercise determination and resolve, to control her body, and to make it behave in a way that is non-threatening to society, to their families, and especially to their friends, so as to avoid being bullied. Okay.

This conversation explains why and how food and discussions around food are always connected to both racial and economic injustice, even though we may believe this is all a recent phenomenon. Societies are still affected by thought patterns that either consciously or unconsciously imbue white societies with positive characteristics (such as progressive, active, smart, productive) while Black people and cultures are associated with the opposite qualities (unenlightened, lazy, unintelligent, unproductive, and non-progressive). In a society where thinness is seen as a measure of self-control, the opposite is interpreted as a lack of restraint. Heavy bodies are read as morally weak. And when you combine these ideologies with racial signifiers, the result is public opinions that correlate being overweight with being lazy, undisciplined, and morally bankrupt. In his essay "The Origins of Black Body Politics," communication scholar Ronald Jackson sets out to address the question of how Black bodies first became a "problem." He argues, "Black bodies were inscribed with a set of meanings, which helped to perpetuate the scripter's racial ideology. Through these scripts, race gradually became its own corporeal politics."[62] These "scripts" extended to cultural products like food, clothing, music, cars, and other material goods. Stereotypes and images that sought to denigrate African American men, women, and children using foods such as chicken and watermelon were—and, as I have discussed, continue to be—pervasive, perpetrated in large part through popular culture. As Jackson explains, narratives like these that socially assign Black bodies to an "underclass" had their origins in the institutions of "slavery and the mass media." Today, this includes social media, with its ability to reach vast audiences with haste. Sabrina Strings offers a similar point of view in *Fearing the Black Body*:

The Racial Origins of Fat Phobia when she suggests the current fat-phobia bias was born not of the medical field but of the racial scientific literature of the eighteenth century that claimed fatness was "'savage' and 'black.'" To this end, she maintains that the phobias about fat have always already been infused with a racial dimension, debunking the notion that slimness is all about "empirical medical findings." Strings argues that fat phobia is more in line with Bourdieu's concept of "social distinctions." She writes, "The elites of society have used the denial of food, along with 'social censorships which forbid coarseness and fatness, in favor of slimness' to prove the superiority of those who sit atop the social hierarchy."[63]

What these scripts reveal is that Black people's bodies are inscribed with and socially constructed by race meanings and representations, thus rendering them politicized in their apparent differences. From slavery to the present, representatives of state power—slave masters, police, and others imbued with the authority to regulate behaviors and enforce order—have sought to control African American minds, bodies, and spirits. African American cultural expression—food, dance, language, clothing—is often considered outside the bounds of civility and morality and thus in need of regulation by the state. This is why white people believe they can shoot Black men for playing loud music, or for not moving aside when they walk on the sidewalk, or for any other everyday action that ordinarily would not cause a person to even look twice.[64] In these kinds of scenarios—and in the one that opens this book where the Black female D.C. Metro worker is surveilled and reported on while eating on the train—Black bodies are devalued and read as unruly and always out of control, an ideology not far removed from a master/slave dichotomy.

These kinds of perceptions have always surrounded Black communities. The messages might be delivered in different ways, but the implication is always the same. This is why I thought it prudent to open this chapter with a remark from the 2020 film *Cut Throat City*. In this film, three young Black men struggle in the aftermath of Hurricane Katrina. Following the hurricane, as people try to reclaim their lives, their homes, and their families and to find their way forward, these young men become even more locked in the cycle of poverty that prevented them from evacuating the city. Though the hurricane waters have receded, the ones that engulf their lives continue; the young men are in despair. Blink, the main character, is an aspiring artist who is working on a graphic novel he calls *Cut Throat City*. He becomes defeated and disgruntled after he is denied a chance to publish his work, and he and his family are denied FEMA benefits because his wife works a low-wage job and thus makes a dollar or two more than what is allowed. Blink looks to make fast money with little or no success. In fact, most of his attempts to get ahead are thwarted or end tragically, with his friends getting killed one by one. In a moment of intense realization, Blink says, "Katrina has always been with us; it has a bunch of different names." Though a fictional character, Blink has never lied. Katrina has always been with Black folk and it has always had a bunch of names, many of which I have already discussed. Most of these names are informed by misguided beliefs, propelled in no small way by the surveillance of Black people's bodies, which leads to a constant reading of African American communities as always lacking and always in need of help, even when none (or little that will actually change our lives for the better) is forthcoming.

These kinds of perceptions fuel the beliefs that wholeness and health are not in the interest of Black communities. For instance, it is not accurate that African Americans dislike exercise. But when we do not work out in the "right" places, wear the "right" clothing, or do the "right" exercises, then it is assumed we do not care about our health. For example, at the end of the online photo essay of Latrisha, one of the last photos we see before she is jumping for glee at having completed the FitNut program is her on the floor grimacing as she attempts to do a sit-up. The caption reminds us that by the time she leaves elementary school, she hopes to also leave behind the cruel teasing and being called "King Kong." The juxtaposition of the caption and the image implies that Latrisha just needs to get herself in gear and do these sit-ups so she can achieve her goal. She needs to let these volunteers help her control her body so she is more acceptable to her friends and those who tease and bully her. She needs, in other words, to put in that work. Unbeknownst to Latrisha, her inability to do the exercises recommended by FitNut and other volunteer health projects can easily be interpreted by *Washington Post* readers as a personal failure. Omitted from this conversation—and perhaps not even considered or presented to Latrisha—are the numerous ways she might enjoy getting exercise that do not require the grimacing strain she feels she needs to put herself through so that others will like her and treat her like a human being. Walking home from school with her friends at a brisk pace is but one example.

When our bodies are saddled with a few extra pounds, it is always easy to assume that we eat too much and that our kitchens are too unhealthy. But rarely is it considered that our diseases are exacerbated by the vicissitudes of life and myriad systemic inequalities. It is only occasionally considered that our neighborhoods still may not be safe, even when they are not riddled with gunfire. As we know from living in the United States, a midday jog, for a Black man or woman, can easily become our last outing in life, even when it is in a familiar community. Little consideration seems to be given to the ways that socioeconomics can constrain our physical and emotional movements, not just the ability to relocate but also moving about in our everyday lives.

Some of these issues came to light in May 2012 when literary scholar Alice Randall wrote an op-ed for the *New York Times* titled "Black Women and Fat," in which she claimed Black women are fat because "we want to be" and it is the way our men want us.[65] I followed the heated discussion online, as the article generated a lot of controversy. The online responses to the piece illuminated the many sides of the argument, including acknowledgment that the issue is multifaceted and much too complex for an op-ed to allow Randall fully to "speak her truth." As a result, many readers felt that her point of view came across as oversimplified and that the newspaper chose a headline that was more of an attention-grabber than a reflection of what Randall wrote. On one listserv in particular the responses ranged from arguments for doing away with the notion that Black women's bodies are all the same to arguments claiming that Black people, especially Black women, actually do not like to exercise because washing our hair daily is not optimal for our hair textures and styles. In a rebuttal op-ed, sociologist Rashawn Ray pointed to his own research into why there is such a low rate of physical activity among Black women. Among many barriers, Ray identified three that were common among middle-class Black women: little spare time, fewer accessible facilities and green spaces, and male-dominated gyms and public spaces. According to Ray, 25 percent of college-educated Black women are single parents, meaning they have very little spare time for a variety of activities. If lack of time, fewer accessible facilities, and male-dominated gyms pervade middle-class communities, these variables are most likely intensified among lower-class and working poor Black women, who have even fewer material resources.[66]

Randall's position was not a new one, as the discussion in chapter 1 illustrates. Ava Purkiss, scholar of American culture and women's studies, explained in an interview that there is a long history of "intraracial black fat contempt." She said, "Historical evidence shows that black women did not accept fatness with open arms as some imagine. Black men were also critical of fatness and decried fat black women in the public sphere." Addressing this issue in another context, Purkiss explained that she began her thesis research project assuming

> that health would be the only motivator for black women to participate in exercise because, in the early 20th century, black women experienced high rates of infant mortality, maternal mortality, tuberculosis, and infectious diseases. But during my research, I also found that black women used very alarming language to encourage themselves and others to exercise. They describe [other Black] fat women as lazy, sluggish, ugly, abnormal—and those are cited in primary sources. . . . So, a key takeaway from this 20th century cultural exercise is that black people, particularly black women, are not immune from fat-shaming. Fat disdain functions as a way for black women to challenge these racist ideas about their "excessive bodies."[67]

The comments from myriad chatrooms and groups addressing Randall's op-ed revealed that Black women's body image, fat or slim, was still very much a vexed issue. But the online discussion also revealed that many African American women actually do exercise.

Prior to the publication of Randall's op-ed, an organization known as Black Girls RUN! (BGR) was established. Most likely being intimately familiar with the barriers mentioned above by Rashawn Ray, BGR operates within and around the misconceptions about Black women and exercise. Under the banner "Of Course Black Girls Run," the organization writes,

> There's a huge misconception that black women don't run. In 2009, Black Girls RUN! was created to tackle the growing obesity epidemic in the African American community and provide encouragement and resources to both new and veteran runners. . . . The goal of "Black Girls Run" is to encourage and motivate black women to practice a healthy lifestyle. We want to serve as a fitness resource for runners and gym rats alike, as well as provide tips and commentary on staying active and maintaining a healthy lifestyle. We want to start a movement to encourage ALL women to get off the couch and get active.[68]

GirlTrek is another organization started by two African American women college friends in Los Angeles, California. The two began their organization in 1996 by bonding over "2Pac, Nikki Giovanni, and their inability to say no to smothered pork chops." They said GirlTrek was never an "'aha moment' but a shared belief in radical acts of self-care." This self-care movement now encourages others to walk toward "freedom," as Harriet Tubman did. Its goal is to encourage Black women and girls to fight for injustice and walk to heal their bodies at the same time. Their website says, "Wherever there's injustice you can find GirlTrek on the frontlines. We walk to heal our bodies, inspire our daughters and reclaim the streets of our neighborhood." Their web page also includes the following definition of the term "GirlTrek":

GirlTrek
\gûrl-'trek\

- (v.) To lace up our sneakers and walk each day as a declaration of self-care!
- (v.) To heal our bodies, inspire our daughters, and reclaim the streets of our neighborhoods.
- (v.) To reestablish walking as a healing tradition in Black communities as tribute to those who walked before us.
- (n.) A health movement organized by volunteers across America to inspire one million by 2020.[69]

As I frequently reread the *Washington Post*'s coverage of Latrisha, I could not help but wonder if she had been introduced to either of these organizations, as both are nationwide and BGR has a very active and large following in the DMV area. While there is nothing wrong with volunteer organizations like FitNut, the exercise program that Latrisha completed, once the program ended what would she do? What is the follow-up to ensure that she continues to remain active, whether walking, running, yoga, Zumba, or any other exercise?

I thought about all of this as I considered the options available to this young girl and other Black children like her. How could Latrisha continue to enjoy the foods that are appetizing and culturally relevant to her without overeating? And even if she does overeat occasionally, who is teaching her to balance this kind of consumption with regular exercise and other forms of self-care? And perhaps most importantly, who is helping Latrisha to assess her mental, emotional, and social health and offering her some kind of necessary assistance? Another, more fruitful, long-term paradigm may be to let Latrisha know that it is perfectly fine to indulge in the kinds of foods that she likes. She does not have to live her life in dichotomies—choosing either this *or* that. There are a number of ways that she can have both and still be healthy. Teaching Latrisha and her godmother that they can bake instead of deep-fry or panfry fish, chicken, lamb, tempeh, tofu, spinach, and portobello, might be one option. Introducing them to different combinations of vegetables—succotash for example (butter beans, corn, and maybe tomatoes), sweet potatoes, eggplant, carrots, cauliflower, and so many other vegetables can be introduced to provide a variety of tastes and textures. Introducing salads with lemon, oil, red wine vinegar, spices, and other ingredients that are lower in calories might be another option. And they absolutely can still have the monthly indulgence that is rich with culinary tradition by using less calorie-dense ingredients or recognizing the higher calorie meal and thus eat less of it. Finally, cooking larger amounts and freezing the leftovers for the week might help to also reduce some of the added stress of midweek meal preparation. Forcing Latrisha into an either/or situation—in any part of her life—already primes her not to succeed, because few of us live our lives in this way. Most of us live in the in-between of contradiction, which makes us what singer, songwriter, and actress Jill Scott calls "beautifully human."

Rejecting the either/or dichotomy seems to be at the heart of the My-Pyramid Program, which has been reconfigured to reflect the food cultures of different racial and ethnic groups in America. Based on the recommendations set forth by the *Dietary Guidelines for Americans*, the most recent version of which was released in 2020, the food pyramid can guide individual food choices. Nowadays, the guidelines suggest adapting the pyramid to fit one's cultural beliefs and practices, whether it is in choosing tortillas or rice from the grains group or choosing beans, tofu, and turkey wings from the meat and beans group. Using these newly developed models will begin to lessen some of the divisions that foster the notion that there is or needs to be a separation between one's cultural background and their food consumption habits. Today, many organizations are teaching and advocating for food policies that recognize an additional need to work with extended families—such as grandmothers and other women who may head families (and thus have a different historical experience of cooking certain foods)—instead of focusing solely on individual family members. Organizations like the Food Trust are raising awareness about the lack of supermarkets in many urban communities—Philadelphia, New York, Chicago, and Washington, D.C., among others. They are also crafting life strategies (dietary and those related to physical activity) in neighborhoods lacking affordable food sources, green spaces, and facilities. They are doing all of this in such a way that gives power to those in the community, a point to which I will return in the final chapter. These organizations are doing what they can by using a perspective of "corrective and restorative action" that is grounded in culture and biomedical science. I call the approach "corrective and restorative action" because Harris and Nowverl found in their 1999 study that before the 1960s, African Americans had the best dietary habits in the U.S., notwithstanding ethnic, economic, social, cultural, and environmental differences, because we relied upon our own homegrown foods and our communities to sustain us.[70]

Creating healthy bodies requires a redefinition of the food stories that impact African American culture. But it also requires that we push back against acts of sacralization that seek to attach scriptures to racially motivated points of view and other historical perceptions that seek to keep us bound in a Katrina-esque state of racial, cultural, economic, and psychic trauma. Redefining and pushing back is part of the work that helps us to heal bodies as well as minds. Healing occurs when we take into consideration the whole person: the cultural, biomedical, economic, and social being. If we accept this as true and use our humanistic selves, then we can intervene in questions of nutrition and food policy by discouraging people from demonizing and degrading the foods that help communities "to keep on keepin' on." This corrective and restorative work, however, is far from simple. Not only does it require the voices of those who work in the humanities to inform food policies, but it also requires individual and communal responsibility on the part of all people. There is no one formula for all people, and there cannot be. We would be foolish to believe that there is such a solution. But in working together to really help foster change as humans, whether activists, policy makers, or academics, we can enable children like Latrisha Avery (who did lose fifteen pounds in 2008) to reduce their predisposition toward obesity and enjoy the pleasures of eating the foods that aid in their overall well-being. We can offer her more than the limited choice of tuna on a bed of lettuce, on the one hand, or fried chicken, candied yams, and potato salad, on the other.

The approach I am proposing requires that we be open to self-reflection and self-examination about the ways in which we communicate with individuals and communities that we "want to help." What is at stake for us in our lending a helping hand? To whom do we owe a report for the work that has been funded and how will we describe our success and that of those with whom we work? Are we willing to be honest about our investment in power structures that, from the outset, may doom a project to failure? There are many ways that families feed themselves. Not all healthy eating begins or ends with growing one's own food, driving to the organic market, buying and eating locally, or even shopping at particular food markets. As I discuss some of these issues in the final chapter of this book, we must consider the differences between our intentions and the impact they actually end up having. Doing this kind of work looks to be the most humane and liberating solution if we are going to honor the food choices and decisions of African American communities.

CHAPTER 4

Eating in the Meantime

Expanding African American Food Stories
in a Changing Food World

Is it right for a fellow shopper to police how another feeds
her family and shame her for how she does it?
—R. Bentley, "Shaming at the Grocery Store: The Perils of
Shopping with Food Stamps"

Being a vegan is easy. All you have to do is . . .
—Seminar attendee, southwestern United States

Putting your hands in the soil is like "heaven on earth."
—Audience member, Midwest symposium

The worst kinds of racist aren't the ones who hate us.
The worst are the ones who want to come save us.
—*Black Beach*

I was at a seminar on the intersection of health, diet, and culture for African Americans when one of the speakers mentioned that some of the elderly clients that visit her service center do not take their medication because they do not have food. The costs of health care and prescriptions make it almost impossible, at times, for these elders to the afford both, and by the middle of every month they are in a quandary and must make difficult choices. These are hard decisions to make at any time, and certainly at the end of one's life cycle. Around the same time as the presentation, I had been working for some time on a theory about shopping at dollar stores, so the co-panelist's information resonated very strongly with me. It was my hope to include the essay in my coedited publication *Taking Food Public: Redefining Foodways in a Changing World*, but my arguments just were not hanging together as I would have liked. I spoke to a colleague about the article and shared my thoughts; while she was encouraging, she also cautioned me that some food products in the dollar store are expired and/or imported and thus maybe would not be the best source of nourishment. The comments of my co-panelists, however, rapidly brought my attention back to the argument that budget stores might be a useful option for people to consider for a number of different reasons, from convenience to economics, accessibility to creativity.

When my daughter was in elementary school, it seemed we were always attending birthday parties or holding celebrations of one kind or another. In the absence of a party-supply store, the local Dollar Tree became my go-to place to shop. It had everything: seasonal decorations, gift bags, crafts, paper goods, school supplies, bleach, and other miscellany for my household. From a budgetary perspective, I could maximize my shopping in one stop—I could get twenty items for just over twenty dollars. Over time, this local value mart began to make the one-stop shopping experience even more convenient by expanding their line to include food products such as bottled water and a host of dry goods. It was a subtle change, this expansion into food products. And yet it was a change that was both welcoming and troubling. As a wife and mother, it could make my often-tedious errand runs relatively shorter. As a food scholar, however, it made me ask, Who buys food from the dollar store? As I noticed the inventory increase to include such as items as wheat bread, bagels, and English muffins, I also noticed the installation of refrigeration. The next thing I knew, the dollar store was offering everything from turkey bacon to eggs, cheese, and frozen vegetables. My curiosity was heightened, and the question began to resound even more loudly: *Who is buying food from the dollar store?*[1] More to the point of this discussion, why had no one considered the role of the value market as an immediate option for getting food? At a time of rapidly changing sources of food supply (and demand), how are these stores being used to reduce dimensions of food insecurity? And thinking more broadly, I began to wonder what other venues could enable people to purchase food economically, especially when everyone was decrying food deserts, far and wide. Why was the local budget store not an option? These questions led me to consider how we can empower people to eat and live how they want and need to without imposing shame or policing them. Using two distinct venues that are most likely considered polar opposites of health—budget stores (that is, dollar stores, bodegas, corner markets, convenience stores, fast-food outlets) and farmers markets—this chapter is designed to encourage readers to consider a variety of stores, markets, and networks. These food spaces can challenge how we think about accessing food and also can allow people to exercise food choices without making them feel bad about their decisions. And lastly, this discussion hopes to broaden the conversation about a topic that is polarizing, because it assumes an either/or option or what philosopher Lisa Heldke refers as a "paper or plastic" mentality.

In the previous chapter, we saw how Latrisha Avery found herself in a quandary of paper or plastic thinking. She was presented with the choice to eat the foods that reinforced her cultural traditions or choose a salad of raw vegetables. Part of the chapter's discussion was designed to open the conversation, so that we could see and consider the many options potentially available to Latrisha. Availing herself of many options is exactly what Pennsylvania native Elizabeth Fisher has done by shopping at the Dollar Tree market. Growing up, Fisher was one of five kids in Conshohocken, Pennsylvania. Because there were constantly growing children, her family would frequent thrift shops. So she grew up appreciating the bargains available at stores that some might have considered unconventional. This conscientious frugality extends to food products for Fisher. It is not surprising then, that as she cares for her eighty-eight-year-old mother Fisher turns again to an alternative store for food products. In an interview with the *Philadelphia Inquirer,* Fisher tells Annette John-Hall, "My friends used to make fun of me all the time, but it was OK. . . . Those places were like my Neiman Marcus." A friend confirms this longstanding practice of Fisher's when she says, "Whether it was clothes or items for the house, Fisher had a knack for making her things 'frugally fly.'" According to the *Inquirer* article, Fisher uses the ingredients she purchases from the dollar store to create "gourmet meals" and shares her knowledge in a cookbook titled *Dining with the Dollar Diva: Divalicious Menus with Ingredients Costing $1 or Less.*[2]

It was affirming to realize that at least one other person found the dollar store to be a place from which they could get food. For Fisher, this is especially important, because she is able to help her aged mother by picking up goods at the local Dollar Tree. Fisher indicates that while shopping for placemats and glasses, she also picks up dry good ingredients that she combines with leftovers from her mother's refrigerator. One of Fisher's main meals is Salisbury steak, with creamed spinach, macaroni and cheese, and tea biscuits. According to Fisher, the meal "pays homage to family sojourns to the old Horn & Hardart Automats in West Philly, those giant vending machines where you'd pull the food out of the glass mail slots." Fisher's respect for the

Figure 4.1. Food products at the Dollar Tree in Laurel, Maryland, 2011. Photo by the author.

automat foods of West Philly speaks to another kind of culinary cultural tradition—the foods of our youth. Sometimes we want to re-create the foods that we grew up eating because they bring us comfort. Fisher is able to do this, or get close to doing this, and saves money in the process. Though Fisher does not indicate how many of these items were purchased from the Dollar Tree, she makes the overall point that there are options available, depending upon where your store is located. But what I particularly appreciate about Fisher's story is that it moves beyond an either/or set of options. Rather, she engages in multiple possibilities. Fisher encourages others to buy what they can from dollar stores—especially ingredients like beans, rice, and spices—but also meat and vegetables where they are sold. For those stores that do not sell such items, she encourages buying from "farmers' markets or on the sale aisles in discount supermarkets like Aldi."[3] Taking her mother's fixed income into account, Fisher embraces a combination of alternatives, including ones that involve relying on fixed-price budget stores.

The Dollar Tree in my neighborhood is large, which is perhaps why it is able to provide refrigerated items. On one of my many visits to the store, both to shop and to observe, I saw that they not only had frozen vegetables but also one-dollar rib-eye steak, brown rice, pasta, condiments, spices, bread (wheat, white, and buns), and canned goods. How is it not healthy to have a

Figure 4.2. SNAP (food stamps) is accepted at
the 5 Points West-Food market in Birmingham,
Alabama, 2012. Photo by the author.

meal of brown rice or pasta and vegetables along with baked chicken, fish,
or something else already in the refrigerator? The Supplemental Nutrition
Assistance Program (SNAP), or the food stamp program, provides food-
purchasing assistance for low- and no-income people living in the United
States. Are farmers markets and grocery stores the only food sites where
EBT/SNAP is acceptable? Many other stores (dollar stores, Target, Walmart,
even gas stations) now take SNAP and offer some of the same foods that are
available at grocery stores. The next time I went to the major grocery store,
about a mile away from the value store, I noticed they had a freezer bin in the
middle of the meat section with seafood and fish, also selling for one dollar
per package. What Fisher's experience reveals is that it is possible for some
dollar stores to be used as a food source. And she demonstrates that it may be
especially helpful for those who are living with limited funds, like the elderly
citizens who visit my colleague's service center.

Fisher is not alone in her stores of choice for grocery shopping. Nor is the
dollar store option being accessed only by those on a fixed income. In a 2011
article for the *New York Times Magazine*, Jack Hitt writes:

We are awakening to a dollar-store economy. For years the dollar store has not only made a market out of the detritus of a hyperproductive global manufacturing system, but it has also made it appealing—by making it amazingly cheap. Before the market meltdown of 2008 and the stagnant, jobless recovery that followed, the conventional wisdom about dollar stores—whether one of the three big corporate chains (Dollar General, Family Dollar, and Dollar Tree) or any of the smaller chains (like "99 Cents Only Stores") or the world of independents—was that they appeal to only poor people. And while it's true that low-wage earners still make up the core of dollar-store customers (42 percent earn $30,000 or less), what has turned this sector into a nearly recession-proof corner of the economy is a new customer base. "What's driving the growth," says James Russo, a vice president with the Nielsen Company, a consumer survey firm, "is affluent households."[4]

It is interesting that so many of the people leaving comments about Hitt's article said they would not purchase food from any of these stores because the products are "cheap." I was curious to ask if they would purchase the same or a similar good from a local market. Moreover, I was intrigued by Hitt's conclusion that the new consumer at these stores is "affluent." I wonder to what degree affluence is relative in this context. I have been in the dollar store when people of all races, ethnicities, and, at least by appearance, socioeconomic statuses, were shopping for everything from toiletries and sundries to orange juice, coffee, milk, and bread. I recall being in Target, and the customer in front of me had a full cart of groceries. She paid for the items with her Target red card. I know this both because I saw the card and the cashier was relatively indiscreet. When I exited the store, I noticed the woman was putting her groceries into the trunk of a Mercedes SUV. There is absolutely no way of knowing her socioeconomic status by this display of materialism. But given where the store is located in the county and the other shoppers who were there that day, by all appearances this shopper was a person of some means.

In an effort to assess whether people of different economic statuses were shopping at dollar stores, I asked this question of one of my graduate classes, where we tend to see a cross-section of students from various backgrounds. Several people responded to my query, but one response that struck me in particular was from a student in my course Feminist Cultural Criticism of Diasporic Texts. Though living in Maryland at the time, the student originally hailed from the West Coast, a point that might affect the kinds of foods that are sold at the dollar stores she is used to. When asked what kind of discount stores her family visited, she replied, "99 Cent Only Stores." She explained, "My family has bought all kinds of foods from 99 Cent Only Stores (the purple chain one), including fresh, packaged, and frozen." She went on to voluntarily list food from each of these categories: pot pies, seafood, garlic bread, mini quiche, ice cream, butter, milk, canned goods, sardines, and much more. Most likely, this student would not describe herself as affluent, but her family had the financial ability to shop elsewhere and still found this kind of store most affordable. She explained that after living on the West Coast for some time, many adult members of her family eventually moved to the Midwest in order "to become homeowners but that resulted in an even tighter budget for some of them. . . . All of my family members (3 different households) . . . live within a 10 minute drive of at least two or three 99-cent stores and all have one less than 5 minutes away." And though these stores are useful for making some purchases, not all "carry fresh and frozen food items." The student finished her written comments by sharing, "My family is price-conscious so price matters, but even my college educated twin brother, who is doing very well financially, still prefers the bargain produce these stores have to offer."[5] What would it mean for food freedom and liberation if we encouraged people to access food how and from where they are able? We seem to herald foragers, back-to-the-landers, and dumpster divers for their ingenuity, but we are willing to look down upon people who access food from the dollar store because we define it as "cheap" and somehow unwholesome.

This latter notion of wholesomeness, along with the requirement of the healthiness of the food, are the twin weapons for issuing shame and culinary policing. Because we all operate out of our own experiences, we can often miss the nuances of how shopping in places like the dollar store and other budget outlets enables those who do the shopping to accomplish more than just purchasing food. For example, once I was in the company of a food advocate who strongly believed in agricultural education and outreach. As we were talking, she began extolling the virtues of her work and why her message was a necessary one for helping communities of people relieve hunger. At one point during our conversation, I told her that farmers markets were not necessarily a feasible shopping option for many people. She sharply responded, "Everyone deserves fresh food." "Absolutely," I said, "but that is not my point." How we obtain foods is of interest and importance to me. It is critical, for me, that we not insist that there is only one correct way of

Figures 4.3a and 4.3b. Seafood items selling for $1.00 and halal
meats at reasonably affordable prices at a local major grocery chain.
Laurel, Maryland, 2011. Photos by the author.

obtaining food. We continued to banter while driving to our destination.
Along the way, we happened to pass a busy shopping center that had a variety
of stores including a Walmart, a Rainbow (an urban-centered clothing store
for women and girls), and a Dollar Tree. As my driver continued to argue
her point, I could not help but think of the many errands I had to run when
I returned home, and the number of tasks I could accomplish in one hour

or so just by going to the three stores we just passed, or even one of them. Alternatively, the thought of needing to figure out the time and location of the next farmers market and how it would fit within the scope of the many other things I had to do was daunting, to say the least. I explained to my companion how I, as a middle-class Black women, would find relief in the option of large stores with varied merchandise. After I said this, we rode in silence for the rest of the trip, each of us lost in our own thoughts, perhaps thinking about the privileges in our own lives.

I was not angry with my driving companion so much as I was frustrated and tired by the need to share continuously this kind of information in order to help people check their privileges. I am perpetually amazed by the freedoms enjoyed by so many who choose to tell Black people how we should practice our food cultures. It is clear they most often have little or no clue about our cultural history, heritage, sustainability, or even about how we manage life on a day-to-day basis. These advocates are determined in their zeal to impress upon me the need to acquire "fresh" food. And they feel justified by their outrage to impress upon me that I, as a human being, have a right to have this freshness in my life. Yes, of course I do! But what my companion and others seem to miss is that it is also my right to acquire food and other goods in ways that works best for me, even if that means going outside the confines of what others consider acceptable. But some people get this. In the article "The Buck Shops Here," Ronette King explains that not only are dollar stores now being frequented by those "with incomes greater than $70,000" but also that they appeal to customers "who might not want to traipse across a huge store and its accompanying parking lot just to pick up a few items."[6] And this is especially the case when you are busy with families or live alone. It is absolutely true that everyone deserves to have fresh food. And it is also absolutely true that people need to be able to eat what they want and get their food from where they need while they are in the "meantime" of their lives—that is, while they are waiting for things to change or improve.

This is one of the many reasons I dislike the question "How do we get people to stop eating at McDonalds?" When asked this by a young African American woman during a panel in California, I responded, "Why is that your concern?" It was not my intention to be flippant, but I asked out of genuine curiosity. I wanted to know if the question was being generated because of a family member or close friend. Her lack of response suggested this was not the case but instead that she most likely intended to play the role of culinary police. This was problematic for multiple reasons, not least of which was that one of my colleagues was in the audience. Prior to the event, she had shared with me that on their way to the event her family had to stop off at McDonald's to grab something for her daughter to eat. Perhaps it was the fact that my colleague was coming to an event about food and culture and we were on the West Coast that led her to admit that she felt guilty. But this was unfortunate, because as a single, professional mother, I understood the stress of moving from pillar to post with a child in tow, trying to get work done, and manage life—with or without a partner to help.

McDonald's should always be an option. And for some people, it is a good option but not necessarily for the reasons you might believe. I teach a course called Food, Trauma, Sustainability. This is an experiential or hands-on course for students that begins by identifying an organization that has a problem we want to help solve. We are an undergraduate class, and we cannot effect a lot of change given that the course only runs for about four months, from February to May. But we try to tackle at least one manageable concern that will benefit the organization. A lot of time is taken to help students recognize how and why empathy is important when dealing with people and communities. Understanding how and why people think in particular ways about food goes far toward our being able to identify various strategies to arrive at solutions. The first year I taught the course, our "client" was Meals on Wheels, a volunteer organization active throughout the United States that helps seniors and the elderly address hunger and isolation. It was then that I learned that, in addition to having to choose between resources (food or medicine), many elderly do not eat because they are lonely and have no one to eat with. Enter McDonald's, Burger King, and perhaps other fast-food or low-cost eateries that offer dollar menus and/or free coffee and other foods to seniors. In the article "'Our Hearts Are Hurting': Elderly Chinese Isolated as SF Dim Sum Restaurants Shutter in Pandemic," Megan Zhang writes,

> Ever since [Cheung Yinching and her husband] immigrated to America, they have looked forward to this regular tradition as a chance to connect with other members of the Chinese American community—sharing good news about their lives, commiserating over woes, and enjoying the company of trusted confidantes. But when the onset of the [COVID-19] pandemic in March brought the implementation of social-distancing guidelines and indoor dining closures to their Mission Bay neighborhood, what was once an imperative weekly ritual came to an abrupt halt. . . . Dim sum is a well-loved breakfast and lunch tradition among much

of the Chinese diaspora. . . . It's the togetherness that the dim sum par-
lors afford that [Cheung Yinching] misses most. . . . "It's like the bridge
has broken. The world has turned upside down."[7]

Though dim sum is a far cry from fast food, this gathering of elders mirrors
many at quick eateries during the breakfast hour all across our nation. So
common is the practice that in New York a group of Korean patrons were
being kicked out of a McDonald's in Queens for "milking their stays over
$1.09 coffees, violating the restaurant's 20-minute dining limit." Following
a protest by community leaders and residents over this treatment of the elders, a truce was made when the customers agreed to vacate by peak hours.[8]
What is most important for this discussion is not just the similarities that
exist among racial and ethnic groups but the commonality that exists among
elders at this stage in their lives—their need for independence, access, and
community.

Michael Kimmelman, the author of "The Urban Home Away from Home,"
explains that as he dug deeper to understand why the Korean seniors were
attracted to that particular McDonald's location, he learned several things
but especially that access was key. Kimmelman writes that most of these
older city residents either can no longer drive or no longer own a car. Moreover, the close distance meant they could walk together to the meeting place.
They rejected senior centers, because they wanted the freedom to roam
as they pleased. So, in addition to access, independence matters. And, of
course, another factor was budget; most of these outlets offer inexpensive
food. Alongside these reasons are others: these establishments have heating
and air conditioning for the changing seasons, and they are equipped with
bathrooms. One last motivation may be the most important: gathering at
these establishments means the seniors do not have to eat alone. Kimmelman writes, "People don't want to be alone. So, they find a sense of belonging
in what they think of as their neighborhood, which tends to shrink as they
age." He goes on to explain, "McDonald's is a ready-made NORC. The official
name is Naturally Occurring Retirement Communities. . . . Despite . . . many
disgruntled patrons who find nothing charming about people they consider
space hogs, McDonald's is the NORC that has bound together the elderly
Koreans. Most of them didn't know one another until they visited the restaurant. They were drawn there by proximity and price, and they have stayed
for the companionship."[9] This is not only a New York phenomenon, nor is
it particular to Koreans or Asian Asians. Throughout the summer of 2020,

during the COVID-19 pandemic I would often see groups of elders socially distancing in the parking lots of McDonald's and Burger King restaurants, continuing their communal time. It was generally during the breakfast hour, when I would be running errands to the grocery or dollar store, that I would encounter these groups. Sometimes it was just men. Other times it would be men and women enjoying a sense of commensality or social engagement with food. And pre-pandemic, on many mornings while in Hyattsville, Maryland, grabbing a cup of McDonald's coffee, I would see clusters of white and Black seniors having breakfast. Closer to my own reality, my dad and one or two of his clergy friends gather each morning for coffee, breakfast, and community news at their local fast-food outlets.

Here again is where the issue of complexities in food choices comes into play alongside race, gender, and even age, location, space, and place. Most likely, none of these matters emerge when conversations take place about eating healthy and avoiding fast food. And perhaps even more ironic is the fact that some of those same "disgruntled patrons" and people who want to stop folks from eating at fast-food outlets will celebrate farmers markets for the ways in which they encourage community. In situations such as these, the food is often secondary to the communal benefits. So the shaming and policing that takes place is really due to ignorance about social and cultural relations around food as much or more than it is about the foods themselves. I recall reading an article once about a man proposing to his fiancée in a McDonald's. The African American man indicated that the restaurant was where he and his girlfriend had first met, and so the space became a site of romance. Though I do not remember any other details of this particular incident, any Google search today will reveal the frequency of such occurrences—people proposing with chicken nuggets, Big Macs, and even french fries. What is compelling about the marriage proposal I reference is not the food but the location as a site of memory. Similarly, in 2019, a South African man proposed to his fiancée at KFC. As the proposal circulated on social media, strangers came out of the woodwork to help the couple—from wedding planners to musicians to an official South African Audi dealer who volunteered to help get the couple to their honeymoon.[10]

Another frequently asked question that I tend not to like centers on either starting a community garden or a farmers market in a particular neighborhood. For one, this is not my area of expertise, so I would not attempt to address the question. But I do tend to respond by asking if the query has been posed to members of the community for whom this "resource" is being considered. Most of the time the question is asked by white women who are motivated by good intentions but have not done the necessary work in the community to see it all come to completion. I encounter this very often, but one instance in particular stands out. While in Illinois for a presentation, my mentor and I were walking to our destination when we passed an organic corner market. I took a detour into the store, hoping to support a small business that was nestled on the edge of the local African American community. As I walked about the sparsely filled store, a white woman came from a back room to ask me if I needed anything. We struck up a conversation and talked about my visit to the university for an evening presentation. She then went on to ask me if I had any suggestions for how she could get more African Americans to visit the store, since that was her primary purpose for opening in the area. I responded by asking her if she had gone into the community to let them know she is there. She replied that she had not. I then suggested that she might want to contact some of the local houses of worship where primarily African American people attended service. She thanked me and as I left, I noticed a few dark-spotted bananas and several kiwi but no collard greens or sweet potatoes. In short, the place had no Black food energy!

Organic markets, health-food stores, and farmers markets are curious sites in my studies on food. Whether I happen upon them while out for a walk or am more deliberate in seeking them out because I intend to shop, sometimes I enjoy going to these places for the variety and options, but not the prices. These spaces are instructive for helping people to understand food inequities while also being valuable sources for food acquisition. But they are not the be-all and end-all that they are often touted to be by well-intentioned advocates. In fact, these sites for food shopping can be outright problematic. On another occasion, I was in a southern city to deliver a presentation, and my host took me to a local farmers market located in the epicenter of the city's downtown. Among the many other reasons for our visit, I recall the market organizers had applied for and received a grant, partially to appeal to a neighboring African American community, who had been displaced by gentrification. I explained to my host that I saw this effort as an undeniable symbol of white guilt and that thus the market on its face was problematic. Moreover, the goal of the grant was to get African American customers to come to the market—another obvious and fundamental flaw in the application. Because, similar to the Illinois example above, if your intent is to appeal to a group of people, the first thing you do is find alliances among the community of people with whom you are seeking camaraderie and make the effort to go to them. It may take months or even years before an invitation is extended, but what you do not do is ask them to come to you.

As we walked and chatted during the pre-opening setup, I noticed that most of vendors were selling the same kinds of foods: free-range eggs, pesticide-free produce, responsibly raised meats like grass-fed beef and pasture-raised pork. There was a variety of swiss chard, snap peas, bok choy, carrots, and kohlrabi. Lots of kohlrabi. And there was a table that held literature and hardware for taking EBT/SNAP. As I walked through the market watching the vendors set up, I thought to myself, Where are the African American retailers who look like the people to whom they are trying to sell? More importantly, where are the foods familiar to most African American people—maybe half of the intended audience and those to whom the grant was directed? What I saw was a "yes"/ "and" scenario. African Americans do eat swiss chard and bok choy, (YES!)/(AND) I was curious about the absence of sweet potatoes, collards and other greens, squash, cabbage, leeks, purple peas, peppers, and so on. I was searching for the foods more familiar to various classes of African American people.

In an article by Kristen Aiken, "'White People Food' Is Creating an Unattainable Picture of Health," the author quotes Natalie Webb, a Black registered dietician and nutritionist in the D.C. area: "My clients absolutely associate healthy eating with eating like white folk."[11] Webb goes on to say, "I think it stems from what people see in marketing and what they associate healthful eating with, and it often doesn't include foods they're familiar with. . . . When you change folks' food—especially people of color—it's like you're asking them to change who they are. . . . That's why it's so important as a dietician to start where folks are and introduce foods that are going to be familiar but maybe in a little different way." Charmaine Jones, another Black D.C.-based dietician, is also quoted in the Aiken article. In a short paper she wrote titled "Do I Have to Eat Like White People?," Jones describes the belief that "white people food" is salads, fruits, yogurts, cottage cheese, and lean meats—the standard low-fat, heart-healthy foods promoted by the *Dietary Guidelines for Americans*. But what few people may realize is that these guidelines are put out by a fourteen-member advisory board. This board, which dictates what the average American should eat to maintain a healthy lifestyle, sometimes has very little to no representation from non-white racial and ethnic groups. Another contributor to the Aiken article, Erica Bright, a forty-five-year-old management analyst who sought Jones's help to make some dietary changes, sums it up perfectly: "The thing that bothers me about eating healthy is that in the media, people appropriate different ways of eating to different people.

. . . And so I don't necessarily feel like black people eat as unhealthily as people would assume that we do. If you think about Italian food, which I love, it's just as fatty [as soul food], but it doesn't have that same reputation." Bright rightly points out that the origins of southern food took root at a time when it was necessary to cook with less-than-ideal ingredients. She explains,

> Some people think all black people eat is chicken and collard greens, and that's not necessarily true. However, out of utility and necessity, we ate a lot of that down South back in the day because that's all that was available. It's not like we didn't know what carrots or Brussels sprouts were. . . . Stereotyping is extremely frustrating. We all have to find an approach to food that still respects and honors our culture. We can still respect our ancestors for how they had to eat out of utility. Now, I have a lot more choices than they did. I shop at Whole Foods, I can go to Trader Joe's.

Baruch Ben-Yehuda, the owner and CEO of Everlasting Life Restaurant, an African American vegan restaurant in the D.C. metropolitan area, also contributed to the article. Ben-Yehuda observes, "African-Americans might say, 'I don't want to eat like white people.' . . . However, at the end of the day, it's not eating like white people, it's actually eating the way we used to eat before we were brought to this country." All of the comments here are spot-on. I also contributed to the Aiken article and emphasized,

> I don't think there's such a thing as white people food. . . . But I think there are foods that have been assigned to black people, and there are foods that have been more in line with white communities. And I think soul food is largely what gets short-handed as black people food, and things like veganism and vegetarianism get short-handed as white people food. Quite frankly, African-American people have been eating "white people's food" since we arrived on this continent. But a lot of folks don't know that because the food we tend to get associated with is almost always soul food.

At the same time that there is no such thing as "Black people's food" or "white people's food," there are markers that say to potential customers, "You should shop here." Let me explain. As I walked further along the farmers market path during my visit to the southern city, I came upon the sole African American stall, a worm farmer or vermicomposter. This, too, struck me as odd, given that at least part of the intention of the grant was to attract African American customers. Not only was he at the very end of the curved pathway (probably because of what he was selling), but he also had no actual food. So it was not just the fact that there were no purple-hulled peas, jams, pickles, melons, peaches, lopes, oversweetened cakes and pies, and few vendors of color, but the space did not have *the feel* of a market meant to welcome African Americans. There were no soaps, hair products, jewelry, or clothing, all items frequently found at Black-run markets. Rather, the environment of the farmers market was sterile—meaning there was no sense of what I call *Black food energy* to signal "You are welcome here."[12]

What is Black food energy and where does it come from? Food is a significant component of cultural sustainability, as I have discussed to some extent in previous chapters of this book. It is one of the many life rituals that help us to reinforce our social and cultural norms. More than mere sustenance, food rituals and customs, as ingredients and in processes of preparation, are symbolic for what they convey about who we are—our racial and ethnic identities, in particular. It is from cultural sustainability that we get Black food energy. Black food energy can be hard to explain, but one may know it when they experience it. It is why the combination of macaroni and cheese, collard greens, and fried chicken is familiar to many Black people, though these are arguably not "Black foods." It is the sound of funk, soul, hip-hop, and maybe even trap music playing while Black people sell Afrocentric clothing, Black art, and pumpkin and sweet potato pies, lemon pound cake, or bean pies. It is the smell of gumbo cooking or shrimp and crab legs with butter, hot sauce, and vinegar, while the game is on, the kids are loud, and the sounds of Marvin Gaye waft in or the Migos blare in the distance—all of which is only complete with a spades game in progress.[13]

When you are surrounded by Black food energy, you know what it is. There are versions to the ways in which it plays out because Black people have styles to ourselves and our food cultures. We eat shrimp and grits, jambalaya, caviar, fried chicken, Cobb salad, tofu, seitan, eggplant, cabbage, broccoli, cauliflower, carrots, peppers, avocado, kale, Brussels sprouts, collard greens, bok choy, waakye, jollof rice, red red, Savoy cabbage, and gai lan. But even more than this, Black food markets are where networking takes place, where plans are made, where ideas about political action are discussed, and, historically, where insurrections are formulated. Black food energy, as I see it, is when women at the marketplace are talking about selling chicken. But they are really talking about other news, because we are complex like that. We are masters at riffing and borrowing, improvisation, and flow. We are shaped by multiple histories and experiences of personal agency, and these in turn effect how we move about the world. These histories—food and otherwise—are informed by our regions, socioeconomic statuses, genders, families, religions, and more. Now, this may sound somewhat reductionist, because lots of Black people shop at different kinds of farmers markets that do not have the kinds of vendors mentioned above. But in the DMV at least, what gives those markets Black food energy is the people themselves. For example, in Prince George's County, Maryland, which boasts one of the largest populations of African Americans of varying socioeconomic statuses in the state, Amish markets are a weekly, biweekly, or monthly ritual. Lots of Black people from all walks of life descend upon the market from Thursday to Saturday to get food—already prepared dishes, orders from the deli, a brilliant array of vegetables, desserts, dry goods, and more. These kinds of smaller markets are intimate spaces where you are likely to run into a neighbor as well as a foe. But for certain you will find food items that you can name, many of which are reasonably affordable, and that you will know how to cook. And here is what is smart: the markets are located in areas that are heavily populated by Black people. And while the other elements—music, jewelry, and so on—are not present, there is enough community engagement within the walls of the market to make it appeal to a broad swath of Black people. Word of mouth is a powerful advertising mechanism. These markets have been around long enough that their reputations precede them, and most Black adults, and perhaps some children, know that the Amish market is open every weekend.

Understanding the ways in which cultural sustainability works is especially important when we set out to do good food work in communities. No doubt we do so with the intention of doing good, but we should be constantly monitoring our impact. Sometimes our goals land well, and sometimes they land with a thud so heavy it disrupts everything and turns situations upside down. Perhaps this is because we did not tap into the Black food energy, or we did not connect the foods to the histories and the contexts that inform who and where African American people are. Without an understanding of the historical contexts of the foods African Americans eat and their nutritional and cultural value, the work that is done in the name of social justice and equity could land organizations in quagmires similar to the one that had the lone African American vendor who sold composting worms. This suggestion is especially necessary in areas that have been gentrified.

Urban renewal and land redistribution is nasty business, and it has been going on ever since Black folk first owned land. Perhaps today it is recognizable to current generations because, literally almost every day, a parcel of land or a store goes from Grandma's house to a college residence hall, or Mr. Coles's mom-and-pop grocery store becomes the latest luxury apartment building. This encroachment forces urban Black people away from the city center, where they have access to public transportation and various other services that enable them to go to work (even when it is low-paying), take care of their health, and attend school and community functions. Urban renewal turns properties into unaffordable housing, drives up property taxes, and infuses the landscape with people who look different and engage in activities that exhibit freedoms that most Black people do not have or even recognize. Zoning laws are changed, bank loans are denied, and African American people are encouraged or forced to sell lifelong properties for a minimum offer, only to see the same property possibly split into multiple units and rented for exorbitant prices. New white citizens claim public space as their own, the same spaces that used to be frequented by Black and Brown people—who are now exiles in a familiar land. Durham, North Carolina, reporter Thomasi McDonald, in writing about one locale in that city, argues, "This is the inverse of 20th-century white flight, when white people fled racially mixed urban regions, leaving them impoverished, for suburbs and exurbs. . . . The anger and frustration felt by Black residents who are being priced out of the city is understandable." In the words of community activist Lamont Lilly, who is intimately familiar with the goings on in that city, the people moving their way in and buying up Black people's property are "'colonizers' with little regard for how their presence is uprooting a community that has been cheated out of a fundamental birthright: the sanctuary of a home."[14] Families are being destroyed by this insidious practice, and with it affluent gentrifiers are devastating cultural habits and behaviors.

White politics creates blight and then swoops in (through an "urban land rush") to recover and improve the damage. Except the recovered land is not intended for the African Americans who have suffered from the neglect; it is for the new denizens, who are deemed more deserving and worthy. Here, I would remind readers of the concept of "secondly" spoken of both by Mourid Barghouti and Chimimanda Adichie: "If you want to dispossess people, the simplest way to do it is to tell their story, and to start with 'secondly.'" Make it seem as if you are saving Black communities by buying up their blighted property as opposed to admitting that the properties are "blighted" because of intentional divestment, and you will understand the point of "secondly." North Carolinian urban planner Nate Baker explains it this way:

For decades, the inner city typically referred to historic residential neighborhoods where low-income, Black, and working-class people lived. . . . But the inner city also encompassed neighborhoods that were walkable, close to transit, and near services. . . . These areas . . . were 'notorious' for both public and private disinvestment, but as investment shifted to downtown and market preferences shifted toward walkable places, the inner cities that whites once fled became the natural locations for revitalization. Gentrification now means that any efforts to make neighborhoods better threatens the ability of low and middle income residents to remain where they are. . . . Imagine the injustice of living in neighborhoods neglected by society for decades only to be forced out of your neighborhood by the very investments that residents needed all along.[15]

Though Baker and Lilly are referring to a major city in North Carolina, they could very well be describing Washington, D.C., Nashville, Houston, or New Orleans, as well as smaller rural communities where lifelong town dwellers are now being forced out into the countryside by the expansion of white businesses, colleges and universities, and new and improved (but unaffordable) housing units.

It is into this morass that farmers markets enter as an imagined culinary panacea. We talk about food as if it is the great equalizer, a cure-all for all that ails. Now, gentrified cities have what the Duke Sanford World Food Policy Center rightly identifies as "a 'foodie' culture lauded in publications such as the *New York Times*, *Bon Appétit*, and *Southern Living*, among many other newspapers and magazines. Microbreweries, fair trade coffee shops, artisanal food trucks, and other hallmarks of foodie culture often serve as gentrification's leading edge by signifying that a community is ripe for investment. Gentrification changes what food retailers can exist in the local food environment, sometimes creating 'food mirages,' where high quality food is priced out of reach of longtime residents. There is also the issue of who is able to participate in this flurry of food entrepreneurism."[16] From Baltimore to Seattle, Sacramento to Miami, Alexandria to Farmville, Charlottesville to Detroit, the story is the same, and it was written on the landscape of the farmers market that I visited that day with my presentation host.

The last several decades have witnessed a proliferation of data, from the social sciences in particular, about the existence of "food deserts." As Steven

Bitler and Marianne Haider suggest in their review of the literature, the conversations have ranged from concerns over insufficient quantity/quality of foods, to systematically higher prices for these foods in certain geographic areas (that is, few healthy food venues in poor areas), and fewer chain supermarkets in lower-income neighborhoods and those heavily populated by African American and Latino peoples. The now familiar, but quite contentious, term "food desert" is at its most basic the inability to access healthy and nutritious food, a definition supported by the 2008 Farm Bill.[17] But some studies have suggested that while there are many places devoid of the kinds of grocery stores that are preferred, there are some smaller stores in communities that have shelf space devoted to fruits and vegetables. For example, using a market-basket price survey, Judith Bell and Bonnie Burlin found that "the red line of economic discrimination extends throughout the low-income consumer infrastructure, with dramatic effects on low-income consumers and their neighborhoods." The result of such discrimination is that while large national chain stores in low-income neighborhoods help to keep food prices low, their absences creates dramatically higher prices for the consumer because, in part, there is less competition. Even though some smaller stores do carry fruits and vegetables, the operating costs for independent, inner-city grocers tend to be much higher. But often, these corner stores and bodegas or ethnic markets serve low-income and elderly residents. Bell and Burlin also found the "complete lack of willingness among wholesale distributors to deliver in low-income areas" to be another mitigating factor.[18]

Arguing along similar lines, sociologist Julie Guthman, cites three additional red-line issues as primary causes for food blight in low-income communities:

1. Racist insurance and lending practices
2. White flight—and with it the flight of a particular market base
3. Neoliberal restructuring of urban space—disinvestment and unemployment—leaving in its wake intense poverty in some situations.

One solution to this blight—aside from the obvious need for more food outlets—is the creation of food security projects like CSAs to combat these discrepancies. But Guthman, among others, argues that these projects often assume knowledge, access, and cost are the primary barriers to more healthful eating. Guthman states: "Much of the on-the-ground work is focused on donating, selling (at below market prices) or growing fresh fruits and vegetables, and educating residents to the quality of locally grown, seasonal and organic food."[19] With these solutions, however, there are a lot of assumptions being made in these initiatives (aimed largely at African Americans). Most of these projects are also sparse—aimed at specific (mostly urban) areas. Take for instance Will Allen's Growing Power, which had as its stated mission, "[to transform] communities by supporting people from diverse backgrounds and the environments in which they live through the development of Community Food Systems. These systems provide high-quality, safe, healthy, affordable food for all residents in the community." Then there is Peaches and Greens, the roving truck fruit vendors that sell fresh fruits and vegetables at fair prices and provide kitchen and regular dairy demonstrations in the Detroit, Michigan, area. In some locales the roving truck makes sense because of both the ways that residents are spread out and the dearth of transportation to get people to the food stores. In this way, Peaches and Greens is like the arabbers of Baltimore, who would use horse and cart to peddle their wares to customers. Peaches and Greens goes further; they also have community gardens where volunteers grow greens, tomatoes, and other vegetables to help stock the trucks. The food also is offered at a neighborhood produce market, and organizers work to persuade liquor stores and corner markets to stock their vegetables.[20] These solutions—fruit and vegetable pushcart vendors in New York, truck vendors in Detroit—are necessary because many residents have limited public transportation options. As a result, they have a difficult time getting to farmers markets or stores in outlying suburban areas.

Individually, several cities have come up with options in order to help those who are struggling with obesity, diabetes, and other illnesses tied to diets high in calories and sugar. These communities are circumventing the larger industrial food system by trying a variety of ways to solve the problem. In a recent *New York Times* op-ed, David Bornstein pointed out that in Highland Falls, New York (population 4,000), residents had to drive eleven miles to access the nearest store. The town offered a weekly bus service for about two years, until a local couple, Lisa Berrios and Albert Rodriguez, decided to open a supermarket called MyTown Marketplace. With the help of funds from the New York Healthy Foods and Communities initiative, they were able to get the store up and running.[21] Though the prices are sometimes higher than those at the store eleven miles away, having a market that is accessible and that caters to the local community is worth the extra cost. This example suggests that the problem of food insecurity not only affects low-income communities but many neighborhoods that lack big-box stores. Bell and Burlin suggest other reasons for the creation of such alternatives:

Low-income consumers' typical spending patterns also drive up operating costs for supermarkets. Generally, low-income consumers make
smaller purchases but shop more frequently, since their budgets must be
constructed around each paycheck or the distribution schedules of government assistance programs (e.g., food stamps). Transporting groceries
on public transportation or on foot also limits the size of low-income
consumers' purchases. This high volume of shoppers making smaller
purchases drives up operating costs and requires adjustments, such as
modernizing checkout lanes to speed check-out. However, if grocers
lack the resources for such changes, their customers must tolerate the
resulting inconveniences. Finally, small stores' limited storage capacity
also increases their operating costs because it reduces stores' abilities
to take advantage of the lower wholesale prices associated with large
orders.[22]

Relatedly, in her research on the Deanwood neighborhood in Washington,
D.C., Ashanté Reese deftly explains the ways in which Black residents engage in self-reliant solutions to accessing food from growing their own food,
trading and bartering, to using hucksters and vendors, small grocers, and
community markets. In *Black Food Geographies*, Reese is clear about the
self-sufficiency and ability of Black residents. But she is equally clear that sub-
par and limited resources undergird this need, illustrating that Black people's
lives require several alternatives both by necessity and by choice.[23]

In these examples, not everyone is able to or wants to employ the same
methods. As Erica Bright from the Aiken article plaintively says, "We all have
to find an approach to food that still respects and honors our culture." Why,
then, can this model of alternatives and finding different approaches not be
extended to the conversation on how Black people get food? Julie Guthman
similarly asks this when she speaks to changing the discussions around food
projects. Rather than focusing on why African American neighborhoods reject or accept such traditional alternative food projects, she suggests that we
reframe the question: rather than ask why Black people won't participate, we
should question "white desire to enroll black people in a particular set of food
practices."[24] Here, Guthman is referring to the constant discourse pushing
local food eating and, more importantly, buying local food from farmers
markets. As I discussed in other chapters of this book, immigrants and migrants need to eat too. What are they to do when their cultural foodways are
not accessible locally? To be sure, there are lots of different ways to eat locally,

but sometimes it is not always clear that those who are suggesting this option understand these nuances.

Along these lines, another mantra often touted is the need for residents to participate in growing their own food. The urgency of this goal as an essential project for many food activists has been reinforced over and over to me. On the one hand, it is a form of "eating in the meantime" when we encourage others to grow their own food. The element of self-sufficiency is not lost. The beauty of the growing is not eclipsed. This became even more clear to me after presenting my research at a college in Missouri, when an audience member approached me and proceeded to admonish me for not encouraging people "to put their hands in the soil." In her estimation, growing one's own food was akin to "heaven on earth." Time did not permit me to engage in the necessary self-reflexive response, "Why would you think that?" or "Say more about that." So I gently clarified for her that producing one's own food is not always a welcome task given the racialized histories of people's relationships to landscapes and landmass in the United States. Again, I turn to Guthman, who cites Jeffrey Romm's essay "The Coincidental Order of Environmental Injustice" to explain that even while homesteaders were given free land, African Americans were forced into sharecropping: they were denied their forty acres and a mule. With slogans like "Keep California White," Chinese and Japanese Americans were denied land ownership and citizenship; Native peoples had their lands appropriated and lives obliterated; and the "Californios were disenfranchised of their ranches."[25] Agricultural racial segregation was and continues to be an issue for people of color. And on a personal, smaller scale, growing food can be hard work, and not everyone has the time, interest, or patience to do it. The problematic part of this audience member's thinking was in her logic of right/wrong, moral/immoral eating. I encounter this a great deal and often find it difficult to help those well-intentioned advocates to recognize how they are coming across. They are blinded by their need to "help," and so I am often approached with preconceived notions about what is best for Black people and asked to cosign onto these racialized food practices that are not informed (or approved) by the communities that advocates are trying to save.

It is a culture of assumptions and, to some extent, arrogance in which food tourism is one of the latest trends. The rhetoric tends toward insisting on a particular set of beliefs in which organic, local, and fair-trade eating is the refrain, as if this way of eating justifies and purifies one of all sins. The rhetoric is so loud that it turns a blind eye to displacement, theft, and the outright taking of Black people's land, opportunities, and right to make their own decisions about where, how, and what they want to eat. Lisa Heldke's observation is as urgent and notable as a billboard surrounded by flashing red lights. She writes, "Would-be ethical food *consumers* approach every alternative food campaign as a kind of moral-social-ecological litmus test. To be a good person, you must eat 'vegetarian/eat vegan/eat organic/eat local/eat biodynamic/eat fair trade/eat authentic/eat . . .' I applaud these individual efforts to challenge the industrial agro-food system; I do not applaud their tendency to reduce moral life to a set of rigid choices that if made correct can, 'make me good.'"[26] These food campaigns should not be just an effort to challenge the industrial agro-food system. These campaigns should also be willing to join with Black people in protecting against the cultural erasures and sanctioned ignorance that seeks to declare our lives inconsequential, deviant, and unruly. This is not to suggest that all food activism has run amok. There have been a number of worthwhile projects on individual and community levels. But what I am advocating for here is food choices that recognize Black people also have personal values. So some Black people may choose to buy foods branded as organic, natural, grass-fed, local, fair trade, etc., as an expression of their health consciousness or personal politics. And some may not. But what is for sure is that these privileges will not make broader systemic changes in the industrial food system without more explicit connections to the social movements that address the root causes of the food inequities, such as racial justice, land justice, worker justice, and immigration justice.[27]

That day at the southern city farmers market, a lot of this historical and contemporary context was swirling through my mind as I walked around. As I took it all in, I thought about my presentation the next day and the growing dis-ease of these racial food projects that kept insisting Black people partake in them all while failing to accommodate Black people. It is this unease that makes a culinary cultural landscape like a farmers market "contested" and "nervous." It is one thing to fantasize about Black people coming to the market; it is another thing for us to be there, because our presence disrupts the landscapes. When we show up and ask for or about certain foods, we disrupt the landscape because the assumptions about what we eat can be called into question. When we pull out cash, credit cards, EBT, and other forms of payment, we disrupt the landscape because preconceived notions of who we are and what we can afford can force people to question their assumptions. I thought about all of this as I prepared my remarks.

The next day, I shared my observations during my presentation, and my remarks were met with mixed levels of understanding. Upon request, my host shared with me some of the comments left by those who attended the symposium. One commenter said, "That is *awesome*! If we can't push the envelope here, with this group of people, when can we? And if our organizing is too weak to be able to withstand some challenges and strong feelings, then we are not doing real change work." As my host and I debriefed over email, he wrote, "So they were saying things around 'I didn't get it' and 'so is this good or bad?' Instead of shifting to more complex thinking, they reacted as though it was a dialectic—this thing that I think is good she is telling me is actually bad."[28] These speaking engagements rarely allow for follow-up conversations where participants and I can talk and unpack my comments. But "not getting it" is part of the continuous education individuals and groups have to do when they want to work with those outside their own communities. It requires reading and talking with people until it is gotten. The energy that is used to write grants, or to start a garden in someone else's community, or to open a corner market in a majority African American community, or to tell people that they need to eat healthier, is the same energy that should be used to understand the larger issues of how food is rooted in systemic racism, segregation, discrimination, gentrification, and cultural history. It is not hard to get, but it does take work!

This lack of effort, or incomplete follow-through, is further revealed by the lack of the presence of Black food energy. In her article "We Got Our Own Way of Cooking: Women, Food, and Preservation of Cultural Identity among the Gullah," sociologist Josephine Beoku-Betts argues that in the eyes of white society or "under the pressure of dominant cultural practices," cooking and food preparation "may be viewed as a measure of gender inequality and women's subordination." But "in marginalized cultural groups," food preparation can be a window into understanding "the construction and maintenance of tradition."[29] Beoku-Betts's point is similar to that made by anthropologist Brett Williams, who studied tamale-making among Tejano women (discussed in chapter 2). When it comes to food, cultural cannot be dismissed. Consequently, if you are going to be a food provider, advocate, or activist around food for Black communities, it is important to know about Black culture and history. Take, for example, the Black Farmers' Market, a collective that reemerged across the nation in the early 1990s. This particular program actually was seeded back in the 1970s by the Reverend Al Sampson of Fernwood United Methodist Church in Chicago, but it has taken some time to grab a foothold. Now the movement is rapidly gaining momentum among Black farmer cooperatives from Arkansas to Virginia. Similar models exist in Baltimore, Oakland, Indianapolis, and North Carolina.[30] In addition to the shared goal of enhancing food access, these markets promote greater self-sufficiency and entrepreneurship, while simultaneously building and boosting community. Among the many kinds of fruits and vegetables that some of the farmers bring to the many market are muskmelons, cantaloupes, yams, red, yellow, and orange peppers, green bell peppers, cucumbers, yellow squash, cabbage, zucchini, tomatoes, greens, and corn. Herbs include basil, fennel, oregano and mint. At the Richmond, Virginia (RVA) markets there are a variety of vendors including "a mix of growers, purveyors and artists." Also sold are jams, cakes, and confections. One of the stated purposes of the RVA market is to fly in the face of the data that suggests "the typical farmer is a 58-year-old white male who has been farming on his land for over 20 years."[31] Because less than 5 percent of American farmers are Black, it is necessary for Black people to create their own spaces to provide support. Accordingly, "While intended to support and uplift the Black community, the [RVA] market, which is held on the third Saturday of each month through November, welcomes growers of all levels from commercial farms to backyard ventures, as well as people of all colors. We're not excluding anyone at all, but it's for us to have that space, so we know it's there."[32] And having that space is important. Again, it is not a cure-all but a necessary corrective and restorative action.

Crystal Taylor, a vendor from North Carolina, described to Grace Abels of *Facing South* some of the challenges that Black growers frequently face. Taylor, a co-organizer of Black August in the Park and the Black Farmers' Market in North Carolina, spoke of the competitive, rigid, expensive, and overall difficult process of getting into a farmers market: "When they have restrictions on what they can sell, what they can't sell, and things of that nature, it makes it hard for farmers that don't have all the resources and opportunities that white farmers have." Samantha Foxx, a grower from Mother's Finest Urban Farms of Winston-Salem, said that at white-dominated markets, African American and racially and ethnically different vendors can feel like the space is "flat-out unwelcoming." She further remarked, "I mean, it's a traditional setting, you know, is a nice way to put it. . . . I've had people who come by me, and I'm like, 'Hey, how are you doing?' And they don't even look my way. Even if we have the best things to offer, they don't even want to consider what we have."[33]

Foxx's experience played out in downtown Washington, D.C., following the police killing of George Floyd and the Black Lives Matter protests that took place in the city. In 2020, Freshfarm, a local farmers market organization that sponsors the trendy, upscale Dupont Circle market, indicated that they took an anti-racist stance by promoting Black vendors in their network. Toyin Alli of the food booth Puddin' took them to task by pushing back on their claim. Alli wrote on her Instagram feed, "Please refrain from using my business to demonstrate [your] 'inclusiveness' when I know y'all not about that life!" In an interview with *Forbes* magazine, Alli shared that of "the roughly 150 vendors at Freshfarm, only 15 or so are Black and that in the seven years she had been applying, [she] had been repeatedly denied, without explanation, one of the coveted spots at the Dupont Circle market." The *Forbes* article goes on to state, "[Alli's] impression was that spots were awarded based on tenure and financial stability, but efforts to show her business's financial viability were never enough."[34] This is just part of what happens in the "farm to table" journey when anti-Black racism seeps onto the dinner plate. It is rendered invisible to keep all of us feeling good about our food. We all want to believe that food practices are filled with kumbaya moments, when the reality is that food brings out the most vile, racist, unequal, inequitable parts of humanity.

I am not a farmer, but I concur with how Samantha Foxx describes many non-Black farmers markets: "A traditional setting, you know, is a nice way to put it." What Foxx and the other Black sellers were describing is that energy that I also found missing during my visit to the southern city farmers market I visited the day before my presentation. Alli's experience in Dupont Circle may explain why there was only one Black vendor at the market I visited, or it could be the competitive, restrictive nature of the rules that Crystal Turner described. Either or both of these observations may also explain more about why the lone Black vendor was at the end of the pathway. Though this seller seemed perfectly fine to be alone while he was setting up, I did wonder about the seeming absence of community for him—both in customers and among the other vendors. This kind of noticeable absence did not seem to be existent during the Black Farmers' Market program. According to the articles by Gray, Mellon, and Abels, these market spaces cultivate a family-reunion style atmosphere where people network, gain exposure to new clients, and heighten representation of people's merchandise. This attempt to increase awareness was not just about the freshly picked food but also about exposing people to agriculture. These Black farmers market spaces are environments of empowerment that reach well beyond the vegetable leaves and tables of tomatoes.

In reading about Black farmers markets as environments of empowerment, I thought back to when I walked along the pathway that took me past stall after stall at the southern city farmers market. In addition to there being only one Black vendor, at the time I visited the market, there were two Black people walking unhurriedly from one end of the market to the other. Most likely this was because the vendors were still setting up and had not officially opened for business that day. The customers were a man, who appeared to be aged by the vicissitudes of life, and a younger-looking African American woman. They did not seem to be a couple, however, but more like an older gentleman and his daughter or a social worker and her client. As they approached the EBT/SNAP table, upon which sat a Trader Joe's bag and a mason jar filled with clear liquid, I watched them and wondered how much he would be able to purchase at this place, given the ratio of his monthly allotment to the costs of the items for sale. How much pasture-raised pork, grass-fed beef, or free-range chicken could he buy using his SNAP benefits? Who would cook the kohlrabi and radishes for him? What kind of meal would be made? I thought all about this in the context of my being told that part of the grant application was to appeal to the displaced African American consumers. If this was the case, then the optics of the market were way off in terms of the vendors and the foods they offered.

For me, this assessment was further cemented by the casual appearance of the Trader Joe's bag and mason jar sitting on the EBT/SNAP table. No doubt the twentysomething woman staffing the table thought nothing of it as she laid down the bag that contained the food stamp supplies and the mason jar holding what was presumably her water. But, as one who extensively studies and teaches about how we use objects and their many meanings, I read these innocently placed things in a very different way. Trader Joe's is a boutique grocery chain founded in 1967 by Joe Coulombe in Pasadena, California, with just over 500 locations throughout the United States. Its average customer makes over $80,000 a year and, one may assume, is highly educated. In their *Business Insider* article "Meet the Typical Trader Joe's Shopper," Dominick Reuter and Heather Schlitz quote from Coulombe's memoir, in which he indicates his target customer is "over-educated and underpaid with a taste for whole-bean coffee and fresh brie, rather than 'the masses who willingly consumed Folger's coffee, Best Foods Mayonnaise, Wonder Bread, Coca-Cola, etc.'" This "younger, married, college-educated person earning over $80,000 [is a] typical customer [who] visits Trader Joe's 13 times per year—and picks up 15 products for a total cost of about $47 per trip. . . . Shoppers tend to choose pre-made foods like frozen dinners and salad kits, as well as brands like GT's Living Foods and Volpi cured meats."[35]

And then there was the mason jar. Historically, the mason jar was used for canning and preserving vegetables and fruits. As a common household object, it could very well have also been used for holding food items or drinks. In today's cultural moment of "hipness," however, the mason jar has a new meaning. In the article "Authenticity, Repurposed, in a Mason Jar," Claire Martin writes, "Several years ago, the simple Mason jar was more likely to be found in the nooks of grandmothers' pantries than on retailers' shelves. It was salvaged from near extinction by businesses eager for a homespun aesthetic in a sturdy, affordable package—many of them hoping to lure the millennials who have fetishized the jars in photographs on Instagram and Pinterest." So while a hundred or even seventy years ago the jar was used out of necessity, the turning point for contemporary use came around the 2008 recession, according to Chris Scherzinger, president and chief executive of Jarden Home Brands, which currently makes Ball- and Kerr-brand mason jars. As more people began to return to the "core of their roots," they also began having "an aversion to processed food" and intensifying their focus "on self-sufficiency and eking out as much value as they could from what they bought—and at a reasonable cost." Moreover, this younger generation wanted to take more control over their environment, including knowing where their food comes from and how it is made. Scherzinger sums it up this way: "[With] the personalized food movement, 82 percent of Jarden Home Brands' customers have their own gardens, and many patronize farmers' markets. . . . They want to get their hands dirty; they want to be involved in the process, selection and the making of their food. . . . And canning is an extension of that." Chief among this customer base are millennials. According to Laura Gordon, vice president for marketing and brand innovation at 7-Eleven, for millennials the jars are a "combination of simplicity and an emotional, fun nostalgia." Gordon goes on to say that 7-Eleven sells the jars in an effort to court younger consumers. She concludes, "We really do believe the millennials are striving for a combination of what's real and also that moment of going a little bit against the grain so they can show their individuality."[36]

When I gave my presentation the day after visiting the farmers market, I mentioned my impromptu experiences there, not knowing the young woman who managed the EBT/SNAP table would be there. She did not take kindly to my remarks and, in fact, was visibly upset by the time I finished my overall discussion. It was not my intention to hurt or shame anyone. However, doing this kind of community work will elicit emotional responses because it tears at the fabric of who we are or think we are morally and ethically. And the truth of dealing with other people's hard-core realities—especially Black people's realities—is that it will make you check your privilege. If this makes you uncomfortable, well, then you have more work to do on yourself before you try to help someone else. I had not seen the article on mason jars back in 2015 when I visited the southern city farmers market, but I did not need to. I knew enough to know back then that millennials' use of mason jars was "a thing" and that it, along with the Trader Joe's bag, shouted "upscale" and "hip," both of which were mirrored on the landscape of the farmers market that day in the southern city. And whether or not the older Black man saw or paid attention to the random items, I did, and both of those things together sitting on that EBT/SNAP table signaled to me, "You don't belong here; you can't afford this."

It is possible that the haggard-looking Black man I saw that day at the market did, like the typical Trader's Joe customer, make over $80,000 a year and was very well educated, but my lived experiences of being Black in America told me this was not the case. He looked like life had beaten him down to where, at least on that day, he was using food stamps. When my friend and I left the area, the man and his companion were sitting on a picnic table across the street from the market. As we drove away, I felt sad, very sad, at the situation that had him waiting for this place to open to buy food that most likely would not satiate him in body, mind, or spirit. I was also very angry and annoyed by the audacity of this group of people to use the African American community, people who had been forced out of their homes and away from their stores, their playgrounds, and their neighborhoods, as pawns to lure in grant money. By all appearances, the grant writers had absolutely no intention of catering to Black people. At the very least, they were grossly misinformed about what would appeal to this particular customer base. As we drove away and on to our next event, I grew despondent as I also wondered if anyone there actually cared. I made notes about the market all the while wishing there had been farm stalls with names such as Sankofa, Puddin', Freedom Farm, Mother's Finest, Fertile Ground, or other monikers, attended to by people with faces that would have signaled, "You are good here."

I have thought about this experience many times and replayed it time and time again in my head. As I was working on this chapter, I again thought back to it and realized that part of what bothered me then, and so many times since, was the feeling of disempowerment that surrounds the farmers market space. It is the exact opposite of what Abels heard vendors in the Black Farmers' Market initiative describe as one of their goals. As I was writing, I had to consider my own most recent visit to a local farmers market. This was a new venture since I had relocated. Though everything about the market screamed, "You won't like it here," I thought I would give it a try since I was in the mood for some new and different kinds of veggies. Because the market was reopening during the COVID pandemic, there were a lot of rules and directional signs. One of the first things I noticed as I exited my car was that pretty much everyone had their own reusable bag—from Whole Foods, Wegmans, or Trader Joe's; with a local library logo; or with other demarcations reflecting their owner's life, habits, and behaviors. I returned to my car and retrieved my own reusable bags, including one that had an image of Tiana, the only African American Disney princess, from Walt Disney Pictures' forty-ninth animated feature film, *The Princess and the Frog*. The bag had been gifted to my daughter when we all excitedly went to see the film, and now I use it to convey my own messages of Black girl-ness (despite the fact that it is a Disney product). With the bag in hand, I thought to myself, "Okay, here we go."

Before I knew it, I had spent upwards of fifty dollars for only a couple of items that would last my daughter and me maybe a couple of days. I had gotten most of the way around the loop when I thought, "I have to stop or I will be broke when I leave here." I also knew I would definitely be stopping by Food Lion on the way home to get all of the "real" things I needed from the store. I also stopped buying because there were only a few customers and one vendor who looked like me, and the vendor was selling homemade fruit juices. Though there was a voter registration booth, someone selling coffee, and a booth run by a local Asian food restaurant, all the other vendors looked racially the same and sold pretty much the same foods, with an exception here and there of flowers or meat and poultry. I asked myself, Where are the Black and Brown farmers? I mean, in all of the DMV, there were none who could be invited to participate in this weekly market experience? Surrounded by numerous bumper stickers that read "No farms, no food," I thought, So Black people don't eat? In the apocalypse, will we all die because there are no Black farmers? Looking around, one would think this is the case. The setting would have been the perfect place to yell out the words of Toyin Alli of the food booth Puddin', who was repeatedly denied access to the D.C. farmers market: "Y'all not about that life!" White food activists talk a good game, but when the rubber meets the road, oftentimes Black farmers are left out of the conversation.

I thought about all of this when I read Gerrit Marks's op-ed in the *Washington Post* about being a longtime vendor at the 32nd Street Farmers Market in Baltimore, Maryland. His excitement is palpable when he writes,

> So the markets have been my life. Even during those bone-chilling winter days when I wondered if I'd ever get warm again, I still would not trade the work for the warmth and security of the cubicle. . . . The mechanics of the markets, the setup and teardown, are something of a well-rehearsed and choreographed ballet. The first trucks rumble into the darkened space between 4:30 and 5 in the morning. . . . "Real estate" is at a premium, but everyone has his space. Boundaries are respected; tents and tables mark the layout of each stand. No fights break out, no shouting matches—we all know where we belong.[37]

This sense of belonging is exactly what Toyin Alli was seeking from the Dupont Circle market in Washington, D.C., and it is what was missing for me at the new farmers market that I shopped at with my Tiana bag. It was also what was missing for me at the southern city farmers market in 2015. How many Black and Brown vendors have been left out of finding their place of belonging at these food spaces where premium real estate is offered, but not to them? How many times do Black and Brown farmers and vendors get told there are no available cubicles because boundaries have to be respected?

Here is where the research of sociologist and professor of environmental justice Monica White is instructive. In her book *Freedom Farmers: Agricultural Resistance and the Black Freedom Movement*, White details the history of African Americans and agriculture in this country, beginning with enslavement and the vast amount of knowledge, foods, and seeds that the enslaved brought with them across the treacherous Middle Passage. She reminds readers that in the nineteenth century newly freed African Americans were denied their promised forty acres and a mule by the federal government, which instead took the millions of acres of land—which had been stolen from American Indian and Indigenous peoples—and gave it to white homesteaders. This move created generations of wealth for white Americans while it simultaneously thrust generations of Black and Brown people into cycles of poverty from which we are still trying to extract ourselves. Coming out of enslavement, with the promised opportunities thwarted by President Andrew Johnson, most African Americans were forced into sharecropping. This was another arrangement that enabled white planters to garner considerable wealth while saddling Black families with debt-inducing poverty that, in many cases, has lasted for generations.[38]

In their study on regional and income differences in the African American diet, Ellen Harris and Alvin Nowverl state that before the 1960s, African Americans had the best dietary habits in the United States, despite ethnic, economic, social, cultural, and environmental differences, because we relied on the land to feed us. This was largely due to necessity and because we had few options. It was also because over time some African Americans had been able to purchase and own land. In an article for *Mother Jones* magazine, Leah Penniman, codirector of Soul Fire Farm in upstate New York and author of *Farming While Black*, describes how "Black farmers innovated methods that remain at the core of sustainable agriculture today." Chief among these innovators was George Washington Carver, a pioneering professor at the historically Black Tuskegee Institute (now Tuskegee University) in Alabama, who developed hundreds of products using peanuts but also championed crop rotation on cotton farms. Penniman explains, "Carver . . . wanted farmers to grow peanuts . . . because he was trying to convince them to plant nitrogen-fixing legumes into diverse crop rotations, which would improve the soil in a region that had been burned by decades of mono-crop cotton farming."[39] Carver went on to develop an information-dissemination system known as the movable school, which was essentially a horse-drawn carriage outfitted with all the latest gadgets and tools to help farmers who could not get to the agricultural experiment stations set up by the United States Department of Agriculture, an idea that has given rise to the modern-day extension program.

In the 1920s, there were nearly a million Black farmers working on over 40 million acres of land. Today, we make up only about 1.4 percent of the nation's farm owners, and we tend less than 5 million acres of farmland. This is due in so small part to a history of racist policies that denied federal farm subsidies to African Americans. It is also due to the rise in the Ku Klux Klan, which meted out white supremacist violence in Tulsa, Oklahoma; Rosewood, Florida; and countless other locales about which we have little or no recollection or information. These towns were entirely destroyed by the white violence, and the Black residents were driven out. Black land was stolen, like that in Manhattan Beach, California, which was originally owned by Charles and Willa Bruce, an African American couple. The Bruces created a lucrative seaside resort called Bruce's Beach Lodge. In the 1920s, at the request of white residents, the city of Manhattan Beach seized the beachfront property and forced out all the Black families. The Bruces had their resort stolen and generations of wealth and fortune along with it. In October 2021, the governor of California, Gavin Newsome, signed a bill that would give the land back to the Bruce family, the descendants of whom are Black and American Indian. As we had our lands stolen and our opportunities for wealth denied, the value of land continued to grow in to the twenty-first century, making it "prohibitively expensive" for new Black farmers and those seeking to reclaim stolen lands "to break into agriculture, meaning that white dominance of farmland maintains plenty of momentum."[40]

Black Americans have always had to fight racism, and we have done this at the ballot box (or in order to be able to go to the ballot box), with lawsuits, and with violence. We have always had to fight for even the smallest pieces of land, though we helped white people in this country grow wealthy by working the very land that we have been denied. Erin White of the Community Food Lab, a group based in Raleigh, North Carolina, that works to design a more equitable food system, explains the urgency and necessity of the Black Farmers' Market initiative this way: "We need to understand that the entire agricultural system in the U.S. is built on the exploitation of Black and Brown people."[41] This is one of the many reasons why cooperative strategies like the Black Farmers' Market initiative is key. These spaces make it possible for Black people to enjoy economic, cultural, and emotional empowerment. And we have always used these strategies of self-help and cooperative economics. In chapter 1, I mentioned historian Kelsey Bates's account of the African American community in Gee's Bend, Alabama, who found themselves in severe and dire straits after the white merchant who had been providing loans so Gee's Benders could purchase agricultural supplies passed away. Shortly thereafter, the African American residents had their agricultural equipment violently seized. According to Bates, the African American community survived by entering a collective whereby they shared food, information, supplies, money, and other resources.

Looking at similar situations from a food studies point of view, Monica White and Priscilla McCutcheon detail how Black farmers formed organizations and cooperatives to create alternative systems in which to farm and market their products, increasing their self-sufficiency. These acts led not only to economic self-reliance but also to the ability to practice cultural sustainability. For example, in late 1967, Mississippi voting rights activist Fannie Lou Hamer started the Freedom Farm Cooperative (FFC) to create collaboratively maintained community gardens in an effort to reduce reliance on white merchants and increase access to food. According to White, the FFC dedicated a large portion of their acreage "to subsistence crops and kitchen crops, where co-op members planted greens, kale, rape, turnips, corn, sweet potatoes, okra, tomatoes, string and butter beans." They also had a catfish cooperative and land for grazing cattle and planting cotton, soybeans, and wheat. With the income from these cash crops, the organization was able to help people pay their mortgages, buy much-needed supplies, receive educational and retraining opportunities, and access health care and disaster relief. By availing themselves of the help offered by the FFC, families were not only able to eat, because they had a pig bank, where they raised and bred pigs to help feed people, but also community gardens, a commercial kitchen, and a tool bank. Black families were able to send their children to a Head Start program, work at and secure clothes from a garment factory, or participate in a sewing cooperative. Many were able to find shelter in low-income, affordable housing units, which supported the needs of African Americans who were fired or evicted for exercising the right to vote. This cooperative enterprise, which went on to inform contemporary Black agricultural self-sufficiency efforts in places like Detroit, Chicago, Milwaukee, New York City, and New Orleans, is a foundational example for "current conversations regarding the resurgence of agriculture in the context of food justice/sovereignty movements in urban spaces."[42]

Around the same time that the Freedom Farm Cooperative was established, in the late 1960s, the Federation of Southern Cooperatives / Land Assistance Fund was founded to provide financial, technical, and cooperative assistance to Black farmers and landowners. And in 1995, the National Black Farmers Association was formed in Virginia to advocate for the rights of Black farmers. It was a key player in *Pigford v. Glickman*, in which Black farmers sued the U.S. Department of Agriculture for racial discrimination in providing loans and other assistance. Winning the $2 billion settlement was just the beginning. The fight continues. Black communities continue to use such agricultural strategies "as the basis for resistance [in fighting] for the right to participate in the food system as producers and to earn a living wage in the face of racially, socially, and politically repressive conditions."[43] The Black Farmers' Market is, by and large, a product of Hamer's early initiatives because even today, cooperative economics is both needed and necessary.

I want to be clear not to romanticize the food and community-building process, so that "Black" is synonymous with "good" and "white" with "bad." As I have discussed throughout this book, though we usually find collaboration among and between groups working for social, cultural, and economic change, intraracial conflict is also a thing. Just because we are all Black or African American does not mean we do not have to put in critical effort when doing activist or community-building work. Our complexities as people inform our relationships to power—how we exercise it, resist it, entertain it, and live in it. Power is heterogeneous, dynamic, ever-changing, productive, unproductive, and inhibiting. It can manifest itself through food interactions as forcefully as a violent blow or as subtly as a gentle breeze. We would do well, then, to recognize that power has its own metalanguage, which is another reason that cultural sustainability practices are important. These practices allow us to engage food and power on our own terms, even when the odds are not in our favor and when our food interactions are policed and shamed. Because everyone likes the familiar. And when we do not know what something is or how to control it and make it do what we want it to do, we ridicule it. We shame it. We shun it. Again, sometimes our intention is to help improve people's lives by inviting them to come get good, new, fresh, or "better" food. Sometimes it is to encourage people to eat "healthier." Often, however, it can all fall flat when we do not do the necessary research on the community and when we do not take time "to read the room."

One final example may serve to illustrate this last point. I had been invited to speak at a university in the Southwest, and when a church organization heard I was coming they asked if I could also meet with them. The church group was trying to figure out how to encourage their congregation to eat "healthy." In particular, they had concerns about how to garden, because the task was overwhelming to a number of them but they had repeatedly been told it was "the thing to do." So a luncheon meeting was set up, and on the menu were baked chicken, rice, vegetables, salad, iced tea, and dessert. After some brief introductions, and once everyone had had a chance to get lunch, I began explaining my work in churches and other community organizations and the primary arguments that I would be laying out later that day at the university talk. After I finished my brief remarks, but before we began discussing the concerns of the attendees, a local community leader was given the floor to share a couple of food experiences with the luncheon group. The speaker explained that a family member of hers had survived a major health scare and that prior to surgery she had vowed to the family member that when they recovered, their family would become vegans. Gone, she explained, were her "beloved cheese" and other tasty foods. In their place were vegan ingredients and recipes. To be sure, we applaud those who make dramatic or even mundane changes to their lives to prolong their health, and those in attendance said as much. But for some, the hand-clapping and back-patting turned to disapproval when the speaker began to admonish the other attendees for not adopting the same or a similar stance. Even as our plates, filled with chicken bones, sat before us, it felt like we were castigated for being omnivores. We were told, "Being vegan is easy. All you have to do is . . ."

My mind drifted off because it more or less went into overdrive at hearing her comment. I felt especially attacked as I sat there, having flown hundreds of miles with a fourth grader in tow, deadlines swirling on my calendar, my bank account low. For a brief moment, I felt like a bad mother. Little did she know that in addition to juggling the normal stuff in my life, I had started my trip by purchasing tons of vegetarian snacks because my daughter had announced earlier that week that she was no longer eating meat. Knowing she would be hungry throughout the long days of travel, I had purchased lots of different items on short notice, not knowing whether we would have refrigeration, whether she would like them, or whether (or when) she would change her mind again. Days later, with many of the snacks gone or simply considered "nasty," I wondered how I could sustain such a lifestyle, having experimented with several options and blown almost eighty dollars on munchies. I thought all of this as I simply responded, "It's all relative, no?" as I looked closely at the speaker and realized she spoke vehemently about preserving life even as she wore a smart-fitting leather skirt.

The point here is not to be snarky or facetious but highlight how contradictions can and do surround us when we speak with zeal about food practices that enthrall and excite us. Often, an advocate mounts a soapbox not from malice but out of a strong desire to see others enjoy the same privileges of health and welfare that the advocate is experiencing. Of course, this is one perspective. Another perspective recognizes that every culture has spokespeople who see it as their duty to inform us of the best way to live. From First Lady Michelle Obama's organic garden to policy proposals that tax soda consumption to Julia Robert's meal-based healing on the big screen, food is a site of American political, social, and cultural fixation. Increasing attention has been paid to processes of food production, distribution, acquisition, and consumption that tend to operate apart from but within conventional food systems or industrial monoculture.[44] These ideas and terms have been made popular by a few (primarily white but also some Black) men and women whom the media has appointed as the national spokespersons or cultural intermediaries on food production and consumption. They can also be self-appointed and socially appointed experts who see themselves as imbued with the power to instruct others on the correct way of eating. These spokespeople often vie for the ability to decide what foods are and are not acceptable, whose voice should and should not be heard on the subject, and which modes of food acquisition should be sanctioned and which are to be disdained. And as Lisa Heldke points out, often these admonitions come with a particular tone of moral certitude.

One reason it seems that it is possible for these cultural intermediaries of food to convince Black people of the "best" and "right" food culture is because so few people really know the intricate aspects of Black history, let alone African American food histories. Some advocates in the food movement see the solution as "turning away from all edible food-like substances," as Michael Pollan terms them, and embracing the "fresh, local, and . . . organic" by tapping into alternative food networks (AFNs)—farmers markets, co-ops, community-sponsored agriculture sites, and the like.[45] Alison Alkon and Julian Agyeman point out that making the choice to engage with these particular kinds of food outlets is a means of voting "with your fork." Though generally small in scale, these sites of food production, acquisition, and consumption are multifaceted and variegated. They are spaces where not only can fresh food be obtained but a sense of connection can be established, affirmed, and maintained with the people, places, and processes involved with growing and supplying food. Sometimes engaging with these spaces is also a vote for environmental sustainability and biologically diverse polycultures because they avoid synthetic pesticides and fertilizers.[46] All of this is in line with the conversation above that speaks to the sense of belonging and disbelonging that can exist in these food outlets.

Similar to Alkon and Agyeman, Julie Guthman, in her revealing essay "Bringing Food to Others," shares that some alternative food networks tend to cater primarily to those who have the wealth to participate in them. These consumers have the cultural cachet and capital to indulge in eating niche products—free-range eggs, chickens, bison meat, fifty-dollar turkeys, arugula, artichokes—and so on.[47] These purchasers of what Guthman calls "yuppie chow" have similar backgrounds, values, and proclivities and have produced their own monoculture. This kind of consumer most likely shops at food outlets inclusive of, but not limited to, the kinds of boutique grocery stores and farmers markets that I discussed in regard to my visit to the southern city market. In some instances, these are experiences of food tourism, an example of which was captured in Tracey Middlekauff's 2011 *Urbanite* essay, "Romancing the Farm: Farmers Lure City Folk with Promises of Pastoral Bliss." As this phenomenon was emerging, Middlekauff wrote that the adventure was designed to lure "city folk with promises of pastoral bless." She said, "This is not your grandmother's farm festival. These well-heeled adults have each plunked down $50 to attend the festival, hosted by the farm's fashionable owners." Today there is an entire cottage industry devoted to farm food tours where people can "go behind the scenes to meet the makers and taste the wide array of artisanal food and libations coming from our local food shed."[48] It is possible to get caught up in the thrill of such an experience— celebrity chefs, country air, beautiful-looking and good-tasting food and drink, and lots of socializing. Like using mason jars to reclaim a sense of nostalgia, going on an outing to a farm re-creates a sense of an agrarian past that was a more innocent time—for some. In 1999 chef, artist, and former model Jim Denevan founded the organization Outstanding in the Field, in which chefs and farmers collaborate to provide a star-powered event for "people [who] are drawn to stories about a more innocent time in the nation's rural past." Middlekauff quotes Denevan: "Before the 1950s, there would be a harvest, and the community would come together as a reward and share in it for free. . . . Now people feel separated from that. And they'll pay to be reconnected to that lost sense of belonging."[49] There it is again, that sense of belonging that is connected to food. While there is no indictment here of people who have the financial means to participate in these events, which provide a sense of inclusion, engender warmth, and offer good food to boot, this kind of outing is somewhat hypocritical. Some of the same doctors, foodies, and maybe even nutrition advocates who will criticize poor, African American, full-figured Latrisha will go to these kinds of events and drink and eat themselves into a fatty liver at $180 per person. Why is this cultural experience considered better eating than a Sunday meal that consists of collard greens, fried chicken, and macaroni and cheese?

There is another concern here, that some visitors may leave this event confusing real life with this very well curated performance. I said as much when Middlekauff interviewed me for her article: "People love that [harvest] story. . . . The trouble is, it's not based in fact. We cherish the idea of citizens of small farming towns sitting down together to share the fruits of the harvest, but in reality, many people couldn't even get close to the harvest." Middle-kauff elaborated on my view by writing that I "call[ed] these present-day farm experiences 'performances,' not true representations of the harsh real-ities of farm life, because they don't expose people to farms that are barely surviving—those that can't afford the time or resources to gussy up their property and make it visually appealing and tourist-friendly." My point was that these events represent one kind of farm-to-table experience. But, just like tourists who visit Colonial Williamsburg or historic Wild West towns, you are getting a performance, not reality. Places designed to celebrate the colonial era, for example, are devoid of the smell of urine and feces, or any of the other unpleasantness of living in the actual era. These spaces omit all of the things that give rise to death, disease, and other unpleasantries—so visitors receive an idealized view designed for the tourists' enjoyment. This is what makes the event a culinary tourism experience; you indulge in the foods of a culture without immersing yourself in the actual culture. Middlekauff concludes, "Williams-Forson adds that there's nothing wrong with paying for a farm dinner or wanting to spend some time in a rural environment. '[You can] have that fantasy—if you can afford it,' she says. 'But know that what you're getting is a culinary invention. Let's not act like it's more than it is.'" Again I ask, other than the price tag, what makes these experiences richer than an African American family reunion at the family homestead, where the aunties and uncles play good music, enjoy lots of laughter, drink good drinks, and eat heartily from tables lined with well-smoked barbecue?[50]

In the same way that an authentic past (a very loaded phrase) is sought in the mason jar, it is looked for in the farm experience. When people gathered for the Tomato Festival hosted by farmer Steve Goertemiller and his partner Anita in Maryland in 2012, the event was highly in demand. Tracey Middle-kauff indicated that Anita believed the event was so popular because these days "farms are few and far between. We're losing farmland, and people want their kids to experience it." Steve added, "People are tired of this plastic so-ciety, where nothing is real anymore."[51] Again, this point of view echoes the unspoken conversation around the Trader Joe's bag and mason jar sitting on the EBT/SNAP table at the southern city farmers market. In both situations, many of those who celebrate farm life or "real food" have gained from de-cades of gentrification due to redlining, redistricting, easily acquired loans, capitalism run amok, and a reduction in government control and spending. It is interesting because while many of these partakers nostalgically want to reconnect to a past that was more real than plastic, there are many more women and people of color who never want to return to the period when America was supposedly at its greatest.

It is curious that there is this strong need to marry nostalgia with ruralism and agriculture in order to reclaim a sense of innocence. What does this mean? Innocence for whom? And how far back is the past? Because there is little that America can speak of as innocent when the early twentieth century bore witness to African Americans sharecropping and being lynched, Japanese Americans being forced into internment camps, American Indians being annihilated or thrust further onto reservations, and Latinos being subjected to mass deportations, along with so many other injustices. This is why I say that food is so mired in gender, race, and class that the reality of it is hard to dissect. Ignoring this so we can focus only on the feel-good aspects of food means that we erase the realities of many people's lives. There are a lot of people for whom this is a new kind of foodie experience that is very eye-opening. However, the mid-twentieth century ushered in several social movements, from civil rights to ashrams, communes, and 1960s counterculture, in which people were eating from the land, producing and preparing food with their own hands. Far from romantic, it was a hard time, as we know from the work of organizations like Fannie Lou Hamer's Freedom Farm. While foodies and advocates are urging us to cook slow and cook at home, they forget that most people of color were eating from the land in the not-so-distant past. Even fifty years ago we would grow okra, peas, potatoes, cucumbers, squash, lettuce, eggplant, watermelons, tomatoes, onions, and other produce on the plots of land on which we lived. It is not that today's encouragement to eat by going "back to the land" is not valid; it is that many Black families are very familiar with this way of eating and have been for a long time. And as quiet as it is kept, despite what we see on social media and in popular culture, we still eat these foods, albeit in different ways. For one, we just cannot eat the same way our ancestors did, for many reasons, including changes to the land, climate, and soil. The notion that we should eat only foods that our great-grandparents would recognize is interesting but not altogether realistic.

This latter point was emphasized to me on two occasions. Almost daily in the summertime, my elderly cousin Daut would amble out of her small rambler home across the street from us and wander into the wooded lot beside her house with a brown paper bag. She would emerge about forty-five minutes later with the bag filled to the brim with either pokeweed or cress (which we called crees). I watched her perform this ritual many times, and often after I saw her return to her house I would go over to sit and talk about anything, everything, and nothing, while she cooked the greens. In 1997, around the time I first started studying African American food cultures, Daut was eighty years old and still had a sharp memory. I recorded a conversation with her in which she shared this bit of wisdom:

> Mama never did do no work outside the house. She stayed at home all the time and did housework. She wouldn't go out to work, oh no. She had enough to take care of right there at the house 'cause she had her chil'lun. . . . She just stayed at home and worked. And could cook. Mama could cook. Back then Mama could make some good spoonbread. That's how I learned. We'd eat the spoonbread with poke salad and crees salad. Now crees salad is good, too, and they easy to make. You just put some onions in them and fry 'em. Lawd, girl, you got a pot. Cook some chicken backs—I love chicken backs—strings beans and potatoes, and you have a meal. . . . Girl, that's good there. We had good food back then. Chile, you can't eat that food now, 'cause it would make you sick! Yeah, you can't eat that food like we used to eat when we was coming up. I could take bread and sop 'lasses and grease. Let me do it now. See if it won't make me sick. 'Cause it was fresh then, so we could do it. We would get stuff right out the garden. Papa use to raise a garden and we used to work it.[52]

Even thirty years ago, eating foods from a nostalgically remembered past was all but impossible. I learned so much watching Daut work and listening to her talk—including that poke salat, a dish made from pokeweed, can be toxic to humans if not prepared correctly. But it is not only about the landscape and knowing how and from where your food comes from; you also have to know how to cook particular foods. And when you're planning to grow your own food, you have to have a lot of time and patience for the growing process and give attention to the soil.

I was in the Midwest as a keynote speaker at a conference in 2013 when I noticed an older Black man who sat in the back of the room nodding his head. Though he appeared interested in everything that was being said, he offered no comments of his own, nor did he ask any questions. After seeing him at two or three events, I went over to thank him for coming. As we struck up a conversation, he told me that he really appreciated my points about growing your own food because he was from Trinidad and Tobago and had tried several times, unsuccessfully, to grow some of the vegetables and herbs that reminded him of home. He went on to share that, while he would often work hard to treat and turn over the dirt, by the time he felt the soil was ready for whatever seeds he had, the temperature would have changed, making it impossible for him to carry on. This perspective had not occurred to me. I know that we are all in different regions and should grow various foods accordingly, but I had never considered the problems that American soil and temperatures would pose for someone from outside the country who wanted to plant the foods they were accustomed to.

Many of these nuances are lost on people because we just do not go deep enough in our conversations about food. We tend to stop with our own experiences, which are important and valid but represent only one perspective. This includes the experiences related throughout this book, which is why my goal here is open up conversations rather than provide definitive answers and conclusions. Knowing this, I sat in silence and listened carefully as the activist in the southwestern church group meeting shared her experiences of converting to veganism and urged others to do the same. As she spoke, I looked at the faces of the other luncheon attendees in the room. They had come hoping to be encouraged and to get ideas for how they could maneuver around the forces that kept them feeling trapped in a revolving cycle of endless messages about healthy eating, growing their own food, eating at home, and more. Many of the community faith-based leaders and laypeople who attended the event that day wanted to know how they could grow their own food, not because they wanted to, but because they felt they had to. To help allay some of their concerns, we talked about the usefulness of container gardens and growing herbs in egg cartons. My goal was to reassure them and inspire them to do whatever they could without feeling pressured to do something beyond their capabilities, time constraints, and even desires.

The concerns and worries of this audience were not atypical. People are anxious about food, feeling bombarded by so many different messages from so many different places—social media, cooking shows, magazines, morning and TV talk shows, popular culture, the government, doctors, friends and family members, schools, houses of worship, and even our own minds and bodies. Many of these messages are not incorrect; they just do not go far enough to consider the messiness of people's lives or the ways that food is weighed down by so many issues, most of which are discussed throughout this book. For example, Erin White, founder of the Raleigh, North Carolina–based group Community Food Lab, which works to design more equitable food systems, spoke frustratedly about Black people's "disengagement" from the food system: "We are allowing other interests to build the food system that works for them, and we end up with a food system that doesn't support human health, doesn't support racial equity, doesn't support sustainable land use, or climate responsibility."[53] Though White was not incorrect, there are a host of factors that disincline people from getting involved, age and inaccurate information about the past among them. I experienced pushback and reluctance myself when I tried to encourage members of my house of worship to participate in a community-sponsored agricultural program. CSAs are usually local groups whose members receive weekly boxes or bags of food from one or more farms in their region. The prospect of being able to receive fresh fruits and vegetables without a great deal of thought was exciting for the group of professional, early-thirties church members I talked to. They were even more "down for the cause" when I shared that as a large group we could get reduced prices. But their excitement disappeared when I mentioned the CSA would require us to work the land once a month. It was at that statement that they drew the line. One member said, "Yeahhhhhhh, my people did that work so I don't have to." And there were other murmurs, all of which ended in a resounding no. I understood their rejection of the idea and did not push it further. I knew it would take much more time to unpack their concerns, undo what they had been told, and erase negative perceptions to get them over the line to be in agreement. I did not have the time for any of that, so I did not push, but I did recognize that this is just one of many reasons why it is most prudent to meet people where they are.

Examples such as these illustrate why telling people that eating this way or that is easy if they only do x, y, or z is rarely helpful. People access food in different ways, sometimes in different ways at the same time. And though we may have some critical thoughts and feelings about supermarkets, they still are one of the primary vehicles for food distribution. But even supermarkets are not the sole remedy for many of our food dilemmas. Food activist LaDonna Redmond smartly maintains that access to full-service grocery stores does not guarantee that a person's eating habits will change. Alongside this, Redmond points out the weak position of another popular notion— more grocery stores means more healthy eating. As one article put it, she believes that "many people mistakenly make supermarkets the 'silver bullet' to change food access in urban areas [but] what's really needed is a rebuilt system." Redmond notes, "There should be a plethora of choices as far as how to spend one's dollars and how to best feed oneself. . . . Really focusing on supermarkets is missing the mark."[54] Interestingly, a United States Department of Agriculture study found that "even higher income households do not consume enough fruits and vegetables to meet recommendations, suggesting that other factors besides income play a strong role in fruit and vegetable purchasing behavior."[55] Furthermore, health economists J. Paul Leigh and DaeHwan Kim found that fast-food dining becomes more common as earnings increase from low to middle incomes and that "low prices, convenience and free toys target the middle class—especially budget-conscious, hurried parents—very well."[56] This study and others like it are why I gently pushed back against the young African American woman who asked "How do we get people to stop eating at McDonald's?" during the panel symposium in California. As I have already discussed, eating at McDonald's or any other fast-food restaurant is not necessarily a death knell unless it is done in excess. Furthermore, fast-food eating is not only relegated to the poor and low-income. Middle- and upper-class communities may have fewer and better fast-food options—places like Cava, Chick-fil-A, Panera Bread, and the like—but in the main, people of all income levels consume fast food.

So, if it is relatively unwise to place all the burden on supermarkets for being the root or source of healthy eating, it is equally unwise to blame fast food and bad eating alone for higher rates of obesity and disease among Black people. Given that we all have similar eating habits, regardless of income, what accounts for the health disparities? I turn back to Dr. A. Wilberforce Williams, whose work I discussed in chapter 1. Writing almost a century ago for the *Chicago Defender*, Williams identified then what still persists today: "Statistics show that under the same environments, the same locality, the same conditions as to hygiene, sanitation, housing, and working condition, the same medical care and hospitalization, the health of the Negro compares favorably with the health of other human unities living in similar environmental conditions. Therefore, we do not believe that there is any real Negro health problem." Williams goes on to suggest that "the Negro . . . must become inured and learn the art of mastering and controlling his environmental conditions."[57] Williams might be saddened to know that few situations have changed for "the Negro" at a systemic level that allow us to "master and control" our environmental conditions. To be sure, in a country that touts "liberty and justice for all," equal access to a living wage, as well as the ability to acquire and consume food that is both good to you and for you, should be an inalienable right. But sadly, we know it is not, and often those most affected are the elderly, those with low or no incomes, and those with

Black and Brown skin. Not surprisingly, these groups also tend to suffer dis-
proportionately from tooth decay, obesity, diabetes, hypertension, and other
diseases linked to years of unhealthy consumption of food, alcohol, or drugs,
and lack of exercise. As I shared in the previous chapter, what we overlook is
that most people do not *want* to live their lives in ways that are detrimental
to their health. But when you lack a living wage and affordable housing and
even access to housing in general, your dietary health may be the least of
your worries. The daily stress from centuries of racism, sexism, and gender
inequity, and multigenerational mental health issues, exacerbated by a lack of
health care (affordable or otherwise) may make you feel beaten to the core.

   So, no, farmers markets are not the only answer. Being a carnivore, pescatarian, vegetarian, or vegan is not the only answer. Independent artisan food
producers/chefs and community-owned or community-operated markets
are not the only answer. Food activism in the United States is focused largely
on developing alternatives to the conventional industrial food system, but
this also is not the only answer. To be sure, food movement participants and
activists provide an overwhelming amount of good food information, and
they have important insights, particularly regarding the nature and problems
of industrial agriculture—but this alone is also not the answer. And supermarkets are not the only answer. The answers, options, and variations are as
plentiful as the people who want to exercise them. Some folks will shop at
Walmart, Trader Joe's, and Costco only to go home and pick tomatoes from
their own vines. Some people eat only what they produce and shop only for
spices. Still others eat out every day of the week, despite having a freezer
full of good, homemade food, because their life that week, month, or year
is so overwhelming that the mere thought of putting a pot on the stove or
a container in the microwave might bring them to tears. You get the point!
People have to be allowed to live in whatever ways best fit their life, without
retribution, shame, and judgment.

   There are many solutions, and it will take collective work and action to
recognize that what works for one person or group may or may not work for
others. And it will take even more work to realize that people, Black people in
particular, do not need reforming. And why, in the twenty-first century, are
we trying to reform people's eating cultures, habits, and behaviors? This question leads to one of the many reasons the food movement has been heavily
critiqued. The movement has been characterized by lack of attention to issues
of privilege, race, and class, let alone assuming that others are wise enough
to suggest what everyone else should be eating. In his pointed commentary

on the food industry, agricultural economist Jayson Lusk takes on spokes-persons such as Michael Pollan, Mark Bittman, and Alice Waters and dubs them "the food police." Lusk maintains that this "elite" body of thinkers and writers "think they know exactly what we should grow, cook and eat." He goes on to explain: "The debate is nasty because our freedom is at stake. On one side are farmers who want to work, and consumers who want to eat, as they please; on the other side are self-proclaimed saviors of the food system, who want to make decisions for us. The food elite have appointed themselves our caretakers. They seek the power to steer food production and choice, claiming to know better than farmers and consumers."[58] Though Lusk goes on to suggest uncritically that we need to assume "responsibility for our own health, environment, and pocketbooks," as if that were always easy, some of his points are worth considering.

Another argument offered by Lusk is that organic food is not necessarily healthier or tastier (but certainly more expensive).[59] A similar point has been made by others, including Corby Kummer in his essay "The Great Grocery Smackdown: Will Walmart, not Whole Foods, Save the Small Farm and Make America Healthy?" Kummer's essay, which reinforces points made by Carole Counihan and myself in the introduction to *Taking Food Public: Redefining Foodways in a Changing World*, describes his visit to the grocery section of a Walmart supercenter. The author indicates that he had trouble believing he was in a Walmart because of the "very reasonable-looking pro-duce, most of it loose and nicely organized . . . [laid out] in black plastic bins." Kummer writes that one of the first things he saw when he entered the store was McIntosh apples that came from the same local orchard whose apples he had just seen similarly packaged at Whole Foods. Kummer suggests that in an ideal world people would buy their food directly from the people who grew or caught it, or grow and catch it themselves, on a daily basis.[60] But most of us do not live in this ideal world, or even in locations where getting your food directly from the grower on a daily basis is an option. We do, however, live in a world where sometimes your funds are so short that you have to wait until that day to know whether you will eat, what you will eat, and from where. And in contemporary America, we do live where "food spending rises with income. . . . But the form that the additional spending takes nowadays is food away from home and 'other foods' at the grocery store."[61] And all of this has been upended by the worst pandemic many of us have ever seen, which disrupted supply chains, making the prices for food and other goods even higher than usual. When we recognize these realities, we see that there

Figure 4.4. Walmart sign listing local produce available.
Richmond, Virginia, 2011. Photo by the author.

are multiple factors that affect our food choices and behaviors, and there are just as many that affect our health and well-being.

None of this means we should stop trying to be better versions of ourselves if we so choose. It also does not mean we should stop providing assistance to those who request our help or want to be in community with us around learning new, different, or better (for them) foodways. During the COVID lockdown, numerous social media groups emerged to walk people from the most rudimentary to the more complicated steps of growing, planting, and enjoying green life overall. Facebook groups such as Black Girls Grow Gardens Nationwide, Black Girls Grow in Container Gardens, Sow in Love Seed Exchange, Black Women Who Love Outdoor Living Spaces, and Gardening with Skinny Boy Randy, which welcome beginners and experts, sprang up or saw an increase in membership as quarantine and remaining indoors took away the social components of our everyday life. In many neighborhoods, being locked in and locked down allowed some people to reach out to local farms, whether in rural, suburban, or urban areas. Washington, D.C.–based Soilful City, for example, continued to provide education and employment opportunities to residents in underresourced parts of the city. In partnering with local residents, they aimed "to create community spaces that center around community health and wellness. These spaces use urban gardens as a central meeting space for residents to congregate around physical, mental, and spiritual well-being."[62] And who cannot benefit from a little bit of self-care?

For me, moving to a new space in a new state; dealing with a pandemic, end-of-life care for a family member, a family mental-health crisis, and daily reminders that white supremacy is alive and well; and attending to work-life balance issues all spurred me to seek outlets that acknowledge life and growth. It was never my intention to turn my balcony into a garden with containers that could feed my family. My intention in planting indoors and out was "to find [my] free," both during this viral pandemic and throughout the daily onslaught of messages that seek to discourage me from living my best life free, every day.[63]

EPILOGUE

When Racism Rests on Your Plate, Indeed, Worry about Yourself

In America, it is traditional to destroy the black body—it is heritage.
—Ta-Nehisi Coates, "Letter to My Son"

My early years were spent in upstate New York, where my father worked for the Neighborhood House in Buffalo's Fruit Belt area. The Fruit Belt, which lies outside the city limits, was named for the orchards planted by German immigrants. By the 1970s, the area was home to largely African American communities. My dad was a supervisor of community development, organizing community-based Black activist groups and block clubs like FIGHT (Freedom, Integration, God, Honor, Today). In 1967, in keeping with other efforts around the country, like those of Fannie Lou Hamer, the Black Panthers, and other Black community activists, the *I* in FIGHT was changed from "integration" to "independence" in recognition of Black people's self-sufficiency and self-reliance, amid programs providing drug counseling and weeklong youth camps.

Though my family were outsiders in the Fruit Belt community because we lived in the city proper, it never seemed uncomfortable for us to play with the kids who received federal food aid. We were them, or one paycheck and one thrift store away from being them. I remember the powdered milk and eggs along with the huge rectangular blocks of cheese that lined the shelves of our refrigerator. The food from government assistance is familiar all across America, back then and even more now. In her article "After the Reapers: Place Settings of Race, Class, and Food Insecurity," Eileen Cherry-Chandler recalls her own experience with government food when she was growing up in Toledo, Ohio. She writes, "The boxes and bags are dry goods: corn and oatmeal and powdered milk. The silver cans contain peanut butter, pork and gravy, a beef stew people say tastes pretty good, and powdered eggs. There is butter and an infamous five-pound chunk of yellow cheese [and] the most notorious commodity is a shiny 20-ounce can of pink meat we call 'spam,' although its official label was 'Processed Meat.'"[1] I did not know it then, but in adulthood, as I studied and wrote about food, I found out that we also participated in the East Side Cooperative Organization (ECCO) food co-op, where a bag of food cost $1.25. Born out of the East Side Coalition of Churches and Agencies, ECCO was one of the many grassroots projects that aided in reducing food insecurity. And we were often without enough food for our family of five.

As far as the eye could see or the skin could feel, Buffalo was cold and dreary. Summer came late and winter stayed forever, so gardens were the farthest thing from our minds. But summer meant dandelion wine, which our self-declared hippie neighbors taught our mom to make—they never hesitated to teach us the wonders of edible wild weeds, pottery making, and psychedelic creations of artistic self-expression. Sometime around the age of six, I started sucking my thumb. I don't know why, I just started doing it. One day, I heard my mom tell a friend on the phone that I sucked my thumb because I was hungry. I had no idea I was hungry. Hunger was the last thing on my mind—I think. I didn't feel hungry. Or at least I don't recall that I did. But I remember feeling ashamed, so I tried to stop the habit. We lived near the Buffalo zoo. We cooked out in the summer months and ate at smorgasbords after Sunday church, so I didn't know I was hungry. I remember when our family diet changed because my dad developed diabetes. Gone were white bread and gravy. Now we were eating tuna fish, frozen peas, and lots of salads. I had an all-around eclectic set of foodways—northern, southern, sometimes abundant, and sometimes lean. It was during the lean times that I learned the most about food shaming. On Saturdays, we went to Ms. Flood's for dance, an activity our family could afford because of the owner's generosity. At lunchtime, the three of us—my sisters and me—ate peanut butter and jelly, while our dance companions ate burgers and fries from the McDonald's next door. The smell of seared hamburgers and onions hung in the air like a heavy perfume, and the longing of a child unable to enjoy their taste was like a filthy stench. Sometimes our dance friends laughed, and it made the pain of lack all the more real. But there were three of us, and oftentimes there was only one of them. Our parents did the best they could, which made Friday nights at Henry's, a fast-food burger joint, all the more special.[2]

The stories, recollections, and theorizations in this book are a reflection of many years of thinking about the ways in which Black people have been shamed and sometimes shame others through food. The themes I introduced at the outset have repeatedly resurfaced throughout this book, like multiple spokes on a wheel. At times my thoughts might appear redundant and at other times the argument may not go far enough. But that is okay, because the point of this book is simply to get us talking about another facet of Black food life. It is not my intention to offer answers here. Instead, this book offers a window into a way of thinking and perhaps also gives people permission to push back on the rhetoric of what they must do to eat "right."

The experiences recalled here happened over approximately fifteen years, while I traveled the world as a scholar and a speaker. Often, we engage in conversations where the value of the informational exchange reveals itself later rather than sooner. That is what happened to me with many of the topics covered in this book. The constellation of engagements I had been having formed a trend and a trajectory that I began to track. As I saw the same conversations taking place on television talk shows, in classrooms, almost everywhere, I realized some of it was mimicry because the refrain appeared to be the same: we are an obese nation; Black people eat poor food; soul food is bad; Black people are food insecure; Black people should grow their own food; Black people need supermarkets, need to eat more vegetables, need to eat less fast food, need to be or do this thing or that thing. And while there was all this talk about food, very few people were attaching systemic inequality and centuries of race and class discrimination to this material object. It was as if the two were not intricately intertwined. They are—and, as I have illustrated here, overwhelmingly so.

But many African Americans, indeed Americans in general, do not want to acknowledge this correlation as if the present does not have a past. We want to leave behind the legacies of slavery and freedom without restitution, though their burdens continue to manifest today in the lack of generational wealth among broad swaths of Black people (most often unless we are politicians, entertainers, or athletes). It is simple and convenient to believe that slavery is a vague period in history that happened long ago, as if it does not represent real people or events of trauma. But Ta-Nehisi Coates reminds us,

Enslavement is not a parable. It is damnation. It is the never-ending night. And the length of that night is most of our history. Never forget that we were enslaved in this country longer than we have been free. Never forget that for 250 years black people were born into chains— whole generations followed by more generations who knew nothing but chains. You must struggle to truly remember this past. You must resist the common urge toward the comforting narrative of divine law, toward fairy tales that imply some irrepressible justice. The enslaved were not bricks in your road, and their lives were not chapters in your redemptive history. They were people turned to fuel for the American machine. You cannot forget how much they took from us and how they transfigured our very bodies into sugar, tobacco, cotton, and gold.[3]

And you cannot forget that on Black people's bodies are written our food legacies—centuries of trauma and desecration, but also centuries of triumph and agency. We do not have the privilege of living in ignorance of the past, present, or future and the ways in which slavery permeates every aspect of our lives including our food cultures. As much as we seek to resist the over-determination of this history, it continues to creep into our daily lives, precisely because we want to ignore it. And it is this shared history as Black people that unifies us across socioeconomic status, political affiliation, and worldview, whether we acknowledge it or not.

This book, then, centers African American people, because we have long been demarcated as unwritable, destroyable, bendable, and irredeemable, and our food cultures have not gone unaffected. In the context of this book, race serves as a unifying social category transcending social status, world-view, and other demarcations of intragroup difference. And while this is the case, we all have different proclivities when it comes to food. While someone in California might be comfortable eating Vienna sausages from the dollar store, someone from Baton Rouge might ask, What is that in that can? And while casseroles might be the thing for those living in Missouri, the only casserole you may want to see in North Carolina is macaroni and cheese. The overpriced lobster roll in Martha's Vineyard might not be an issue for someone used to enjoying the sandwich or who can afford it, but for the Minneapolis fisherwoman some hot fried walleye with coleslaw and a beer will do just fine. How and what people eat are intensely personal and central to the daily fabric of their lives. These issues and the conversations that surround them must be approached with respect for that complexity and with a sense of humility for what people are going through and what factors into their decisions. There should be no judgment!

I had to impress this point about judgment upon my students. Having gotten tired of hearing remarks from my college-aged students about how people do not want to be healthy so they do not eat healthy, I began teaching a documentary film I was introduced to in a marketing email. *Good Meat* is the story of Beau LeBeau, a member of the Oglala Lakota Nation in South

Dakota. As a teen he had been one of the most celebrated athletes on the Pine Ridge Reservation, but at age thirty-six he was overweight, diabetic, and "angry at the world." In addition to the many ills he saw plaguing his community—tuberculosis, alcoholism, suicide, and homicide, not to mention missing women and girls—his mother had recently died from complications related to diabetes. That's when Beau made the decision to work with a Rapid City physician to restore his health by eating a traditional Lakota diet.

It took tremendous effort. For one thing, Beau had to find out more about the traditional diet, and then he had to get a buffalo. In order to do this, he had to secure permission from the United States Department of the Interior, which owns the lands on which the buffalo roam. Beau found out that the expense involved in getting permission, hunting, and having the buffalo cleaned and butchered was not sustainable. Secondly, when Beau and his relatives went to prepare the soil for tilling so he could grow traditional foods, they discovered that the further down they dug, the harder the red clay dirt became, making it impossible to grow anything, let alone foods representative of the culture. And then there were the social and cultural aspects of the diet. At one point in the documentary, Beau discusses a dilemma that's all too familiar for many, especially those who are food insecure. His family could use their SNAP cards to buy the fresh fruits and vegetables that the government brought onto the reservation—which were expensive and few in quantity, but they would be gone within a couple of weeks. Or they could make the ninety-minute drive to the Walmart in Rapid City, where they would have more options and could use their SNAP cards to buy more groceries while spending less money. Beau said his sisters were often influenced by his nieces and nephews, so they often chose to go to Walmart, where they would buy foods high in sugar, salt, and fat, making it difficult for him to stick to his diet plan. Lastly, few of Beau's family members were willing to try the new diet with buffalo meat at the center, making his own perseverance a bit more challenging. Despite the obstacles, however, over the course of six months Beau lost more than seventy pounds, reduced his cholesterol, and stabilized his blood sugar so it stayed well within the safety margins established by the American Diabetes Association.[4]

In addition to using the documentary *Good Meat*, to bring home the challenges of eating and sustaining local food diets, I required my students to participate in a locavore challenge. In the early 2000s, I learned that some communities would come together and challenge one another to eat locally for a period of time. After reading about this, I thought it would be a good way for students to see whether this task was as easy as they thought or as difficult as some people had been saying. To add an element of tension, students were asked to budget between thirty and fifty dollars for the week's worth of food. In reality, this might be seen as not enough money for some, and for others it can be considered a lot, especially if you plan on this amount every week—it's almost $200 per month. The cost of the assignment was added to the syllabus as another textbook in order to help students budget and/or prepare for the task. They could eat only food grown within a 150-mile radius of College Park, Maryland, though they were allowed three foods from outside this radius known as "freebies" or "Marco Polos." To help them stay accountable and to document the experience, we used the Canvas platform, where students could blog their experiences within the walls of the online classroom space. Students were required to make at least three entries and respond to other people's posts as well. This was very successful because students began to help one another by sharing details of their trips (plural) to the store, farmers market, and homes of relatives in search of food that was locally sourced. They were also careful at times to include pricing information, especially if a place was expensive or somewhat unreasonably priced for their low student budgets.

I participated alongside the students. To prepare them for what to expect, I tried to go to the farmers market, the grocery store, or other nearby food outlets first and then report back to them about possible options and pitfalls. For example, one spring I went to the farmers market the weekend it opened in College Park. As I was in the market to buy some strawberries, I was looking for the small berries in green cardboard pint-sized containers. What I found were strawberries in a plastic container packaged by Driscoll's, a brand sold in our local grocery store. When I asked the vendor why they had a brand name and not locally grown berries, she told me it was too early in the season for local berries, so they only had the commercial brand. Seasonality is a thing. In the classroom prep for the assignment, we talked about the challenge of using citrus like oranges, lemons, and limes, because these foods are not locally grown. But we had not considered that strawberries would be an issue. We made several assumptions because lots of fruits and vegetables are available to us in grocery stores regardless of the season.

Each time I assigned the project (for classes in the fall and the spring) students learned a lot that they previously had not considered. For one, they found out exactly how many foods are not grown within our 150-mile radius, meaning they had to think long and hard about their three freebie foods. Would it be beer or orange juice, fruit or spices? Secondly, they found out they had to be meticulous in their planning and not make assumptions. At first, the assignment was set up to last five days, but that requirement quickly had to be adjusted as students found out that if they did not create a daily plan, they would go hungry. For example, students often shared that they woke up late and rushed straight to campus, believing they could find something on campus to eat at the campus food co-op, the dining hall, or *somewhere*. They found out the hard way that the campus food co-op had very few, if any, options to accommodate the assignment. One male student awoke too late on the weekend to get to the farmers market, so he decided he would survive all weekend on Domino's pizza and marijuana, because the vendors of each claimed their products were harvested locally.

This lack of awareness about local foods extended to language. As in the case above where the student ate pizza and smoked weed all weekend, many students found out the limits and elasticity of the phrase "local eating." There are differences between the terms "local" and "organic," a point many of them had never thought about. Only once they were on campus with nothing to eat did they discover that just because something is labeled "organic" does not necessarily mean it is also local, and vice versa—local does not necessarily equate to organic. One student explained how they came to this realization:

> Yesterday my partner . . . (who is doing the challenge with me) and I went to the co-op to get some food to hold us over until the farmers market on Sunday. We headed straight for the produce, where they had items labeled as either "organic" or "local." I was curious about exactly where the local stuff was from so I ended up finding the produce person, a nice man by the name of Adam who gave us a tour through the produce section and told us exactly where everything was from. At the co-op food must come from within 100 miles away to qualify as local. Our only local produce options were apples, tomatoes, and some squash. All of the produce was organic but none local, except for some small variety packs with things like onions, peppers, and mushrooms already cut up (maybe for a stir fry or soup?) for 5 bucks a pop. We grabbed some apples and headed towards the milk and eggs. I'm lactose intolerant so the local milk was pretty much of no use and the soy/almond milk wasn't local. We did grab some buttermilk to use for cooking but put it back because it had salt and some other probably-not-local ingredients.[5]

This student was fortunate in that there were some safeguards built into the store—all local foods had to be within a 100-mile radius. At some stores, employees could not provide any details about where the food came from.

There were a number of students who were very successful. They were able to find locally harvested foods by going to several different venues—farmers markets, organic markets, grocery stores, and their grandmother's pantry. Some of the students who were able to find the foods in the store and at the market were able to get some new and interesting items, but they also ran out of money very quickly. And they usually left the market with only enough food for the weekend. Pretty soon, frustration and even anger persisted; they were hungry, having been confined by the strictures of the experiential assignment. One student blogged:

> For breakfast which I normally do not eat but on this new food diet I find myself to be hungry more often than not. I made two scrambled eggs and had a glass of milk. I really wish I had purchased some freshly made juice but I could not allow myself to spend more than two dollars on juice. . . .

> **Day 2**
> I did enjoy one of my Marco Polo's which was a DiGiorno pizza for lunch. I was too lazy to cook which I find happens often lately with school and work. . . . I realized that this was a very challenging task for me; I did not realize that I ate out as much as I do. I also realized that the food that I purchased taste so much better. It's not that the groceries did not last me the entire project, I just wish I had more options than what I did for the amount of money I spent.

At least one or two students got sick over the course of the assignment and found that by going home to their grandmother, they were able to get homemade foods made from her garden.

By the end of the three days, most students had reached the limits of their tolerance for the experiment. Only then did I ask them to consider how much more a family might feel when their food options are restricted all in the name of good and healthy local eating. One student summed it up this way:

> Being single and carless in College Park I knew that this was going to be a challenge. I thought about the kinds of foods I normally cook, Japanese and Italian, and thought about how I could alter recipes and such to make it fit with the challenge. I also normally cook vegetarian. . . . Of course, most of my Japanese pantry is not even remotely local (since it was mostly filled with stuff I had mailed home right before I left Japan), so I had to sayonara to Nihon-go ryori. And I was really craving some Japanese kare raisu (curry with rice) too. Italian could work, but after

Marco Polo-ing the pasta (ironic, no?) and the wild Sicilian oregano my housemate brought back with him, it was going to be tough. This really touched on Dr. Williams-Forson's point about locavores not taking culture into consideration. . . . With so much going on in my life, I just didn't have the time to go into the city to my usual places. I also didn't have time to wait on the buses, either. So, I went ahead and bit the bullet and rented a Zipcar for two hours ($25.00 . . . yikes) and planned to buy everything except produce (I'm going to wait till the College Park Farmers market tomorrow) in bulk. This also meant having to plan for five day's worth of meals. I pretty much had to resign myself with the fact that I was going to be eating some iteration of the same meal over and over again.[6]

This student is not alone in their frustrations. Though we have always lived in a transnational world, where the flows of people, products, capital, and ideas creates and characterizes global capitalism, now more than ever we are seeing this manifested on our foodscapes. Across the United States, the foods that several cultures have in common can be found in specialty ethnic markets, from Los Angeles to Bar Harbor. Foods like jasmine rice, palm and other cooking oils, maggi cubes, beans and legumes, soy sauces, lemongrass, ginger, tamarind, and a host of meats and vegetables offer a counter-reality to narratives that tout local eating as the apex of good food habits. Some people have pushed back on my assertions, arguing that I should not be encouraging people to consume foods from the places most convenient for them because those places are "unhealthy." But as this book has argued, unhealthy to one person may be lifesaving to another. It should be clear by now that there is no one-size-fits-all solution and that food is much more multivariant than we would like to believe. Given this, it makes sense that we should think in terms of smaller, less traumatic and dramatic changes that people can implement. Perhaps then people will be more likely to consider making more changes over time rather than massive overhauls that at the outset can set people up to fail.

We are in the middle of an era where food shaming, food policing, and food dictating will have a profound effect on future generations. And here I need to be abundantly clear that that this book in no way suggests that we should stop striving to live healthier in all aspects of our lives. Of course we should. And we *should* all be able to live in a way that our culinary lives are in sync with our cultural practices. And we *should* all be able to live in a place where we can breathe clean air and drink clean water. We *should* all work jobs that pay us a living wage so we do not have to work ourselves to death at multiple jobs to bring home a decent paycheck. We *should* all receive affordable health care that includes serious attention to our mental health. We *should* all, whether we live in Utah or Maine, Texas or southern Maryland, be able to walk around and not have to worry about white supremacy violence. And we *should* care about all kinds of violence as much as we care about Black on Black crime. We *should* all be able to participate in yoga classes that welcome bodies of all sizes and jog at all hours of the day and night, where we do not feel that publicizing our whereabouts might bring about unwanted violations of our body, mind, and spirits.

We *should* be able to grow and eat the foods of our ancestors without having to contact the Department of the Interior or fearing that the ground is full of red clay making it virtually impossible to grow anything. And we *should* all be able to bite into a bright-red, plump tomato with the telltale markings of having come straight off the vine, or taste the sweetness of a freshly picked peach and eat it with the sticky nectar dripping down our hands. But, sadly, we do not live in this kind of world. So how do we eat in the meantime? What do we eat in the meantime? Where do we eat from while we wait for these changes to come? These are some of the conversations this book is opening up for discussion, in addition to all the others that are currently going on. And they are critical conversations that we need to engage; we ignore them at our peril.

Food shaming is universal, so I hope this conversation is instructive for other cultures who might want to investigate how food shaming affects their community. But this book was written to speak directly to Black people and those we encounter on a day-to-day basis (or everyone else), because we have a lot of undoing and unknowing work to do. We have a great deal of work to do to know "our Black history," a point made long ago by a young girl briefly featured in the posthumously completed documentary *Black Is . . . Black Ain't,* by award-winning filmmaker Marlon Riggs. During a conversation that takes place at the Youth Achievement Center in Los Angeles, California, between a young Black girl and two of her friends, she "desperately tries to convince her male counterparts that in order to better understand who they are in American society (and the world), they need to have a sense of their history." She looks at them in bewilderment and pleads with them to understand: "History is more than chains on your ankle and knowing this Black leader and knowing that Black leader. There is much more to history than that. I mean, the thing with Black people is, if you are going to be Black, you don't want to know your Black history? You wanna forget about your Black history?" Though I recounted this scene in my article "Chicken and Chains: Using African American Foodways as a Gateway to Understanding the Diversity of Black Identities" from many years ago, it lingers with me still. As I stated in the 2007 article, "In general, people tend to rely upon very narrow versions of group identity when food is the topic of conversation. But food and the meanings assigned to it, whether cognitive, oral or visual, also has an infinitely greater value—the ability to reveal embedded associations that deeply affect individual and group identities. In this way, foods can serve as both a locus of oppression and liberation."[7]

Black food liberation may start by continuing to reject white racial narratives predicated on power and privilege. As Black people, we have to stop buying into the psychosis that we are somehow not worthy or that our very existence is a problem. When we do this then we can really embrace the conviction that Black people's lives matter, not as a slogan but as reality. We need to start believing that our Black lives matter precisely because our food, our clothing, our cultural expressions, our politics, and our economics, among other aspects of our lives, are important and critical to this country's fabric. We need to start knowing "the whole theory was wrong, their whole notion of race was wrong," as Ta-Nehisi Coates writes, so we can reclaim some measure of comfortability in sustaining the everyday aspects of our cultures and heritages that make us *us*. When we realize that sacralization around the supposed curse of Ham has been used to spin a myth of Black inferiority, then maybe we can relax in knowing we are actually a people of immense creativity and skill, with food as much as anything else. When we realize these things for ourselves, we will better understand what Coates means when he argues, "'White America' is a syndicate arrayed to protect its exclusive power to dominate and control our bodies. Sometimes this power is direct (lynching), and sometimes it is insidious (redlining). But, however it appears, the power of domination and exclusion is central to the belief in being white, and without it, 'white people' would cease to exist for want of reasons."[8] It does not matter, therefore, if people's intentions are noble or good or ethnically right. There is nothing inherently wrong with these goals and these desires. But we need to understand that this righteous nobility stems from privileges and legacies of constantly trying to control our bodies—Black people's bodies—and that in the minds of many, Black bodies are always in need of saving.

But Black people do not need saving. None of us needs saving. What we need is to realize that Black people, like everyone else, are complex in our personhood. So when we take up a cause, when we eschew pork products, or choose to eat in a way that makes others feel uncomfortable, or perform social graces about which others might be less familiar, it is not about "performing whiteness." Usually it is more about asserting a form of cultural capital and class-based performance that can serve, albeit unintentionally, to marginalize the behaviors and interests of some other Black people, who might include the poor, the infirm, and the elderly. But these performances can also be a form of Black transgression, and because Black people are not ever supposed to transgress in any way, shape, or form, it might seem to some that we are acting out, acting womanish or mannish, or performing whiteness. And sometimes we are. Sometimes we are showing off when we take up causes that we know will land us at odds with Black communities. So maybe we all need to slow down and do some healing work.

This curative work is part of the haunting embedded in the Adinkra symbol of Sankofa, from the people of Ghana, West Africa. In Twi, a language spoken by the Akan (Ashanté) people, "Sankofa" translates to mean "to retrieve," "to go back and get it," or "to recover." The Adinkra symbol that accompanies the phrase is multiply represented, but most often it is portrayed as a bird with its head turned backwards while its feet face forward, carrying an egg in its mouth.[9] Black farmers understand the restorative power of food, which is why one of the vendors discussed here named their business after this principle. And that vendor was far from the only one to use this moniker to reclaim the healing provided by food. This healing work is also what Avery Gordon refers to when she discusses

> the willingness to follow ghosts, neither to memorialize or to slay, but to follow where they lead, in the present, head turned backwards and forwards, at the same time. To be haunted in the name of a will to heal is to allow the ghost to help you imagine what was lost that never even existed, really. That is its utopian grace: to encourage a steely sorrow laced with delight for what we lost that we never had; to long for the insight of that moment in which we recognize . . . that it could have been and can be otherwise.[10]

I leave readers with several thoughts. One, food disrupts all the neatness of our lives. There are no easy answers and it can be frustrating to know this but it is true. This is the beauty of being human—we cannot fit neatly into boxes, no matter how convenient it might be for others to think we belong there. Two, if we are not willing to do any of the hard work that is necessary to know more about the communities we intend to write about, speak about, grow with, instruct, heal, and help, then what exactly are we doing? Three, if we are not in the business of calling out our colleagues, friends, coworkers, and even family members when we see them attempting to eliminate histories of communities because they do not fit the right narrative, what exactly are we doing? This is the work of liberation, and it is the work of anti-Black racism. And if you are going to be an ally or advocate of Black people, then you need to have the courage to call it what it is—racism. As my colleague Scott Marlow says, "When we fail to acknowledge or take into consideration the myriad meanings that food occupies in people's lives, we can easily slide over into judgment of their habits and behaviors rather than working to empower them to do what is best for themselves."[11] Yes.

From this standpoint, it is imperative that we begin seeing Black people as resilient, always already living with and resisting trauma, with full bodies that may move in many different ways throughout the world. Begin valuing Black people by not seeing us as unruly or always in need of taming and controlling, but as fully capable as anyone else of contributing to all aspects of society from the kitchen to the boardroom. Change the perceptions that fuel beliefs that wholeness and health are not in the interest of Black communities. This is misguided and wrong, and it propels you in no small part to surveil and try to control. We do not need this. Consider, instead, that when our bodies are saddled with extra fat and/or disease, it may well be that we are exasperated by life, by systems and structures that have taken away our breath for the moment. It is not necessarily that our kitchens are unhealthy; it is that our souls are weary and we need a second to regroup. And when we present ourselves as food professionals, know that we are most likely capable of creating more than just "soul food"—traditional or modern. Though we have shared histories, we are not monolithic or one-dimensional. We are a community of people filled with as many densities, destinies, and desires as anyone else. And when you are inclined to worry about us, in the workplace, at school, in our houses of worship, or anywhere else, ask us first what we want, what we know, who we are . . . otherwise, worry about yourself, indeed!

ACKNOWLEDGMENTS

Around 2012, my then department chair Nancy Struna asked me in earnest to describe my next book project. I explained that it was a study on African American domestic interiors but that it would take a while to complete. Given plans that we had for the future of the department, she encouraged me to think about work that I could publish sooner. After I explained my dilemma to a couple of my colleagues, one suggested I think about the presentations I had been giving since the publication of my first book, *Building Houses out of Chicken Legs: Black Women, Food, and Power*. The more I thought about it, the more I began to see patterns and linkages. It has been a long while since those initial conversations, but I am nonetheless grateful for the scholarly wisdom of my colleagues in the Department of American Studies at the University of Maryland, College Park, especially Christina Hanhardt and Nancy Mirabal. They are all among the smartest and most generous scholars one is likely to ever meet. This thanks includes staff members Julia John, Tammi Archer, and Dana Persaud, whose patience and assistance over time have been unparalleled. The Arts and Humanities Dean's Office, led by Bonnie Thornton Dill, awarded me an ADVANCING Scholarship Initiative early in the writing process for a book workshop. As a result, I was able to benefit from the wisdom of Fath Davis Ruffins, Jennifer Wallach, Elizabeth Englehardt, Carole Counihan, and Jessica Walker. I am honored to have my book be among the final manuscripts shepherded by Elaine Maisner. She has never failed in her wisdom and guidance, and I am forever grateful that she welcomed the recommendation and introduction by our late friend and colleague, Dr. Gladys-Marie Fry. The UNC Press team is a joy to work with; thank you all for your patience and guidance and for choosing excellent readers and reviewers. I am deeply thankful to all the students who participated in the locavore challenge over many semesters of teaching. In particular, I am grateful to the students who took Race, Class, Material Culture; Food, Trauma, Sustainability; Advanced Material Culture; Individualized Advanced Food Studies; and Critical Cultural Feminism/Womanism of Diasporic Texts. Your experiences, though they were for a classroom assignment, were enlightening and beneficial to my thinking deeply about local issues.

Thank you to Holly Reed, National Archives and Records Administration Still Picture Division; Elsa Barkley Brown, Michelle Rowley, Faedra Carpenter, Mary Corbin Sies, Jason Farman, Ken Albala, Melanie DuPuis, Amy Ferrell, Bill Ferris, Marcie Cohen Ferris, Jessica Harris, Martin Manalansan, Toni Tipton Martin, Leni Sorenson, Rebecca Sharpless and Rafia Zafar, Kenyatta Graves, Ashaki Goodall, Maria Inez Valezquez, Shoji Malone, and Melissa "Mia" Reddy contributed in different ways to the development of this project by sharing experiences, allowing me to think through ideas and talk them out even when they sounded disorganized and disconnected. I am especially thankful to my colleague Tracey Deutsch, who, along with a team of excellent food studies scholars and graduate students at the University of Minnesota, invited me to be a part of an interdisciplinary collaboration. Tracey heard more about this project, food shaming, and food policing in one weekend than anyone probably ever wants to know. Thank you! Doris Witt, whose work on African American food studies I have long admired, made it possible for me to hear the profound comments of Lisa Heldke. The concept of "paper vs. plastic mentality" opened up so many ways of thinking about this project. Thank you, Lisa!

Thank you to all of my colleagues who invited me to speak and thus unbeknownst to either of us provided the material for this project. I owe you a huge debt. Special thanks to Stephen B. Thomas, Craig Fryer, and the UMD Center for Health Equity; Father Joseph A. Brown; Rachel Black; Miriam Harris; Belinda Wallace; LuAnne Roth; Natalia Lee, Kimberly Johnson; Michael Di Giovine; Tara Powell; Charles Ludington; Todd Romero and the Gulf Coast Food Project; Meredith Abarca; Paula Johnson, Kavitha Sankavaram; Ashley Young, and the food history folks at the Accokeek Foundation, National Museum of American History; Sydney Daigle and the Prince Georges County Food Equity Council; Natasha Bowens; Derek Hicks and the Wake Forest School of Divinity; Melissa Harris-Perry; Bryant Terry and MOAD; Scott Marlow and Rural Advancement Foundation International— USA; Joan Bryant; Mary Nucci; Naa Oyo Kwate; the Graduate Association of Food Studies; the Gender Studies Program at Notre Dame University; the Weissman Center at Mount Holyoke, Kameelah Martin; Amy Farrell; Wendell Smith; Desiree Lewis; Krystal Mack; and Galerie Myrtis.

I appreciate my steady accountability partners, Pier Gabrielle Foreman, Maurice Wallace, Andrea Williams, Daina Berry, and Jacqueline Goldsby, who offered invaluable feedback as well as encouragement for the last several years. Kimberly Nettles-Barcelon, Monica White, and Ashanté Reese are my sisters in Black food studies, and I appreciate their brilliance immensely.

Elena Abbott, of Inkblotter, read through drafts of this manuscript page by page and her feedback was invaluable as a writing editor and coach. At a time when I thought this book held no promise, she was able to show me the golden nuggets and the threads that were yet to be pulled. I am thankful too for the proofreading eye of Jassmyn K. Paxton.

My soror Sheri Stanford traveled with me to Erfurt, Germany, to hear me talk about African American foodways. Her travel knowledge is unparalleled. Without her foresight, critical portions of this manuscript would not have been written. Also thanks to my soror Barbara Wadley-Young, who has been patient through my cancellations because . . . "the book." Thank you for asking me important questions that are useful for sharing with so many different audiences.

To my sisters along this life's journey, Philipia Hillman, Elena Temple, Jacquie Harris, Sandra Tee Rice, Mona Brown, thank you for always having my back and for supporting me through this academic journey from undergrad to professorship. I appreciate y'all. My family, Rev. James S. Williams and Lyllie B. Williams, who gave me the foundations for so much in this life and for exposing us and modeling community engaged work and for always working toward Black liberation. My sisters, Jamantha Williams Watson and Omega W. Wilson, who laughed when I first ordered blue-corn pancakes and are now asking me if I know Tracye McQuirter's *By Any Greens Necessary*, love y'all. Continue to "produce your thoughts, and may God strengthen you in spiritual awareness and the struggles of our people!"

Heartfelt thanks to John W. Simpson Jr., who has been my confidant, critic, supporter, and motivator. Thank you for knowing when to push and when to fall back. Thank you for bringing light to some really dark days and for sharing in the frustrations and for bringing the laughter. Most of all, thank you for reminding me not to take myself too seriously but also celebrating with me in the joyfully serious moments. I appreciate you, immensely.

And last, but only because she is the most important, thank you Abena-Ann Seven, my road dog, sounding board, and daughter-bestie. You have come of age with this book, and your experiences—your growth, your struggles, your triumphs—have made you an amazing young person. Through my journey and your own journey, you are finding your purpose and will hopefully continue your goal and our family legacy of educating others. I look forward to reading your first book. Thank you for allowing me to be an example of one way to be a MommyPhd!

NOTES

Introduction

1. Janelle Griffith, "An Author Reported a Black Metro Worker for Eating on a Train. Now She Might Lose Her Book Deal," NBC News, May 12, 2019, https://www.nbcnews.com/news/us-news/author-reported-metro-worker-eating-train-now-she-might-lose-n1004716.

2. There are several different versions of this memo, depending upon which *Washington Post* article you read. Some indicate the memo used the language "cease and desist"; one indicates Metro transit police are "to stop." Either way, a memo apparently went out earlier in May advising that no infractions should be noted.

3. I had a well-meaning friend tell me that for all I knew about African American food, I missed a fundamental observation—we ate scraps while enslaved. Despite his education and cosmopolitan worldview, he, too, had bought into the myths of African American food history. On the concept of African Americans "making do" with whatever they have to create ingenious culinary delights, I am grateful for numerous discussions with food and religion scholar Derek Hicks, including his pointed comments during my presentation at "Half the Sky, Half the Earth: A Conference on Women, Faith, and Food," Food, Faith, and Religious Leadership Initiative, at Wake Forest University School of Divinity, Winston-Salem, North Carolina, in March 2014.

4. Gordon, *Ghostly Matters*, 3.

5. Warren Belasco's *Appetite for Change* was originally published in 1989, and it considered the rise of the "countercuisine" of the 1960s. Eating "healthy" meant Red Zinger and other herbal teas, granola, and other foods considered new and "revolutionary." Today's discussions are a resurgence, as Belasco's updated edition remind us. Eating vegetarian and vegan have been around for a long time.

6. This reflection is in no way an attempt to denigrate social workers. On the contrary, this book is being written to engage in conversations with them and to encourage them to understand cultural dynamics even as they perform work that is laborious and draining as much as it is rewarding and necessary.

7. Halloran, *Immigrant Kitchen*, 41–45.

8. Using self-ethnography or autoethnography is one reason I go back and forth between using "African Americans" (in third person) and "we" as a means of inclusion. This method enables me to use anecdotal and personal experiences while connecting them to wider cultural, political, and social meanings and understandings.

9. These are common approaches I use in most all of my research, which is informed by several methods, including personal narratives and ethnography. "Thorny terrains of power" refers to the ways in which food is an unstable signifier, informed by multiple variables in our lives. Williams-Forson, "Other Women Cooked for My Husband," 459. In addition, see similar methods used to discuss these terrains of power in

Williams-Forson, *Building Houses out of Chicken Legs*; and Williams-Forson, "I Haven't Eaten If I Don't Have My Soup and Fufu," 69–87.

10. Smith, *Decolonizing Methodologies*, 17.

11. Reese and Garth rightly argue that the nation-state has repeatedly proven it does not "provide for or protect Black people," and in fact often institutes more harm than good. Moreover, when stores and other food sites are deemed "unsafe," such labeling can lead to physical violence for people of color who frequent the store as customers. For discussions of state- and community-sanctioned violence in and around food, see Reese and Garth, *Black Food Matters*, 6–7.

12. Csikszentmihalyi, "Why We Need Things."

13. Grosvenor, foreword, xii.

14. The scholarship of Jessica Harris, Toni Tipton-Martin, Adrian Miller, Michael Twitty, and Rafia Zafar, among others, has gone far to correct both the silences and misinformation about the skills and craft of African American culinarians. See also Deetz, *Bound to the Fire*; and culinary historian Leni Sorenson, who maintains a website at https://www.indigohouse.us/.

15. See "Struggles with Body Images Can Start in Elementary School," health enews, Advocate Aurora Health, accessed November 20, 2021, https://www.ahchealthenews.com/2015/08/03/struggles-with-body-image-starts-in-elementary-school/. For more on histories of Black girlhood studies, see Wright, *Black Girlhood in the Nineteenth Century*; and, Chatelain, *South Side Girls*.

16. Kirshenblatt-Gimblett, "Playing to the Senses," 1.

17. Fajans, "Transformative Value of Food."

18. See Lockett, "What Is Black Twitter?," 165–66. In the United States, Black Twitter is considered a network of "culturally connected communicators [who use] the platform to draw attention to issues of concern [and entertainment] to black communities." See Whitelaw Reid, "Black Twitter 101: What Is It? Where Did It Originate? Where Is It Headed?," *UVAToday*, November 28, 2018, https://news.virginia.edu/content/black-twitter-101-what-it-where-did-it-originate-where-it-headed.

19. Williams-Forson, *Building Houses out of Chicken Legs*; among other references, see also William Black, "How Watermelons Became a Racist Trope," *The Atlantic*, December 8, 2014, https://www.theatlantic.com/national/archive/2014/12/how-watermelons-became-a-racist-trope/383529/.

20. Nettles-Barcelon, "Saving Soul Food."

21. Omi and Winant, *Racial Formation in the United States*, 60.

22. Delgado and Stefancic, *Critical Race Theory*, 7–10; Bonilla-Silva, "More than Prejudice," 74.

23. Keeanga-Yamahtta Taylor (@keeangaYamahtta), "Obviously there is a market for this kind of stuff, but the notion that we will end racism . . . ," Twitter, July 14, 2020, https://twitter.com/KeeangaYamahtta/status/1415414709264785408?s=20. Chris Rock told us this in his June 1, 1996, HBO comedy special, *Chris Rock: Bring the Pain*. He said, "There ain't a white man in this room that would change places with me. None of you, and I'm rich!"

24. See Kwate, *Burgers in Blackface*, 4–5.

25. Adichie, "Danger of a Single Story."

26. Barbara Christian as quoted in Marlon Riggs's documentary film *Ethnic Notions*.

27. Grammy Award–winning musician Lizzo, who is both African American and full-figured, took to social media in a tearful pushback against fat-shaming, racist comments following the release of her song "Rumors" with fellow musician Cardi B. Despite Lizzo's having a workout routine that would rival many and being a self-reported vegan, negative comments about her weight, among other issues, apparently flooded her inbox. Emphasizing the positive nature of her music, Lizzo wrote, "I'm doing this shit for the big Black women in the future who just want to live their lives without being scrutinized or put into boxes. I'm not gonna do what y'all want me to do, ever, so get used to it. But what I will do is make great music and be a great artist and continue to uplift people and uplift myself." See Leah Bitzsky, "Lizzo Breaks Down over Fat-Shaming, Racist Reactions to 'Rumors,'" *Page Six*, August 16, 2021, https://pagesix.com/2021/08/16/lizzo-cries-over-fat-shaming-racist-reactions-to-rumors/.

28. Kwate, *Burgers in Blackface*, 5.

29. Kwate, 5.

30. Kendi, *Stamped from the Beginning*, 5.

31. Kendi, 10.

32. See Goings, *Mammy and Uncle Mose*; Lott, *Love and Theft*; Turner, *Ceramic Uncles and Celluloid Mammies*; Pieterse, *White on Black*; Cserno, "Race and Mass Consumption in Consumer Culture"; Williams-Forson, *Building Houses out of Chicken Legs*, especially chapter 2. African American chefs find themselves often having to prove themselves and their culinary skills and as capable of cooking more than just traditional foods considered southern and/or soul. For more on this, see, among many articles on this subject, Sonia Rao, "For Black Chefs, the Fight for Visibility Is Far from Over," *Washington Post*, August 3, 2018, https://www.washingtonpost.com/lifestyle/food/for-black-chefs-the-fight-for-visibility-is-far-from-over/2018/08/03/dcaa4dd2-93f8-11e8-810c-5fa705927d54_story.html.

33. See Toni Tipton-Martin, "The Jemima Code Erased the Work of Black Cooks and Writers. I Had to Break It," *Washington Post*, September 15, 2015, https://www.washingtonpost.com/lifestyle/food/black-recipes-matter-too-why-i-wanted-to-break-the-jemima-code/2015/09/14/00c072ee-5673-11e5-b8c9-944725fcd3b9_story.html. See also Tipton-Martin, *Jemima Code*, xviii–9.

Chapter 1

1. The chef went into the kitchen and sliced off a small piece to share with the audience because most of the audience had no idea what he was describing nor how expensive they are, often between $2,000 and $3,000, or more. See Steffani Cameron, "What Are Truffles and Why Are They So Expensive?," *Wide Open Eats*, November 1, 2020, https://www.wideopeneats.com/so-what-are-truffles-and-why-are-they-so-popular/. I am grateful to my sorority sister Sheri Stanford for the invitation and her feedback on this chapter.

2. Harris-Perry, *Sister Citizen*, 183–84.

3. American Psychological Association, "Interview with June Price Tangney about *Shame in the Therapy Hour*," video transcript, 2011, https://www.apa.org/pubs/books /interviews/4317264-tangney. See also Tangney and Dearing, *Shame and Guilt*.

4. Though it's now a well-worn cliché, when my thoughts first turned to this phrase, it was relatively new and not much discussed, especially in food studies.

5. Alex Kirshner, "Food, Inc.'s Eric Schlosser Speaks as Part of Series," *The Diamond-back*, online edition, July 18, 2015, http://www.diamondbackonline.com/news/campus /article_103c84b0-39e8-11e2-8207-001a4bcf6878.html.

6. Dahn, "'Unashamedly Black'"; Du Bois, "On Being Ashamed."

7. In addition to the mountainous information on enslavement, see also Hannah-Jones et al., "The 1619 Project."

8. Hattery and Smith, *Policing Black Bodies*, 2.

9. For new perspectives on the horrors of the Middle Passage, see Mustakeem, *Slavery at Sea*; and Woodard et al., *Delectable Negro*.

10. Federal Writers' Project, *Slave Narrative Project*, 245.

11. The WPA slave narratives are one of the single most important resources for finding information on African American life during enslavement. Among other sources, see Library of Congress, "The WPA and the Slave Narrative Collection," https://www.loc.gov/collections/slave-narratives-from-the-federal-writers-project-1936 -to-1938/articles-and-essays/introduction-to-the-wpa-slave-narratives/wpa-and-the -slave-narrative-collection/. Also see Eisnach and Covey, *What the Slaves Ate*, 60–61; Armstrong, "Black Foodways and Places."

12. Wolper, *Roots*, episode 1.

13. Most any search for African Americans and food during enslavement will yield a broad number of texts across disciplines. For varied perspectives, consider Bower, *African American Foodways*; Carney and Rosomoff, *In the Shadow of Slavery*; Deetz, *Bound to the Fire*; Edwards-Ingram, "'Trash' Revisited"; Eisnach and Covey, *What the Slaves Ate*; Ferguson, *Uncommon Ground*; Fett, *Working Cures*; Harris, *High on the Hog*; Miller, *Soul Food*; Opie, *Hog and Hominy*; Rice and Katz-Hyman, *World of a Slave*; Tipton-Martin, *Jemima Code*; Twitty, *Cooking Gene*; Yentsch, *Chesapeake Family and Their Slaves*; Wallach, *Dethroning the Deceitful Pork Chop*; Zafar, *Recipes for Respect*.

14. Carney and Rosomoff, *In the Shadow of Slavery*, 72–75.

15. Carney and Rosomoff, 73.

16. Trotter, "Observations on the Scurvy," 18.

17. Carney and Rosomoff address the oral histories of Africans bringing seeds and grains to the Americas in their hair. This did not happen in capture but rather prior to disembarking the ships at its destination. It should be noted, as the geographers explain, that in some cases rice and other grains were used as talisman in hopes of keeping a child safe since mothers did not know if they would continue to stay with their children. In other cases, tucking grains in the child's hair was a means of "bestowing a gift of lifesaving from Africa." See Carney and Rosomoff, *In the Shadow of Slavery*, 76–77.

18. Among many others, see Opie, *Hog and Hominy*, especially the section "The Atlantic Slave Trade and the Columbian Exchange," 1–16; Harris, *Iron Pots and Wooden Spoons*, xvi; and R. Hall, "Food Crops, Medicinal Plants, and the Atlantic Slave Trade."

19. Mustakeem, *Slavery at Sea*, 64–65.

20. See Ed McCree's narrative in Federal Writers' Project, *Slave Narrative Project*, 56–65.

21. In the summer of 2014, I had the privilege of participating in a NEH Landmarks of American History and Culture Summer Workshop on the intricacies of slavery in the colonial Chesapeake region. My contribution focused on foodways of the region and how these K-12 teachers, who hailed from states across the U.S., could implement this information into their curriculum. It was readily apparent how little these educators knew about the institution of slavery—its nuances, layers, and variances.

22. See Alford, *Prince among Slaves*; Austin, *African Muslims in Antebellum America*; Diouf, *Servants of Allah*; Gomez, *Black Crescent*; and Capet, "Created Equal."

23. Khaled A. Beydoun is the Critical Race Studies Teaching Fellow at the UCLA School of Law. Khaled Beydoun, "Ramadan: A Centuries-Old American Tradition," *Al Jazeera*, June 28, 2014, http://www.aljazeera.com/indepth/opinion/2014/06/ramadan -american-tradition-201462714534443176.html. See Alford, *Prince among Slaves*; Austin, *African Muslims in Antebellum America*; Diouf, *Servants of Allah*; Gomez, *Black Crescent*; and Capet, "Created Equal."

24. "African Muslims Enslaved in the United States," Prince among Slaves Project, 2011, accessed July 18, 2015, http://princeamongslaves.org/module/muslimsinus.html.

25. Bluett, *Some Memoirs of the Life of Job*, 26. Also cited in Capet, "Created Equal," 554.

26. On Yarrow Mamout, see "Sites: 16. 3324 Dent Place," Georgetown African American Historic Landmark Project and Tour, accessed November 3, 2021, http://www.gaahlp .org/sites/3324-dent-place/; Johnston, "Every Picture Tells a Story," 418; Diouf, *Servants of Allah*, 87.

27. "Food as Community: Maynard and Burgess Food Habits in Regional Contexts," in Warner, *Eating in the Side Room*, 75. Also helpful are Edwards-Ingram, "Medicating Slavery"; and Franklin, "Enslaved Household Variability."

28. Adichie, "Danger of a Single Story."

29. Williams, *Dividing Lines*, 1.

30. Williams, 2.

31. The literature on social class, socioeconomic status, and diet as well as nutritional sources is fairly extensive, focusing on taste and choice as much as affordability. Among many other readings, see Hupkens et al., "Social Class Differences in Food Consumption"; Latshaw, "Soul of the South"; Engelhardt, *Mess of Greens*, especially chapter 2, "Biscuits and Cornbread"; and Williams-Forson, *Building Houses out of Chicken Legs*, chapter 3.

32. Wallach, *Every Nation Has Its Dish*, 3.

33. In *The Paper Bag Principle*, Audrey Kerr discusses intraracial prejudice and the ways in which myths and colorism intersect.

34. Wallach, *Every Nation Has Its Dish*, 3–4

35. Wallach, *Every Nation Has Its Dish*, 3–4.

36. Wallach, *Every Nation Has Its Dish*, 4–5.

37. "The Change of Food," *People's Advocate* (Washington, D.C.), August 4, 1883.

38. Ulysses Grant Dailey, "Proper Eating," *Chicago Defender*, July 24, 1943, 14. Dr. Ulysses Grant Dailey, renowned African American surgeon and gynecologist, was born on August 3, 1885, in Donaldsonville, Louisiana, and had an illustrious career before his death in 1961. See the Chicago Public Library's collection Ulysses Grant Dailey Papers, https://www.chipublib.org/fa-ulysses-grant-dailey-papers/.

39. Tuskegee Institute, "Experts Accuse Americans of Eating Themselves to Death," *Chicago Defender*, April 22, 1961, 15. Founded as a Normal School for Colored Teachers by Lewis Adams, a former slave, Tuskegee Institute, which has become a university, is best known for being the educational home of Booker T. Washington and botanist Carter G. Woodson. By the mid-twentieth century, its voice had long been considered a major authority.

40. Albert Wilberforce Williams was a prominent physician of internal medicine in Chicago, Illinois. He wrote for both the *Chicago Defender* and the *Chicago Tribune*. He was often considered controversial because he spoke on issues such as sexually transmitted diseases as well as the eating habits and practices of African Americans. See Williams, "Defender Health Editor Looks Back," *Chicago Defender*, May 4, 1935, 24. Also see Encyclopedia.com, s.v. "Williams, Wilberforce A.," accessed December 1, 2021, https://www.encyclopedia.com/african-american-focus/news-wires-white-papers-and-books/williams-wilberforce.

41. "Slum Dwellers Eat Better under Food Stamp Plan," *Chicago Defender*, May 6, 1967, 5.

42. Poe, "Origins of Soul Food in Black Urban Identity."

43. Dahn, "Unashamedly Black," 95.

44. Dahn, 95.

45. Rouse and Hoskins, "Purity, Soul Food, and Sunni Islam," 182.

46. Williams-Forson, *Building Houses out of Chicken Legs*. See also William Black, "How Watermelons Became a Racist Trope," *The Atlantic*, December 8, 2014, https://www.theatlantic.com/national/archive/2014/12/how-watermelons-became-a-racist-trope/383529/; Klein, "Cutting Away the Rind," 73–104; Nneka Okona, "How Watermelon's Reputation Got Tangled in Racism," *HuffPost*, August 2, 2019, https://www.huffpost.com/entry/watermelon-racism_l_5d2dfea4e4b0a873f6428b9c.

47. Williams-Forson, *Building Houses out of Chicken Legs*, 137–40.

48. Sarah Kaufman, Benjamin Peim, and Carrie Melago, "NYC's 'Obama's Fried Chicken' Restaurants Ruffle Feathers," *New York Daily News*, April 3, 2009, https://www.nydailynews.com/new-york/obama-fried-chicken-joints-ruffle-feathers-article-1.359623.

49. Damon Young, "Perfectly Normal Things Black Men Just Know Not to Do Because America Is Racist as Fuck," *The Root*, December 9, 2014, https://www.theroot.com/perfectly-normal-things-black-men-just-know-not-to-do-b-1822522809#! Originally accessed May 3, 2015. When accessed in August 2021, the image of President Obama eating a piece of chicken had been understandably removed and replaced with a stand-alone plate of fried chicken. Initially this book was going to be titled *Don't Yuck My Yum* or *Don't Police My Plate*. Young's article encapsulates the broader arguments of this book and no doubt influenced the first part of this book's title.

50. Young, "Perfectly Normal Things."

51. Associated Press, "Mayor to Quit over Obama Watermelon E-mail," NBC News, February 27, 2009, https://www.nbcnews.com/id/wbna29423045.

52. "All Southerners Like Watermelon," *Life*, August 9, 1937, 21 and 52; Okona, "Watermelon's Reputation."

53. The Farm Security Administration/Office of War Information (FSA/OWI) was started in 1935 to document the activities of the Resettlement Administration (RA) during the era of Rexford Tugwell. Tugwell, an economist, was a member of Franklin D. Roosevelt's inner circle, or "Brain Trust," who helped develop policy recommendations for Roosevelt's New Deal initiative, which was a series of programs, public work projects, financial reforms, and regulations from 1933 to 1939. As part of this initiative, the goal of FSA/OWI was to document loans to farmers provided by the RA/USDA (U.S. Department of Agriculture). Notable photographers like Dorothea Lange, Walker Evans, Marion Post Wolcott, and Gordon Parks were major contributors, along with some others. In total, the Library of Congress's collection includes over 100,000 images from the RA/FSA/OWI. While the photo series are very useful, most often the pictures are of white individuals and communities. For an excellent overview of the collection and its documentation of African American people, see Natonson, *Black Image in the New Deal*, especially chapters 1 and 2. See also Williams-Forson, "Dance of Culinary Patriotism."

54. In 1943, the Department of the Interior (DOI) established the Solid Fuels Administration for War. According to the National Archives, in 1946 the DOI and the United Mine Workers agreed to a joint survey of medical, health, and housing conditions in coal communities. The survey teams went into various mining areas to collect data and photograph conditions that were later compiled into a published report. Some of the photographs captured in this record group are snapshots of miner life from religious activities to their interior lives. The majority of the photographs were taken by Russell W. Lee, a professional photographer who also worked with the Farm Security Administration, while some were taken by the Navy. See National Archives and Records Administration, Records of the Solid Fuels Administration for War, Record Group 245 / 1946–47 / 4,100 item. See also Barbara Lewis Burger, "Guide to the Still Picture Branch Holdings," Research Our Records, National Archives, https://www.archives.gov/research/guides/still-pictures-guide.

55. Bates, "Comfort in a Decidedly Uncomfortable Time," 53.

56. On collective agency, see White, "Freedom Seeds."

57. The Gilliam, West Virginia, mine had 232 employees, 60 percent of whom were African Americans, so there are many other families who can be explored and discussed. Other mining communities mentioned in this record group include Gary Mines of Gary, West Virginia; Mullens Mine, Mullens, West Virginia; and Sipsey Mine of Sipsey, Alabama. See Records of the Solid Fuels Administration for War, Photographs of the Medical Survey of the Bituminous Coal Industry, 1946–1947, Record Group 245, National Archives and Record Administration, Still Pictures Division, Washington, D.C.

58. Ta-Nehisi Coates, "Letter to My Son," *The Atlantic*, July 4, 2015, https://www.theatlantic.com/politics/archive/2015/07/tanehisi-coates-between-the-world-and-me/397619/. Italics in the original.

59. Adichie, "Danger of a Single Story."

60. See the introduction's discussion of Natasha Tynes, who took a photo of a Washington, D.C., Metro employee eating her lunch on the train and uploaded it to social media.

61. Kendi discusses three groups: segregationists, who blame Black people themselves for racial disparities; antiracists, who point to racial discrimination as the culprit; and assimilationists, who argue for laying the blame at the feet of both Black people and racial discrimination. See Kendi, *Stamped from the Beginning*, 2.

62. Lonnae O'Neal, "Ibram Kendi, One of the Nation's Leading Scholars of Racism, Says Education and Love Are Not the Answer," *The Undefeated*, September 20, 2017, https://theundefeated.com/features/ibram-kendi-leading-scholar-of-racism-says-education-and-love-are-not-the-answer/.

Chapter 2

1. There is a growing body of literature that explores African American travel experiences and their linkages to racism and fear. See Lee and Scott, "Racial Discrimination and African Americans' Travel Behavior," 381–92. In addition to the numerous primary sources found in historical newspapers under the search for travel and tourism, there is a plethora of articles available in the contemporary popular press. For additional scholarly starting points, see Denkler, *Sustaining Identity, Recapturing Heritage*; Alderman, introduction to "African Americans and Tourism." On food and tourism in the South including mentions of African Americans, see Stanonis, *Dixie Emporium*; Williams-Forson, "Weary Traveler in a Familiar Land"; and Williams-Forson, *Building Houses out of Chicken Legs*, chapter 3.

2. Derek Alderman has written extensively on travel and tourism among African American communities. See Alderman, introduction to "African Americans and Tourism." Also see Butler et al., "African-American Travel Agents." Some celebrity chefs and travel documentarians have discussed aspects of food and travel in African American communities and many scholars have discussed Victor Green's *Negro Motorist Green Book*. But for one of the most insightful and visually arresting narrative explorations, see Williams, *High on the Hog*. Lastly, see Williams-Forson, "Weary Traveler in a Familiar Land," 44–50.

3. City of Westminster (Maryland), "History of Westminster," https://www.westminstermd.gov/264/History-of-Westminster.

4. Most all of the work by culinary historian Jessica Harris and Frederick Douglass Opie's *Hog and Hominy* offer excellent discussions on African American food adaptations. For more on culinary adaptations among Indigenous and Native Americans, see Mihesuah and Hoover, *Indigenous Food Sovereignty in the United States*. For Italian, Irish, and Jewish communities, see Diner, *Hungering for America*; and Gabaccia, *We Are What We Eat*. Marcie Cohen Ferris offers an excellent discussion of Jewish foodways in the South in *Matzoh Ball Gumbo*. Using South Asian fiction, Anita Mannur explores how immigrants use food to represent Americanization even as they hold affinity for their native India in *Culinary Fictions*; Krishnendu Ray explores similar issues for Bengali immigrants in the *Migrant's Table*. Also see Ji-Song Ku, Manalanson, and

Mannur, *Eating Asian America*; Halloran, *Immigrant Kitchen*; and Brown and Mussell, *Ethnic and Regional Foodways*.

5. Furst et al., "Food Choice."

6. Sobal and Bisogni, "Constructing Food Choice Decisions," s39.

7. Sobal and Bisogni, s37.

8. Sobal and Bisogni, s37; but also see Furst et al., "Food Choice," 251.

9. Sobal and Bisogni, s37.

10. Gordon, *Ghostly Matters*, 4.

11. Gordon, *Ghostly Matters*, 4–5.

12. Bourdieu, *Distinction*, 466–68.

13. Radway, foreword to *Ghostly Matters*, x.

14. Michael Endelman, "'The Wire': You Can't Leave Home," *Entertainment Weekly*, November 13, 2006, https://ew.com/article/2006/11/13/wire-you-cant-leave-home/.

15. Clark-Lewis, *Living In*, 3.

16. Grosvenor, "In the Tradition." Also see Kalcik, "Ethnic Foodways in America," 39; Levenstein, *Revolution at the Table*; Gabaccia, *We Are What We Eat*; and Beoku-Betts, "'We Got Our Way of Cooking Things,'" 551.

17. M. Yanina Pepino, "Our Taste Buds Regenerate Every Two Weeks," *Spirit Magazine Air Tran*, October 2013, 39.

18. Korsmeyer, "Introduction," 12.

19. According to van Andel et al., local plant names reveal that Africans had some knowledge of plant fora in the colonies. They say in some cases, translations are available, and that the name of the plant refers to spicy, salted, oily, and pepper smelling weeds and bark that were consumed. See van Andel et al., "Local Plant Names Reveal That African Slaves Recognized American Plants," E5346–E5347.

20. A notable exception to this statement is Chicago. Many migrants from Mississippi landed in the city, and the *Chicago Defender* extensively documented their food habits and behaviors. For more, see Poe, "Origins of Soul Food in Black Urban Identity." Contemporary New England and the Pacific Northwest also are areas where new studies could be conducted on African American culinary life, from the past to the present. Harris, *High on the Hog*, especially chapters 7 and 8, and White, *Freedom Farmers*, discuss growing as a community-building project in areas in and around Detroit.

21. To be sure, there are many African Americans and Black people, more generally, for whom using this many kinds of spices is discomforting. Most often when I encounter these people, they have a general dislike for cooking, overall. I often read comments that say "salt and pepper is NOT seasoning" on TikTok, Instagram, and other social media where cooking and meal preparation is documented. But even this is a form of shaming, especially for those who are afraid and unwilling to experiment. See Nettles-Barcelon et al., "Black Women's Food Work as Critical Space," 36.

22. Nettles-Barcelon et al., "Black Women's Food Work as Critical Space," 40–41.

23. Nettles-Barcelon et al., 40–41.

24. Nettles-Barcelon et al., 42.

25. Reay Tannahill, *Food in History*, 393. See also Degner, "Reaching Consumers with Novel Foods," 5.

26. Psyche Williams-Forson, "Thanksgiving Dinner," Facebook survey, 2013.

27. Allen and Anderson, "Consumption and Social Stratification," 70–72.

28. Allen and Anderson, 70–72.

29. My analysis of the incident at the museum is not meant to shame my lecture compatriot. Instead, the goal here is to encourage African Americans to check their class and privilege display when it comes to food, just like other forms of expressive culture. And of course this is not the first time that class ideology and food have intermingled or been fused on the culinary battleground. See the extensive set of conversations on food and Black nationalism that have been well covered, for instance, Witt, *Black Hunger*; Wallach, "How to Eat to Live"; Wallach, *Every Nation Has Its Dish*; and Wallach, *Getting What We Need Ourselves*.

30. This is a pervasive perception circulating in the food discussions today. See, for example, Kristen Aiken, "'White People Food' Is Creating an Unattainable Picture of Health," *HuffPost Online*, August 29, 2018, https://www.huffpost.com/entry/white -people-food_n_5b75c270e4b0df9b093dadbb.

31. Walker, "Everyday Use," 317.

32. Walker, "Everyday Use," 314–21.

33. The song title is taken from Lorraine Hansberry's posthumous autobiography, *To Be Young, Gifted and Black*. The song's music was composed and first sung by Nina Simone, with lyrics by Weldon Irvine. It was considered an anthem of the Black cultural movement. This, along with the "Godfather of Soul" James Brown's "Say It Loud, I'm Black and I'm Proud," was critical to the raising the self-esteem of Black people during this time.

34. Williams-Forson, "Take the Chicken out of the Box," 83.

35. Jessica Harris, interview by Shaun Chavis, "Their Gullet: From Someone Else's Kitchen," eGForums, May 10, 2006, http://forums.egullet.org/index.php?/topic/87448 -their-food/.

36. See Wallach, "How to Eat to Live." Wallach is not the only historian to address this issue. Doris Witt before her offers an extensive analysis of Black nationalism and "filth" in *Black Hunger*.

37. Witt, *Black Hunger*, 80.

38. Shortly after our conversation, I sat down and wrote up notes. It was a rich conversation, and I did not want to misrepresent the details since the discussion was somewhat shocking. Moreover, I was unfamiliar with anyone suggesting they eat a "microbiotic" diet, as the student called it, so I was eager to research what it was and why the students on this campus were eating it. She was actually saying a *macrobiotic* diet, which focuses on eating more grains and vegetables, with little or no processed foods or animal and fish products, unless they are organic. For more on this, see "Macrobiotic Diet," CancerResearchUK, updated June 26, 2019, https://www.cancerresearchuk .org/about-cancer/cancer-in-general/treatment/complementary-alternative-therapies /individual-therapies/macrobiotic. Naa Oyo Kwate referred me to the work of holistic diet advocate Annemarie Colbin, PhD, founder and CEO of the Natural Gourmet Institute for Health and Culinary Arts. Colbin offers a thorough discussion of macrobiotic diets, detailing the health and healing benefits of eating as toxin-free as possible.

Poultry is among the foods that should be "seldom" eaten, but there is no mention of total elimination. See Colbin, "Overview of Two Popular Diets," 4. Among other sources, see Shurtleff and Aoyagi, *History of Macrobiotics*; Kushi and Jack, *Book of Macrobiotics*.

39. See Carter, "'Black' Cultural Capital," 137.

40. Zafar, *Recipes for Respect*, 50.

41. Alexander, "Toward a Theory of Cultural Trauma," 1.

42. Alexander, 1.

43. hooks, "Representing Whiteness in the Black Imagination," 345–46.

44. Naa Oyo Kwate, personal correspondence, January 1, 2020, in author's possession.

45. Fufu (pronounced *foo-foo*) is a staple for many West and Central Africans, as well as some residents of the Caribbean. For an excellent conversation about the ways that TikTok has introduced millions of people to this staple food, see Bianca Hillier, "A Fufu TikTok Trend Introduces Millions to a West African Staple," Public Radio International, February 4, 2021, https://www.pri.org/stories/2021-02-04/fufu-tiktok-trend-introduces-millions-west-african-staple. See also Williams-Forson, "'I Haven't Eaten.'"

46. Hawkes is speaking in the context of public planning when he argues for including discussions of culture alongside those involving social, environmental and economic impact. The latter three are known as the "triple bottom line" in economic and financial circles. The theory maintains that there should be multiple bottom lines instead of just one and that companies should focus on people and the environment as well as profits. See Hawkes, *Fourth Pillar of Sustainability*.

47. See Renne, "Mass Producing Food Traditions for West Africans Abroad," in which the author examines foods primarily sold in U.S. specialty stores to consider the ways in which, though technologically different in terms of production and packaging, they nonetheless are used to maintain and culturally sustain aspects of West African lifeways. See also Williams-Forson, "Other Women Cooked for My Husband"; and Williams-Forson, "'I Haven't Eaten.'"

48. Sarah (pseudonym used by request), personal interview, February 20, 2012.

49. Fran Osseo-Asare, "Interview with Dinah Ayensu," *Betumi: The African Culinary Network*, 2018, https://betumi.com/library/http-betumi-com-library-articles-beyond-gumbo-a-history-of-ghanaian-cookbooks-by-fran-osseo-asare/interview-with-dinah-ayensu/.

50. Hillier, "Fufu TikTok Trend."

51. This is true in heterosexual homes as well as lesbi-gay or same-gender households. See DeVault, *Feeding the Family*, 79; Charles and Kerr, *Women, Food, and Families*; and McIntosh and Zey, "Women as Gatekeepers." For food and relationships in lesbian and gay households, see Carrington, *No Place Like Home*; Oerton, "Queer Housewives?" 421–30; Sullivan, "Rozzie and Harriet? Gender and Family Patterns of Lesbian Coparents," 747–67; Bialeschki and Pearce, "'I Don't Want a Lifestyle,'" 113–32.

52. Piercy, "What's That Smell in the Kitchen."

53. Giovanni, "My House," in *Love Poems*.

54. Giovanni, *Love Poems*.

55. Williams, "Why Migrant Women Feed Their Husbands Tamales," 113, 115.

56. Avakian, "Shish Kebab Armenians," 251.

57. Among other readings, for discussions on the intersection of women, food, and power, see Beagan et al., "'It's Just Easier'"; Davies and Carrier, "Importance of Power Relations"; Williams-Forson, *Building Houses out of Chicken Legs*; and Counihan, "Female Identity," 51–62.

58. Naccarato and LeBesco, *Culinary Capital*, 3.

59. Romano, *Intercultural Marriage*, 46.

60. D'Sylva and Beagan, "'Food Is Culture,'" 287.

61. Williams-Forson, "Other Women Cooked for My Husband," 440–41; also see Marjorie DeVault, *Feeding the Family*, for a discussion of such conflicts in food.

62. Mehta, "Culinary Diasporas," 35.

63. Lin, Pang, and Liao, "Home Food Making," 1.

64. Mannur, "Culinary Nostalgia," 11.

65. Williams-Forson, "Other Women Cooked for My Husband," 441.

66. Quoted in Williams-Forson, 442.

67. Williams-Forson, 445.

68. Williams-Forson, 446. Waakye (pronounced *waachay*), or wache, is a dish of rice and beans. The dish is so common in Ghana that when we would go across town to purchase it, the implication was that it was like the Ghanaian version of McDonald's. See Shardow, *Taste of Hospitality*, 85; and Otoo and Otoo, *Authentic African Cuisine from Ghana*. Also see "Queen Elizabeth to Eat 'Waakye' Prepared by Ghanaian Chef," Queensyoungleaders.com, July 2, 2017, https://www.ghanaweb.com/GhanaHomePage /NewsArchive/Queen-Elizabeth-to-eat-waakye-prepared-by-Ghanaian-Chef-554737.

Chapter 3

1. According to History.com, Hurricane Katrina was a tropical cyclone that made landfall along the Gulf Coast in late August 2005. The storm killed a total of 1,833 people and left millions homeless from New Orleans and all along the Gulf Coast of Louisiana, Mississippi, and Alabama. See Sarah Pruitt, "Hurricane Katrina: 10 Facts about the Deadly Storm and Its Legacy," History.com, August 19, 2020, https://www.history.com /news/hurricane-katrina-facts-legacy.

2. David Von Drehle and Jacqueline Salmon, "Displacement of Historic Proportions," *Washington Post*, September 2, 2005.

3. Von Drehle and Salmon.

4. Howard-John Wesley, "The Curse Is Broken" (sermon), All in the Family, pt. 3. February 27, 2021, https://www.youtube.com/watch?v=ruLCn25yraU.

5. Eliza Thomas, "The Curse of Ham: How Bad Scripture Interpretation Inspired Genocide," IMB, June 12, 2018, https://www.imb.org/2018/06/12/the-curse-of-ham-genocide/.

6. Wesley, "The Curse Is Broken."

7. Erikson, *A New Species of Trouble*, 228. Though the storm struck along the coast, my primary focus throughout this discussion is New Orleans because it is the location about which I have the most information and knowledge.

8. Erikson, 229.

9. Erikson, 228.

10. Tee (pseudonym used by request), interview by the author, February 10, 2020.

11. Tee, interview by the author, February 10, 2020.

12. Among the many pieces of information and documentation about Hurricane Katrina, there is now important information on the impact of the disaster on foodways in the Gulf Coast. Aspects of the Gulf Coast Food Project were funded by a National Endowment for the Humanities grant to facilitate the development of food studies at the University of Houston. The Gulf Coast Food Project (http://www.uh.edu/gcfp/) was founded in 2008 to promote the scholarly study of food in the region and its impact upon business and economy, nutrition and health, the environment, and social relations. Marisa Ramirez, "Katrina, Slavery and Food: Gulf Coast Food Project Welcomes Noted Scholar Psyche Williams-Forson" (press release), University of Houston, January 19, 2016, https://uh.edu/news-events/stories/2016/January/119PsycheHIST.php.

13. Joel Anderson, "'It Ain't the Police Who Was Helping Us,'" *BuzzFeed*, July 29, 2015, https://www.buzzfeed.com/joelanderson/how-a-small-time-drug-dealer-rescued-dozens -during-katrina.

14. Wilmarine B. Hurst, "A Lil' Taste of Home: On the Sixth Anniversary of Hurricane Katrina New Orleans Cuisine Reigns Supreme," *New Orleans Tribune*, 2011, accessed April 18, 2012, http://theneworleanstribune.com/wilmarine.htm (page discontinued).

15. Hurst, "A Lil' Taste of Home." I had always heard that red beans on Monday was a tradition becaues laundry day was customarily at the beginning of the week. Because laundry was done by hand it could take all day, so washerwomen and those who did their own laundry would multitask by putting beans on the stove in the morning over a low flame and letting them cook all day. Zatarain's is often mentioned as a local rice brand of choice; Camellia is a frequently used brand of red beans, and Hurst mentions Blue Runner. For those who do not use ham or its bone, D&D and MaBell's seem to be the hot sausage brands of choice. See also "Red Beans and Rice," NewOrleans .com, accessed December 2, 2021, https://www.neworleans.com/restaurants/traditional -new-orleans-foods/red-beans-and-rice/; and Simmons, "Red Beans and Rice," 243–44.

16. Paul Duggan, Dan Morse, and Nancy Trejos, "Area Evacuees Now Hit by Unease, Uncertainty," *Washington Post*, September 26, 2005, https://www.washington post.com/archive/local/2005/09/26/area-evacuees-now-hit-unease-uncertainty/29b56fe1 -0ff3-48a8-8e58-74fc602a9e48/.

17. Sage Policy Group, *The Coming Storm: How Years of Economic Underperformance Are Catching Up with Montgomery County*, April 2018, https://www.empowermontgomery .com/wp-content/uploads/2018/04/Montgomery_County_EM_Final.pdf.

18. Tee, interview by the author, January 10, 2021.

19. Tee, personal correspondence in the author's possession, February 9, 2021.

20. Hurst, "A Lil' Taste of Home." Thomas-Naquin is referring to Double D Smoked Sausage, or D&D, a popular sausage among residents. Many businesses now specialize in shipping foods from the region directly to consumers. See, for example, Louisiana Dry Ice and Shipping Online Store, http://shop.nolafoodshippers.com/main.sc.

21. Tee, interview by the author, January 10, 2021.

22. The written details of Latrisha Avery can be found in Steve Hendrix and Hamil

Harris, "In D.C., Where Kids Live Sets the Tone for Weight-Loss Success," *Washington Post*, May 20, 2008. Most of the online version of the exposé has been sacrificed due to the removal of Adobe Flashplayer, but aspects of the report remain. Because I was interested in Latrisha's story, I captured the images for future use. For the print version, see Lynn Medford and Ashley Halsey III, "Young Lives at Risk," *Washington Post*, May 12, 2008. For the web version, see Jonathan Krim, Jonathan, Stacey Palosky, Nelson Hsu, Sarah Sampsel, and Nancy Donaldson, "Young Lives at Risk," *Washington Post* (online), May 12, 2008, https://www.washingtonpost.com/wp-srv/health/childhoodobesity/.

23. Obesity has been well covered, even in food studies. Both Guthman, *Weighing In*, and Farrell, *Fat Shame*, offer excellent discussions on the topic, generally. Charlotte Biltekoff, *Eating Right in America*, offers a very compelling and convincing set of arguments about cultural politics, eating, and health in American society. Works by Paul Campos et al. and Michael Gard and Jan Wright, among others, caution us about wholesale acceptance of the notion of obesity as an uncontrolled "crisis" or "epidemic" by using terms that are, as Farrell suggests, problematic because they reflect "apocalyptic thinking."

24. See Belasco et al., "Frontiers of Food Studies."

25. Belasco et al., 308.

26. "Different Worlds, One Problem: The Voice of LaTrisha Avery," *Washington Post*. The photo exhibit is no longer available online or in the *Washington Post* archives. I captured the images with the captions for future use in my research. Unless otherwise indicated, the photo captions are attributed to Carol Guzy.

27. Wen et al., "Spatial Disparities," 518–19; Cohen et al., "Public Parks and Physical Activity." See also Moore et al., "Availability of Recreational Resources."

28. Hendrix and Harris, "Where Kids Live Sets the Tone."

29. Walker, *In Search of Our Mothers' Gardens*, xi–xii.

30. Anthony Bradley, "The Marxist Roots of Black Liberation Theology," Acton Institute. April 2, 2008, https://www.acton.org/pub/commentary/2008/04/02/Marxist-roots -black-liberation-theology.

31. Adichie, "Danger of a Single Story."

32. Hendrix and Harris, "Where Kids Live Sets Tone."

33. Hendrix and Harris.

34. Thompson, *Hunger So Wide*, 69.

35. A. Seven Forson, personal conversation, January 14, 2021.

36. Thompson, *Hunger So Wide*, 94.

37. Barghouti, *I Saw Ramallah*, 178.

38. Thompson, *Hunger So Wide*, 94.

39. Erikson, *New Species of Trouble*, 242.

40. Bass, "On Being a Fat Black Girl," 220–22.

41. Cooper, *Eloquent Rage*, 83. Scholar of psychology and human ecology Naa Oyo Kwate reminded me of this admission by Cooper when she asks the question, "Are Black girls ever worth fighting for?"

42. Bass, "On Being a Fat Black Girl," 222.

43. Nettles-Barcelon, "Saving Soul Food," 111.

44. Krieger, "Historical Roots of Social Epidemiology," 899–900.

45. Twitty, *Cooking Gene*, 107.

46. The literature on African American women and domestic work is extensive. My emphasis here is on those who specifically speak to material aspects of these women's lives as they relate to gastronomy. See, in particular, Clark-Lewis, *Living In, Living Out*; Sharpless, *Cooking in Other Women's Kitchens*; and Williams-Forson, *Building Houses out of Chicken Legs*, especially chapter four , "Traveling the Chicken Bone Express."

47. Smith, "Press of Our Own Kitchen Table," 11–13.

48. Weems, *Kitchen Table Series*.

49. Twitty, *Cooking Gene*, 40.

50. Walker, "Nervous Kitchens." Denis Byrne uses the phrase "nervous landscape" to think about how people occupy spaces and thus literally and figuratively make the landscape nervous. This is especially the case when those who are used to holding power in particular spaces have their authority challenged by the introduction of new people with different kinds of access to power. This disruption of the status quo, especially by those considered less powerful in society, makes the landscape nervous. See Byrne, "Nervous Landscapes."

51. Kimberly Nettles-Barcelon et al. discuss the important work of food work as critical space in "Black Women's Food Work as Critical Space," 34–49.

52. Walmsley, "Race, Place and Taste," 44.

53. Carol Guzy, "The Voice of Veronica Gray: Latrisha Avery's Godmother," *Washington Post*, May 20, 2008.

54. Larchet, "Learning from the Corner Store," 406.

55. Tate, *Everything but the Burden*, 1–4.

56. Zafar, *Recipes for Respect*. Several texts that have emerged in the last decade reveal various aspects of African American foodways. They have all filled in the gaps in ways that advance the discussion of African American culture and life. See, for example, Cooley, *To Live and Dine in Dixie*.

57. Reese and Garth, introduction to *Black Food Matters*, 3; Hartman, *Lose Your Mother*, 6.

58. Deepti Hajela and Lindsay Whitehurst, "'I Am a Child!': Pepper Spray Reflects Policing of Black Kids," AP News (online), February 12, 2021, https://apnews.com /article/policing-black-kids-6708e9f229ed9d28b9c60a41ea988b59.

59. Hajela and Whitehurst.

60. Stacy Patton, "In America, Black Children Don't Get to Be Children" (op-ed), *Washington Post*, November 26, 2014, https://www.washingtonpost.com/opinions /in-america-black-children-dont-get-to-be-children/2014/11/26/a9e24756-74ee-11e4-a755 -e32227229e7b_story.html.

61. Hajela and Whitehurst, "'I Am a Child!'"

62. Jackson, *Scripting the Black Masculine Body*, 9.

63. Strings, *Fearing the Black Body*, 210.

64. Nineteen-year-old Aidan Ellison was killed in 2020, as was seventeen-year-old Jordan Davis; both were accused of playing their music too loud. See Katie Shepherd, "A Black Teen Was Fatally Shot Following a Dispute over Loud Music, Police

Say," *Washington Post*, November 20, 2020, https://www.washingtonpost.com/nation/2020/11/30/oregon-teen-shot-music/; Trone Dowd, "Black Teen Killed over Loud Music 8 Years to the Day after Jordan Davis' Death," Vice, November 30, 2020, https://www.vice.com/en/article/n7veyw/black-teen-killed-over-loud-music-8-years-to-the-day-after-jordan-davis-death. On May 20, 2017, Lt. Richard Collins III visited the campus of the University of Maryland College Park with two of his friends. While Collins was waiting for an Uber, a student emerged from a nearby wooded area screaming to him, "Step left, step left if you know what's good for you." Collins refused, and the student stabbed him in the chest, killing him. See Augenstein and Moore, "Guilty: Sean Urbanski Convicted of 1st-Degree Murder in Stabbing Death of Lt. Richard Collins III," WTOP.com, December 18, 2019. https://wtop.com/prince-georges-county/2019/12/how-jury-will-learn-judge-threw-out-hate-crime-charge-in-u-md-murder-trial/.

65. Alice Randall, "Black Women and Fat" (op-ed), *New York Times*, May 5, 2012, https://www.nytimes.com/2012/05/06/opinion/sunday/why-black-women-are-fat.html.

66. Rashawn Ray, "Cause and Consequence in Weight Gain" (op-ed), *New York Times*, June 1, 2012, https://www.nytimes.com/roomfordebate/2012/05/07/women-weight-and-wellness/cause-and-consequence-in-weight-gain.

67. Alexis Miettien, "Interview: Ava Purkiss," University of Michigan LSA Institute for the Humanities, https://lsa.umich.edu/humanities/news-events/all-news/fellows-interviews/ava-purkiss.html. See also Ava Purkiss, "(Re)examining Fat Stigma through Black Women's History," *Food, Fatness and Fitness: Critical Perspectives* (blog), April 1, 2017, http://foodfatnessfitness.com/2017/04/01/reexamining-fat-stigma-black-womens-history/. The work of medical anthropologist Stephanie McClure, who writes on culture and health issues of African American women and girls, is useful here as well.

68. "About Us," Black Girls RUN!, https://blackgirlsrun.com/about/.

69. "Our Story," GirlTrek, 2021, https://www.girltrek.org/our_story.

70. Harris and Nowverl, "What's Happening to Soul Food?"

Chapter 4

1. As distinguished from warehouse clubs and supercenters, which were grouped with supermarkets and grocery stores.

2. Annette John-Hall, "A Timely Book on Eating Cheaply and Healthily from Philadelphia's 'Dollar Diva,'" *Philadelphia Inquirer*, December 21, 2010, https://www.inquirer.com/philly/news/local/20101221_Annette_John-Hall__A_timely_book_on_eating_cheaply_and_healthily_from_Philadelphia_s__quot_Dollar_Diva_quot_.html. According to John-Hall, after Fisher test-marketed the book, Dollar Tree stores, where she had been shopping for some time prior to writing the book, bought 54,000 copies to sell for one dollar each. For another perspective, see Joel Keller, "How to Eat at the Dollar Store," *Black Table*, May 12, 2005, http://www.blacktable.com/keller050512.htm.

3. John-Hall, "Timely Book." Fisher might also benefit from one of the many Philadelphia ShopRite supermarkets owned by Jeffrey Brown. According to Bornstein, who covered Brown in his recent op-ed, "Brown's business model is to locate in densely

populated urban areas, get high volume with lower priced food, and make sure that his stores keep in close contact with the neighborhood. He stocks foods that are in specific demand in each neighborhood. In each store, he also has a community meeting room and a community coordinator. He has a program to hire ex-offenders—now 100 of his 2,400 employees, he said. He's recently added a credit union, which will offer free ATM and check-writing services for customers and a health clinic, with a nurse practitioner." David Bornstein, "Conquering Food Deserts with Green Carts," Opinionator, *New York Times*, April 18, 2012, http://opinionator.blogs.nytimes.com/2012/04/18/conquering -food-deserts-with-green-carts/. By connecting his store to the local community in this way, Brown is expanding upon the notion of "access" and ensuring a returning customer base.

4. Jack Hitt, "The Dollar Store Economy," *New York Times Magazine* (online), August 18, 2011, https://www.nytimes.com/2011/08/21/magazine/the-dollar-store-economy .html.

5. AT, "RE: Dollar Tree Question," classroom response, Feminist Cultural Criticism of Diasporic Texts, January 18, 2011.

6. Ronette King, "The Buck Shops Here," DollarStores by BuckStore Inc. (website), December 5, 2004, http://www.buckstore.com/dollar_store_news_3.htm.

7. Megan Zhang, "'Our Hearts Are Hurting': Elderly Chinese Isolated as SF Dim Sum Restaurants Shutter in Pandemic," *SF Gate*, January 21, 2021, https://www.sfgate.com /food/article/Dim-Sum-family-Chinese-community-15885582.php. Mary Corbin Sies brought this article to my attention.

8. Michael Kimmelman, "The Urban Home Away from Home," *New York Times*, January 28, 2014, https://www.nytimes.com/2014/01/29/arts/design/lessons-from-mcdonalds -clash-with-older-koreans.html.

9. Kimmelman, "Urban Home."

10. Aside from the account I reference, where the African American man proposed to his fiancée at McDonald's, there are countless stories of this kind of wedding proposal. For the South African story, see "Twitter Goes Wild for South African KFC Proposal," BBC (online), November 8, 2019, https://www.bbc.com/news/world-africa-50351433.

11. Kristen Aiken, "'White People Food' Is Creating an Unattainable Picture of Health," *HuffPost*, August 29, 2018, https://www.huffpost.com/entry/white-people-food _n_5b75c270e4b0df9b093dadbb.

12. Special thanks to Kimberly Nettles-Barcelon, Monica White, and Ashanté Reese for shedding some light on these issues.

13. Special thanks to Kimberly Nettles-Barcelon, Monica White, and Ashanté Reese for helping me with these details.

14. Thomasi McDonald, "To Understand How Gentrification in Durham Works, Just Read the Signs," *Indy Week*, September 2, 2020, https://indyweek.com/news/durham /gentrification-durham-signs/.

15. McDonald, "To Understand."

16. Duke Sanford World Food Policy Center, *Gentrification and the Future of Food Justice (2000–2020)*, accessed December 2, 2021, https://wfpc.sanford.duke.edu/durham -food-history/gentrification-future-food-justice-2000%E2%80%932020.

17. See Haider and Bitler, "Economic View of Food Deserts"; Kowaleski-Jones et al., "Alternative Measures of Food Deserts."

18. Bell and Burlin, "In Urban Areas." The authors indicate that some of the practices have been identified and challenged as potentially discriminatory. There was no indication that the issues had been resolved.

19. Guthman, "Bringing Good Food to Others," 432.

20. Though Will Allen's Growing Power collapsed after facing "insurmountable debt and legal pressures," he did some very good work in eradicating lack of access to fresh food, both locally and globally. Steven Satterfield, "Behind the Rise and Fall of Growing Power," March 13, 2018, https://civileats.com/2018/03/13/behind-the-rise-and-fall-of-growing-power/. Peaches and Greens (www.peachesandgreens.org), a mobile produce market, was among the organizations that revived the concept of bringing food to the people by delivering fresh fruit and vegetables to residents of Detroit. This idea mirrors in some respects that of the Baltimore arabbers, the longtime street vendors who sell fruit and vegetables from horse-drawn carts in Maryland. These multigenerational vendors, who have distinctive and traditional street calls, are considered a local cultural institution. See David Frey, "The Last of the Arabbers," Eater, October 8, 2014, https://www.eater.com/2014/10/8/6915565/baltimore-arabbers-fruit-vendors.

21. Bornstein, "Conquering Food Deserts."

22. Bell and Burlin, "In Urban Areas," 269.

23. Reese, Black Food Geographies. While the entire book is a must-read, the reference here is to chapter 1, "Come to Think of It, We Were Pretty Self-Sufficient."

24. Guthman, "Bringing Good Food to Others," 433.

25. Romm, "Coincidental Order of Environmental Injustice," 121–26. See also Guthman, "Bringing Good Food to Others," 436.

26. Heldke, "Staying Home for Dinner," 13.

27. Though the literature on food activism and contemporary food social movements is as vast as it is varied, some worthwhile references to consider include the following: Reese and Garth, Black Food Matters; Reese, Black Food Geographies; Maye, Holloway, and Kneafsey, Alternative Food Geographies; Penniman, Farming While Black; Bowens, Color of Food; McCutcheon, "Fannie Lou Hamer's Freedom Farmers," 207–24; Slocum, "Race in the Study of Food," 303–24; Campbell, "Building a Common Table"; DuPuis and Goodman, "Should We Go 'Home' to Eat?"; and Alkon and Agyeman, Cultivating Food Justice, 2. Rather than rehash the bodies of material written on this subject, I refer to Alkon and Mares, "Mapping the Food Movement," which provides an excellent review of the literature that discusses contemporary food social movements—from local food to community food security, food justice, and food sovereignty. The authors cover the landscape of scholarly and nonscholarly work that is both laudatory of these movements and critical. See also Cadieux and Slocum, "What Does It Mean to Do Food Justice?"

28. Scott Marlow, email to the author, June 29, 2015.

29. Beoku-Betts, "We Got Our Way of Cooking Things."

30. Topher Gray, "From Farm to Food Desert," Chicago Reader, August 19, 2010, https://chicagoreader.com/news-politics/from-farm-to-food-desert/. See also Eileen Mellon, "Let It Grow," Richmond Magazine, July 15, 2020, https://richmondmagazine

.com/restaurants-in-richmond/food-news/let-it-grow/; and Grace Abels, "Black Farmer's Markets Bring Greater Equity to the South's Food System," *Facing South*, July 30, 2020, https://www.facingsouth.org/2020/07/black-farmers-markets-bring-greater-equity-souths-food-system.

31. Mellon, "Let It Grow"

32. Mellon, "Let It Grow."

33. Abels, "Black Farmer's Markets."

34. Jenny Splitter, "Largest D.C. Farmer's Market Repeatedly Denied Spots to Black Vendors, Farmers Allege," *Forbes*, June 15, 2020, https://www.forbes.com/sites/jennysplitter/2020/06/14/racism-dc-largest-farmers-market/?sh=22151e2c575b; Emily Davies, "Dupont Circle Farmers Market Adds New Vendors after Black Businesses Said They Were Denied Access Because of Race," *Washington Post*, June 26, 2020, https://www.washingtonpost.com/local/dupont-circle-farmers-market-adds-new-vendors-after-black-businesses-said-they-were-denied-access-because-of-race/2020/06/25/282aae06-b4a8-11ea-aca5-ebb63d27e1ff_story.html.

35. Dominick Reuter and Heather Schlitz, "Meet the Typical Trader Joe's Shopper: A Younger, Married, College-Educated Person Earning over $80,000," *Business Insider*, September 1, 2021, https://www.businessinsider.com/typical-trader-joes-shopper-demographic-younger-married-earning-80k-income-2021-9.

36. Claire Martin, "Authenticity, Repurposed in a Mason Jar," *New York Times*, August 16, 2014, https://www.nytimes.com/2014/08/17/business/authenticity-repurposed-in-a-mason-jar.html. See also Melissa Fessenden, "How Mason Jars Went from Thrifty to Hip," *Smithsonian Magazine*, September 30, 2015, https://www.smithsonianmag.com/smart-news/how-mason-jars-went-thrifty-hip-180956770/.

37. Gerrit Marks, "Opinion: Area Farmers Markets Have Been My Life. They Are Where I Belong," *Washington Post*, May 7, 2021, https://www.washingtonpost.com/opinions/local-opinions/farmers-markets-vendor-community/2021/05/06/714efb8a-ad10-11eb-b476-c3b287e52a01_story.html.

38. White, *Freedom Farmers*, 3–27.

39. Tom Philpott, "White People Own 98 Percent of Rural Land. Young Black Farmers Want to Reclaim Their Share," *Mother Jones*, June 27, 2020, https://www.motherjones.com/food/2020/06/black-farmers-soul-fire-farm-reparations-african-legacy-agriculture/. Also see White, *Freedom Farmers*; Reid, *Reaping a Greater Harvest*; and, Harris, "Grace under Pressure," 203–28.

40. For information on African American farming statistics, see Lee, *Working the Roots*; Penniman, *Farming While Black*; White, *Freedom Farmers*; Abels, "Black Farmers Markets." Vann R. Newkirk II provides an excellent expose on Black farming and land theft in "The Great Land Robbery: The Shameful Story of How 1 Million Black Families Have Been Ripped from Their Farms," *The Atlantic*, September 2019, https://www.theatlantic.com/magazine/archive/2019/09/this-land-was-our-land/594742/. National Public Radio, among other news outlets, carried the story of Bruce Beach: A. Martinez, "Landmark California Bill Could Help Black Families Reclaim Seized Land," *Morning Edition*, NPR, October 6, 2021, https://www.npr.org/2021/10/06/1043600150/landmark-california-bill-could-help-black-families-reclaim-seized-land.

41. Abels, "Black Farmers Markets."

42. White, "A Pig and a Garden," 20–27. See also McCutcheon, "Fannie Lou Hamer's Freedom Farms," 207–24.

43. White, "A Pig and a Garden," 20–26.

44. Alkon, *Black, White, and Green*, 1.

45. Michael Pollan, "Unhappy Meals," *New York Times Magazine*, January 28, 2007, https://www.nytimes.com/2007/01/28/magazine/28nutritionism.t.html?

46. Alkon and Agyeman, *Cultivating Food Justice*, 2.

47. Guthman, "Bringing Food to Others," 431–32.

48. Tracey Middlekauff, "Romancing the Farm," *Urbanite*, 2011. Sometimes these are impromptu, pop-up food experiences. Other times, these are well-planned public, custom, and even corporate tours that entice you to go behind the scenes while enjoying the farm to table experience. For more on these kinds of outings, see Food and Farm Tours of Northern California, foodandfarmtours.com; Outstanding in the Field, outstanding inthefield.com; Ajesh Patalay, "Mr Jim Denevan Hosts Ultimate Outdoors Dining Experience," Mr Porter (website), September 11, 2021, https://www.mrporter.com/en-us /journal/travel/jim-denevan-outstanding-in-the-field-farm-dinner-interview-9972444.

49. Middlekauff, "Romancing the Farm."

50. Middlekauff, "Romancing the Farm."

51. Middlekauff, "Romancing the Farm." Terms like "authenticity" and "nostalgia" are hotly contested in food studies, especially in the realm of production and among those who see themselves as gatekeepers of cultural and culinary traditions. Among the many articles in food studies examining authenticity, see Heldke, "Let's Cook Thai: Recipes for Colonialism," 175-198; Abarca, "Authentic or Not, It's Original," 4-7.

52. Rebecca Brown, interview by the author, May 10, 1997.

53. Abels, "Black Farmers Markets."

54. La Risa Lynch, "Expanding the Food Desert," *Austin Weekly News*, August 17, 2011, https://www.austinweeklynews.com/2011/08/17/expanding-the-food-desert/. Interestingly, even as we push to return to agro-food systems and away from supermarkets and big-box superstores, many counties are pushing *toward* these retailers. Caryn Abrahams, for example, argues against the norm in favor of a reconsideration of the transformative potential of supermarkets' having the ability to "revolutionize" food economies in southern Africa, specifically Zambia. See Abrahams, "Transforming the Region," most notably 116n1. See also Kwate, "Fried Chicken and Fresh Apples," 32–44.

55. Frazao et al., *Food Spending Patterns*, 6.

56. Kim and Leigh, "Meals at Full-Service and Fast-Food," 307–9.

57. Williams, "Defender Health Editor Looks Back," *Chicago Defender*, May 4, 1935, 24.

58. Lusk, *Food Police*, 25.

59. Lusk, 25.

60. Corby Kummer, "The Great Grocery Smackdown," *The Atlantic*, March 2010, https://www.theatlantic.com/magazine/archive/2010/03/the-great-grocery-smackdown /307904/.

61. Frazao et al., *Food Spending Patterns*, 5.

62. "Our Work," Soilful City (website), accessed December 3, 2021, https://soilfulcity dc.wordpress.com/our-work/.

63. "Find your free" is the motto of yoga instructor, podcaster, "medicine woman of the soul," and wellness healer Rachel Voss, who seeks to heal, educate, and empower. See www.rachelvossyoga.com and @rachelvossyoga on Instagram.

Epilogue

1. Cherry-Chandler, "After the Reapers," 46.

2. Naa Oyo Kwate is working on the history of fast-food burger restaurants and how they remained only in white communities until they were forced by activists to realize the power of our Black economics.

3. Ta-Nehisi Coates, "Letter to My Son," *The Atlantic*, July 4, 2015, https://www.theatlantic .com/politics/archive/2015/07/tanehisi-coates-between-the-world-and-me/397619/.

4. Hurst, *Good Meat*.

5. Student, "Locavore Challenge," 2014, in author's possession.

6. Student, "Locavore Challenge," 2015, in author's possession.

7. Williams-Forson, "Chicken and Chains," 126–27.

8. Coates, *Between the World and Me*, 42.

9. See Adrinka Symbols and Meanings, s.v. "Sankofa," accessed December 3, 2021, https://www.adinkrasymbols.org/.

10. Gordon, *Ghostly Matters*, 57.

11. Many thanks to Scott Marlow, executive director of Rural Advancement Foundation International—USA, for helping me think through these ideas and thoughts.

BIBLIOGRAPHY

Abarca, Meredith E. "Authentic or Not, It's Original." *Food and Foodways: Explorations in the History and Culture of Human Nourishment* 12, no. 1 (2004): 1–25. https://doi.org/10.1080/07409710490467589.

Abrahams, Caryn. "Transforming the Region: Supermarkets and the Local Food Economy." *African Affairs* 109, no. 434 (2010): 115–34.

Adichie, Chimamanda Ngozi. "The Danger of a Single Story." Filmed 2009 in Oxford, UK. TEDGlobal video, 18:33. https://www.ted.com/talks/chimamanda_ngozi _adichie_the_danger_of_a_single_story.

Alderman, Derek H. Introduction to "African Americans and Tourism," special issue. *Tourism Geographies* 15, no. 3 (2013): 375–79.

Alexander, Jeffrey C. "Toward a Theory of Cultural Trauma." In *Cultural Trauma and Collective Identity*, by Jeffrey C. Alexander, Ron Eyerman, Bernard Giesen, Neil J. Smelser, and Piotr Sztompka, 1–30. Berkeley: University of California Press, 2004.

Alford, Terry. *Prince among Slaves: The True Story of An African Prince Sold Into Slavery in the American South*. New York: Oxford University Press, 1986.

Alkon, Alison Hope. *Black, White, and Green: Farmers Markets, Race, and the Green Economy*. Athens: University of Georgia Press, 2012.

Alkon, Alison Hope, and Julian Agyeman, eds. *Cultivating Food Justice: Race, Class, and Sustainability*. Cambridge, Mass.: MIT Press, 2011.

Alkon, Alison Hope, and Teresa M. Mares. "Food Sovereignty in US Food Movements: Radical Visions and Neoliberal Constraints." *Agriculture and Human Values* 29, no. 3 (2012): 347–59.

——. "Mapping the Food Movement: Addressing Inequality and Neoliberalism." *Environment and Society* 2, no. 1 (December 2011): 68–86.

Allen, Douglas E., and Paul F. Anderson. "Consumption and Social Stratification: Bourdieu's Distinction." In *NA—Advances in Consumer Research*, vol. 21, edited by Chris T. Allen and Deborah Roedder John, 70–74. Provo, Utah : Association for Consumer Research, 1994.

Armstrong, Catherine. "Black Foodways and Places: The Didactic Epistemology of Food Memories in the WPA Narratives." *Slavery & Abolition* 42, no. 3 (2020): 1–22.

Austin, Allan D. *African Muslims in Antebellum America: Transatlantic Stories and Spiritual Struggles*. New York: Routledge, 1997.

Avakian, Arlene. "Shish Kebab Armenians?: Food and the Construction and Maintenance of Ethnic and Gender Identities Among Armenian American Feminists." In *From Betty Crocker to Feminist Food Studies: Critical Perspectives on Women and Food*, edited by A. V. Avakian and B. Haber, 257–80. Boston: University of Massachusetts Press, 2005.

Barghouti, Mourid. *I Saw Ramallah*. Translated by Ahdaf Soueif. New York: Anchor, 2003.

Bass, Margaret K. "On Being a Fat Black Girl in a Fat Hating Culture." In *Recovering the Black Female Body: Self-Representation by African American Women*, edited by Michael Bennett and Vanessa D. Dickerson, 219–30. New Brunswick, N.J.: Rutgers University Press, 2001.

Bates, Kelsey Scouten. "Comfort in a Decidedly Uncomfortable Time: Hunger, Collective Memory, and the Meaning of Soul Food in Gee's Bend, Alabama." *Food and Foodways* 20, no. 1 (2012): 53–75.

Beagan, Brenda, Gwen E. Chapman, Andrea D'Sylva, and B. Raewyn Bassett. "'It's Just Easier for Me to Do It': Rationalizing the Family Division of Foodwork." *Sociology* 42, no. 4 (August 2008): 653–71.

Belasco, Warren, Amy Bentley, Charlotte Biltekoff, Psyche Williams-Forson, and Carolyn de la Peña. "The Frontiers of Food Studies." *Food, Culture and Society* 14, no. 3 (September 2011): 301–14.

Belasco, Warren J. *Appetite for Change: How the Counterculture Took On the Food Industry*. Ithaca, N.Y.: Cornell University Press, 2007.

Bell, Judith, and Bonnie María Burlin. "In Urban Areas: Many of the Poor Still Pay More for Food." *Journal of Public Policy and Marketing* 12, no. 2 (1993): 268–70.

Beoku-Betts, Josephine. "'We Got Our Way of Cooking Things': Women, Food, and Preservation of Cultural Identity Among the Gullah." *Gender and Society* 9, no. 5 (1995): 535–55.

Bialeschki, M. Deborah, and Kimberly D. Pearce. "'I Don't Want a Lifestyle—I Want a Life': The Effect of Role Negotiations on the Leisure of Lesbian Mothers." *Journal of Leisure Research* 29, no. 1 (1997): 113–31. doi: 10.1080/00222216.1997 .11949786.

Biltekoff, Charlotte. *Eating Right in America: The Cultural Politics of Food and Health*. Durham, N.C.: Duke University Press.

Bluett, Thomas. *Some Memoirs of the Life of Job, the Son of Solomon the High Priest of Boondain Africa, Who Was a Slave About Two Years in Maryland, and Afterwards Being Brought to Maryland, Was Set Free, and Sent to His Native Land in the Year 1734*. London: printed for R. Ford, 1734. Available online in a digitized version at *Documenting the American South*: https://docsouth.unc.edu/neh/bluett/bluett .html.

Bonilla-Silva, Eduardo. "More than Prejudice: Restatement, Reflections, and New Directions in Critical Race Theory." *Sociology of Race and Ethnicity* 1, no. 1 (January 2015): 73–87. https://doi.org/10.1177%2F2332649214557042.

Bourdieu, Pierre. *Distinction: A Social Critique of the Judgement of Taste*. Translated by Richard Nice. Cambridge, Mass.: Harvard University Press, 1984.

Bowens, Natasha. *The Color of Food: Stories of Race, Resilience, and Farming*. Canada: New Society Publishers, 2015.

Bower, Anne L., ed. *African American Foodways: Explorations of History & Culture*. Urbana: University of Illinois Press, 2007.

Brown, Linda Keller, and Kay Mussell, eds. *Ethnic and Regional Foodways in the United States: The Performance of Group Identity.* Knoxville: University of Tennessee Press, 1984.

Butler, David L., Perry L. Carter, and Stanley D. Brunn. "African-American Travel Agents: Travails and Survival." *Annals of Tourism Research* 29, no. 4 (2002): 1022–35.

Byrne, Denis. "Nervous Landscapes: Race and Space in Australia." *Journal of Social Archaeology* 3, no. 2 (2003): 169–93.

Cadieux, Kirsten Valentine, and Rachel Slocum. "What Does It Mean to Do Food Justice?" *Journal of Political Ecology* 22, no. 1 (2015): 1–26. https://doi.org/10.2458 /v22i1.21076.

Campbell, Marcia C. "Building a Common Table: The Role for Planning in Community Food Systems." *Journal of Planning Education and Research* 23, no. 4 (2004): 341–55.

Campos, Paul, Abigail Saguy, Paul Ernsberger, Eric Oliver, and Glenn Gaesser. "The Epidemiology of Overweight and Obesity: Public Health Crisis or Moral Panic?" *International Journal of Epidemiology* 35, no. 1 (2006): 55–60.

Capet, Race. "Created Equal: Slavery and America's Muslim Heritage." *CrossCurrents* 60, no. 4 (December 2010): 549–60. http://www.jstor.org/stable/24462381.

Carney, Judith, and Richard Rosomoff. *In the Shadow of Slavery: Africa's Botanical Legacy in the Atlantic World.* Oakland: University of California Press, 2010.

Carrington, Christopher. *No Place Like Home: Relationships and Family Life among Lesbians and Gay Men.* Chicago: University of Chicago Press, 2009.

Carter, Prudence L. "'Black' Cultural Capital, Status Positioning, and Schooling Conflicts for Low-Income African American Youth." *Social Problems* 50, no. 1 (2003): 136–55.

Charles, Nickie, and Marion Kerr. *Women, Food, and Families.* Manchester, U.K.: Manchester University Press, 1988.

Chatelain, Marcia. *Franchise: The Golden Arches in Black America.* New York: Liveright Publishing, 2021.

———. *South Side Girls: Growing up in the Great Migration.* Durham, N.C.: Duke University Press, 2015.

Cherry-Chandler, Eileen. "After the Reapers: Place Settings of Race, Class, and Food Insecurity." *Text and Performance Quarterly* 29, no. 1 (2009): 44–59.

Clark-Lewis, Elizabeth. *Living In, Living Out: African American Domestics in Washington, D.C., 1910–1940.* Washington, D.C.: Smithsonian Books, 2010.

Coates, Ta-Nehisi. *Between the World and Me.* New York: Spiegel and Grau, 2015.

Cohen, Deborah A., J. Scott Ashwood, Molly M. Scott, Adrian Overton, Kelly R. Evenson, Lisa K. Staten, Dwayne Porter, Thomas L. McKenzie, and Diane Catellier. "Public Parks and Physical Activity among Adolescent Girls." *Pediatrics* 118, no. 5 (November 2006): e1381–e1389. https://doi.org/10.1542/peds.2006-1226.

Colbin, Annemarie. "Overview of Two Popular Diets: Vegetarianism and Macrobiotics." *International Journal of Healing and Caring* 2, no. 1 (January 2002): 1–10. https://irp-cdn.multiscreensite.com/891f98f6/files/uploaded/Colbin-2-1.pdf.

Collins, Patricia Hill. *Black Feminist Thought: Knowledge, Consciousness and the Politics of Empowerment.* London: Routledge, 1990.

Cooley, Angela Jill. *To Live and Dine in Dixie: The Evolution of Urban Food Culture in the Jim Crow South*. Athens: University of Georgia Press, 2015.

Cooper, Brittney. *Eloquent Rage: A Black Feminist Discovers Her Superpower*. New York: St. Martin's Press, 2018.

Copher, Charles B. "Three Thousand Years of Biblical Interpretation with Reference to Black Peoples." In *African American Religious Studies: An Interdisciplinary Anthology*, edited by Gayraud Wilmore, 105–28. Durham, N.C.: Duke University Press, 1989.

Counihan, Carole. "Female Identity, Food, and Power in Contemporary Florence." *Anthropological Quarterly* 61, no. 2 (April 1998): 51–62.

———. *A Tortilla Is Like Life: Food and Culture in the San Luis Valley of Colorado*. Austin: University of Texas Press, 2009.

Cserno, Isabell. "Race and Mass Consumption in Consumer Culture: National Trademark Advertising Campaigns in the United States and Germany, 1890–1930." PhD diss., University of Maryland, College Park, 2008. ProQuest (3307782).

Csikszentmihalyi, Mihalyi. "Why We Need Things." In *History from Things: Essays on Material Culture*, edited by Stephen Lubar and W. David Kingery, 21–26. Washington, D.C.: Smithsonian Institution Press, 1993.

Dahn, Eurie. "'Unashamedly Black': Jim Crow Aesthetics and the Visual Logic of Shame." In "Visual Culture and Race," special issue, *MELUS* 39, no. 2 (Summer 2014): 93–114.

Davies, Lorraine, and Patricia Jane Carrier. "The Importance of Power Relations for the Division of Household Labour." *Canadian Journal of Sociology* 24, no. 1 (1999): 35–51.

Deetz, Kelley Fanto. *Bound to the Fire: How Virginia's Enslaved Cooks Helped Invent American Cuisine*. Lexington: University Press of Kentucky, 2017.

Degner, Robert. "Reaching Consumers with Novel Foods." Paper presented at the annual meeting of the Research and Development Association for Military Food & Packaging Systems, Inc., Gainesville, Florida, April 1986.

Delgado, Richard, and Jean Stefancic. *Critical Race Theory: An Introduction*. New York: New York University Press, 2001.

Denkler, Ann. *Sustaining Identity, Recapturing Heritage: Exploring Issues of Public History, Tourism, and Race in a Southern Town*. Lanham, Md.: Lexington Books, 2007.

DeVault, Marjorie. *Feeding the Family: The Social Organization of Caring as Gendered Work*. Chicago: University of Chicago Press, 1991.

Diner, Hasia. *Hungering for America: Italian, Irish, and Jewish Foodways in the Age of Migration*. Cambridge, Mass.: Harvard University Press, 2003.

Diouf, Sylviane A. *Servants of Allah: African Muslims Enslaved in the Americas*. New York: New York University Press, 1998.

D'Sylva, Andrea, and Brenda L. Beagan. "'Food Is Culture, but It's Also Power': The Role of Food in Ethnic and Gender Identity Construction among Goan Canadian Women." *Journal of Gender Studies* 20, no. 3 (2011): 279–89.

Du Bois, W. E. B. "On Being Ashamed of Oneself: An Essay on Race Pride." In *The

Oxford W. E. B. Du Bois Reader, edited by Eric J. Sundquist. Oxford: Oxford University Press, 1996. First published in *The Crisis*, September 13, 1933.

DuPuis, E. Melanie, and David Goodman. "Should We Go 'Home' to Eat? Toward a Reflexive Politics of Localism." *Journal of Rural Studies* 21, no. 3 (2005): 359–71.

Durodoye, Beth, and Angela Coker. "Crossing Cultures in Marriage: Implications for Counseling African American/African Couples." *International Journal for the Advancement of Counselling* 30, no. 1 (2008): 25–37.

Edwards-Ingram, Ywone. "Medicating Slavery: Motherhood, Health Care, and Cultural Practices in the African Diaspora." PhD diss., College of William and Mary, 2005. https://dx.doi.org/doi:10.21220/s2-sncj-bn72.

———. "'Trash' Revisited: A Comparative Approach to Historical Descriptions and Archaeological Analyses of Slave Houses and Yards." In *Keep Your Head to the Sky: Interpreting African American Home Ground*, edited by G. Gundaker, 245–71. Charlottesville: University of Virginia Press, 1998.

Eisnach, Dwight, and Herbert C. Covey. *What the Slaves Ate: Recollections of African American Foods and Foodways from the Slave Narratives.* Westport, Conn.: Greenwood Publishing Group, 2009.

Engelhardt, Elizabeth. *Mess of Greens: Southern Gender and Southern Food.* Athens: University of Georgia Press, 2011.

Erikson, Kai. *A New Species of Trouble: Explorations in Disaster, Trauma, and Community.* New York: W. W. Norton, 1994.

Fajans, Jane. "The Transformative Value of Food: A Review Essay." *Food and Foodways* 3, nos. 1–2 (1988): 143–44. https://doi.org/10.1080/07409710.1988.9961941.

Farrell, Amy Erdman. *Fat Shame: Stigma and the Fat Body in American Culture.* New York: New York University Press, 2011.

Federal Writers' Project, *Slave Narrative Project*, vol. 4, Georgia, part 3, Kendricks–Styles. 1936. https://www.loc.gov/item/mesn043/.

Ferguson, Leland. *Uncommon Ground: Archaeology and Early African America, 1650–1800.* Washington, D.C.: Smithsonian Books, 2017.

Ferris, Marcie Cohen. *Matzoh Ball Gumbo: Culinary Tales of the Jewish South.* Chapel Hill: University of North Carolina Press, 2010.

Fett, Sharla M. *Working Cures: Healing, Health, and Power on Southern Slave Plantations.* Chapel Hill: University of North Carolina Press, 2002.

Franklin, Maria. "The Archaeological and Symbolic Dimensions of Soul Food: Race, Culture and Afro-Virginian Identity." In *Race and the Archaeology of Identity*, edited by C. Orser, 88–107. Salt Lake City: University of Utah Press, 2002.

———. "Enslaved Household Variability and Plantation Life and Labor in Colonial Virginia." *International Journal of Historical Archaeology* 24 (2020): 115–55.

Frazao, Elizabeth, Margaret Andrews, David Smallwood, and Mark Prell. *Food Spending Patterns of Low-Income Households: Will Increasing Purchasing Power Result in Healthier Food Choices?* Department of Agriculture, Economic Research Service. Economic Information Bulletin 29-4. September 2007. http://handle.nal.usda.gov/10113/35117.

Furst, Tanis, Margaret Conners, Carole Bisogni, Jeffery Sobal, and Laura Winter Falk.

"Food Choice: A Conceptual Model of the Process." *Appetite* 26, no. 3 (June 1996): 247–66.

Gabaccia, Donna R. *We Are What We Eat: Ethnic Food and the Making of Americans.* Cambridge, Mass.: Harvard University Press, 2000.

Gard, Michael, and Jan Wright. *The Obesity Epidemic.* London: Routledge, 2005.

Giovanni, Nikki. *Love Poems.* New York: William Morrow, 1997.

Goings, Kenneth W. *Mammy and Uncle Mose: Black Collectibles and American Stereotyping.* Bloomington: Indiana University Press, 1994.

Gomez, Michael A. *Black Crescent: The Experience and Legacy of African Muslims in the Americas.* Cambridge, UK: Cambridge University Press, 2005.

Gordon, Avery. *Ghostly Matters: Haunting and the Sociological Imagination.* 2nd ed. Minneapolis: University of Minnesota Press, 2008.

Grosvenor, Vertamae. Foreword to Ntozake Shange, *If I Can Cook/You Know God Can*, xi–xiv. Boston: Beacon Press, 1998.

———. "In the Tradition—Cooking: An Interview with Vertamae Grosvenor." Interview by Judie Moore Smith. Aired February 20, 1984, on WGLT public radio, Illinois State University. Recording in the author's possession.

Guthman, Julie. "Bringing Good Food to Others: Investigating the Subjects of Alternative Food Practice." *Cultural Geographies* 15, no. 4 (2008): 431–47. doi:10.1177 /1474474008094315.

———. *Weighing In: Obesity, Food Justice, and the Limits of Capitalism.* California Studies in Food and Culture, vol. 32, edited by Darra Goldstein. Berkeley: University of California Press, 2011.

Haider, Steven, and Marianne Bitler. "An Economic View of Food Deserts in the United States." National Poverty Center Policy Brief 23 (October 2010): 1–5. Available online: http://www.npc.umich.edu/publications/policy_briefs/brief23/policy brief23.pdf.

Hall, Robert. "Food Crops, Medicinal Plants, and the Atlantic Slave Trade." In Bower, *African American Foodways*, 17–44.

Hall, Stuart. "Cultural Identity and Diaspora." In *Identity, Community, Culture, Difference*, edited by Jonathan Rutherford, 222–37. London: Lawrence & Wishart, 1990.

Halloran, Vivian Nun. *The Immigrant Kitchen: Food, Ethnicity, and Diaspora.* Columbus: Ohio State University Press, 2016.

Hannah-Jones, Nikole, et al. "The 1619 Project." Special issue, *New York Times Magazine*, August 18, 2019.

Harper, Amie Breeze. *Sistah Vegan: Black Female Vegans Speak on Food, Identity, Health, and Society.* New York: Lantern Press, 2010.

Harris, Carmen. "Grace under Pressure: The Black Home Extension Service in South Carolina, 1919–1966." In *Rethinking Home Economics: Women and the History of a Profession*, edited by Sarah Stage and Virginia B. Vincenti, 203–28. Ithaca, N.Y.: Cornell University Press, 1997.

Harris, Ellen W., and Alvin Nowverl. "What's Happening to Soul Food? Regional and Income Differences in the African American Diet." *Ecology of Food and Nutrition* 38, no. 6 (1999): 587–603.

Harris, Jessica. *High on the Hog: A Culinary Journey from Africa to America*. New York: Bloomsbury, 2011.

——. *Iron Pots and Wooden Spoons: Africa's Gifts to New World Cooking*. New York: Scribner, 1989.

Harris-Perry, Melissa. *Sister Citizen: Shame, Stereotypes, and Black Women in America*. New Haven, Conn.: Yale University Press, 2011.

Hartman, Saidiya. *Lose Your Mother: A Journey Along the Atlantic Slave Trade Route Terror*. New York: Farrar, Straus and Giroux, 2007.

Hattery, Angela J., and Earl Smith. *Policing Black Bodies: How Black Lives Are Surveilled and How to Work for Change*. Lanham, Md.: Rowman & Littlefield, 2017.

Hawkes, Jon. *The Fourth Pillar of Sustainability: Culture's Essential Role in Public Planning*. Melbourne: Cultural Development Network and Common Ground Press, 2001.

Heldke, Lisa. "Let's Cook Thai: Recipes for Colonialism." In *Food and Culture: A Reader*, 2nd ed., edited by Carole Counihan and Penny Van Esterik, 327–41. New York: Routledge, 2008.

——. "Staying Home for Dinner: Ruminations on Local Foods in a Cosmopolitan Society." Presentation at the Food, Ethnic Identities and Memory Symposium, University of Iowa, March 24, 2008.

hooks, bell. "Representing Whiteness in the Black Imagination." In *Cultural Studies*, edited by Lawrence Grossberg, Cary Nelson, and Paula Treichler, 338–46. London: Routledge, 1992.

Hunt, Matthew, and Rashawn Ray. "Social Class Identification among Black Americans: Trends and Determinants, 1974–2010." *American Behavioral Scientist* 56, no. 11 (2012): 1462–80.

Hupkens, Christianne L. H., Ronald A. Knibbe, and Maria J. Drop. "Social Class Differences in Food Consumption." *European Journal of Public Health* 10, no. 2 (June 2000): 108–13.

Hurst, Sam, dir. *Good Meat*. Native American Public Telecommunications, 2011.

Imbruce, Valerie. 2011. "From the Bottom Up: The Global Expansion of Chinese Vegetable Trade for New York City Markets." In Williams-Forson and Counihan, *Taking Food Public*, 356–68. New York: Routledge. Originally published in *Fast Food / Slow Food: The Cultural Economy of Global Food*, ed. Richard Wilk.

Jackson, Ronald. *Scripting the Black Masculine Body: Identity, Discourse, and Racial Politics in Popular Media*. New York: New York University Press, 2006.

Ji-Song Ku, Robert, Martin F. Manalanson, and Anita Mannur. *Eating Asian America: A Food Studies Reader*. New York: New York University Press, 2013.

Johnston, James H. "Every Picture Tells a Story: A Narrative Portrait of Yarrow Mamout." *Maryland Historical Magazine* 103, no. 4 (Winter 2008): 404–34.

Kalcik, S. "Ethnic Foodways in America: Symbol and the Performance of Identity." In *Ethnic and Regional Foodways in the United States: The Performance of Group Identity*, edited by Linda Keller Brown and Kay Mussell, 37–65. Knoxville: University of Tennessee Press, 1984.

Kendi, Ibram. *Stamped from the Beginning: The Definitive History of Racist Ideas in America*. New York: Bold Type Books, 2017.

Kerr, Audrey. *The Paper Bag Principle: Class, Colorism and Rumor and the Case of Black Washington, D.C.* Knoxville: University of Tennessee Press, 2006.

Kim, DaeHwan, and J. Paul Leigh. "Are Meals at Full-Service and Fast-Food Restaurants 'Normal' or 'Inferior'?" *Population Health Management* 14, no. 6 (December 2011): 307–15. https://pubmed.ncbi.nlm.nih.gov/21827320/.

Kirshenblatt-Gimblett, Barbara. "Playing to the Senses: Food as a Performance Medium." *Performance Research* 4, no. 1 (1999): 1–30. https://doi.org/10.1080/13528165.1999.10871639.

Klein, Shana. "Cutting Away the Rind: A History of Racism and Violence in Representations of Watermelon." In *The Fruits of Empire: Art, Food, and the Politics of Race in the Age of American Expansion*, 73–104. Oakland: University of California Press, 2020.

Korsmeyer, Carolyn. "Introduction: Perspectives on Taste." In *The Taste Culture Reader: Experiencing Food and Drink*, edited by Carolyn Korsmeyer, 1–13. New York: Bloomsbury Publishing, 2016.

Kowaleski-Jones, Lori, Jessie X. Fan, Ikuho Yamada, Cathleen D. Zick, Ken R. Smith, and Barbara Brown. "Alternative Measures of Food Deserts: Fruitful Options or Empty Cupboards." U.S. Department of Agriculture and National Poverty Center, March 2009. Available online: https://www.researchgate.net/publication/255035861_Alternative_Measures_of_Food_Deserts_Fruitful_Options_or_Empty_Cupboards.

Krieger, Nancy. "Historical Roots of Social Epidemiology: Socioeconomic Gradients in Health and Contextual Analysis." *International Journal of Epidemiology* 30, no. 4 (2001): 899–903.

Kushi, Michio, and Alex Jack. *The Book of Macrobiotics: The Universal Way of Health, Happiness & Peace*. Revised edition. New York: Square One Publishing, 2012.

Kwate, Naa Oyo. *Burgers in Blackface: Anti-Black Restaurants Then and Now.* Minneapolis: University of Minnesota Press, 2019.

———. "Fried Chicken and Fresh Apples: Racial Segregation as a Fundamental Cause of Fast Food Density in Black Neighborhoods." *Health and Place* 14, no. 1 (2008): 32–44.

Lamont, Michèle, and Virág Molnár. "How Blacks Use Consumption to Shape Their Collective Identity: Evidence from Marketing Specialists. *Journal of Consumer Culture* 1, no. 1 (2001): 31–45, https://journals.sagepub.com/doi/10.1177/146954050100100103.

Larchet, Nicolas. "Learning from the Corner Store: Food Reformers and the Black Urban Poor in a Southern U.S. City." *Food, Culture & Society* 17, no. 3 (2014): 395–416. https://doi.org/10.2752/175174414X13948130848386.

Latshaw, Beth A. "The Soul of the South: Race, Food, and Identity in the American South." In *The Larder: Food Studies Methods from the American South*, edited by John T. Edge, Elizabeth S.D. Engelhardt, and Ted Ownby, 99–127. Athens: University of Georgia Press, 2013.

Lee, KangJae Jerry, and David Scott. "Racial Discrimination and African Americans' Travel Behavior: The Utility of Habitus and Vignette Technique." *Journal of Travel Research* 56, no. 3 (2017): 381–92. https://doi.org/10.1177%2F0047287516643184.

Lee, Michele Elizabeth. *Working the Roots: Over 400 Years of Traditional African American Healing*. Oakland, Calif.: Wadastick, 2017.

Levenstein, Harvey. *Revolution at the Table: The Transformation of the American Table*. Oxford: Oxford University Press, 1988.

Lin, Hsein-Ming, Ching Lin Pang, and Da-Chi Liao. "Home Food Making, Belonging, and Identity Negotiation in Belgian Taiwanese Immigrant Women's Everyday Food Practices." *Journal of Ethnic Foods* 7, no. 29 (2020): 1–18.

Locher, J., Yoels, W., Maurer, D., and van Ells, J. "Comfort Foods: An Exploratory Journey Into The Social and Emotional Significance of Food." *Food and Foodways* 13, no. 4 (1999): 273–95.

Lockett, Alexandria. "What Is Black Twitter? A Rhetorical Criticism of Race, Dis/Information, and Social Media." In *Race, Rhetoric, and Research Methods*, edited by Alexandria L. Lockett, Iris D. Ruiz, James Chase Sanchez, and Christopher Carter, 165–213. Fort Collins, Colo.: WAC Clearinghouse, 2021.

Lott, Eric. *Love and Theft: Blackface Minstrelsy and the American Working Class*. New York: Oxford University Press, 1993.

Lusk, Jayson. *The Food Police: A Well-Fed Manifesto about the Politics of Your Plate*. New York: Crown Forum, 2013.

Mannur, Anita. *Culinary Fictions: Food in South Asian Diasporic Culture*. Philadelphia: Temple University Press, 2009.

———. "Culinary Nostalgia: Authenticity, Nationalism, and Diaspora." *MELUS* 32, no. 4 (2007): 11–31.

Maye, Damian, Lewis Holloway, and Moya Kneafsey. *Alternative Food Geographies: Representation and Practice*. Bingley, UK: Emerald, 2007.

McCutcheon, Priscilla. "Fannie Lou Hamer's Freedom Farms and Black Agrarian Geographies." *Antipode* 51, no. 1 (January 2019): 207–24. https://doi.org/10.1111/anti.12500.

McIntosh, Alex, and Mary Zey. "Women as Gatekeepers of Food Consumption." In *Food and Gender: Identity and Power*, edited by Carole Counihan and Stephen Kaplan, 125–44. Amsterdam: Harwood Academic Publishers, 1998.

McQuirter, Tracye. *By Any Greens Necessary: A Revolutionary Guide for Black Women Who Want to Eat Great, Get Healthy, Lose Weight, and Look Phat*. Chicago: Chicago Review Press, 2010.

McQuirter, Tracye, and Marya McQuirter. *Ageless Vegan: The Secret to Living a Long and Healthy Plant-Based Life*. Lebanon, Ind.: Da Capo Press, 2018.

Mehta, Brinda. "Culinary Diasporas: Identity and the Language of Food in Gisèle Pineau's *Un papillon dans la cité* and *L'exil selon Julia*." *International Journal of Francophone Studies* 8, no. 1 (2005): 23–51.

Mihesuah, Devon A., and Elizabeth Hoover. *Indigenous Food Sovereignty in the United States: Restoring Cultural Knowledge, Protecting Environments, and Regaining Health*. New Directions in Native American Studies Series, vol. 18, edited by Collin G. Calloway and K. Tsianina Lomawaima. Norman: University of Oklahoma Press, 2019.

Miller, Adrian. *Soul Food: The Surprising Story of an American Cuisine, One Plate at a Time*. Chapel Hill: University of North Carolina Press, 2017.

Moore, Latetia V., Ana V. Diez Roux, Kelly R. Evenson, Aileen P. McGinn, and
    Shannon J. Brines. "Availability of Recreational Resources in Minority and Low
    Socioeconomic Status Areas." *American Journal of Preventative Medicine* 34, no. 1
    (January 2008): 16–22. https://doi.org/10.1016/j.amepre.2007.09.021.

Mustakeem, Sowande. *Slavery at Sea: Terror, Sex, and Sickness in the Middle Passage.*
    Champaign: University of Illinois Press, 2016.

Naccarato, Peter, and Katherine LeBesco. *Culinary Capital.* London: Berg Publishers,
    2012.

Natonson, Nichols. *The Black Image in the New Deal: The Politics of FSA Photography.*
    Knoxville: University of Tennessee Press, 1992.

Nettles-Barcelon, Kimberly. "Saving Soul Food." *Gastronomica* 7, no. 3 (Summer
    2007): 106–13.

Nettles-Barcelon, Kimberly, Gillian Clark, Courtney Thorsson, Jessica K. Walker, and
    Psyche Williams-Forson. "Black Women's Food Work as Critical Space." *Gastro-
    nomica* 15, no. 4 (2015): 34–49.

Oerton, Sarah. "'Queer Housewives?': Some Problems in Theorising the Division of
    Domestic Labour in Lesbian and Gay Households." *Women's Studies International
    Forum* 20, no. 3 (May–June 1997): 421–30. https://doi.org/10.1016/S0277-5395(97)
    00025-3.

Omi, Michael, and Howard Winant. *Racial Formation in the United States: From 1960
    to 1990s.* New York: Routledge, 1994.

Opie, Frederick Douglass. *Hog and Hominy: Soul Food from Africa to America.* New
    York: Columbia University Press, 2008.

Osseo-Asare, Fran. "We Eat First with Our Eyes: On Ghanaian Cuisine." *Gastro-
    nómica* 2, no. 1 (2002): 49–57.

Otoo, David, and Tamminay Otoo. *Authentic African Cuisine from Ghana.* Colorado
    Springs, Colo.: Sankofa, 1997.

Penniman, Leah. *Farming While Black: Soul Fire Farm's Practical Guide to Liberation
    on the Land.* White River Junction, Vt.: Chelsea Green Publishing, 2018.

Piercy, Marge. "What's That Smell in the Kitchen." In *Food for Thought: An Anthology
    of Writings Inspired by Food,* edited by John Digdy and Joan Digby, 337–38. New
    York: William Morrow, 1987.

Pieterse, Jan Nederveen. *White on Black: Images of Africa and Blacks in Western
    Popular Culture.* New Haven, Conn.: Yale University Press, 1995.

Poe, Tracy. "Food, Culture, and Entrepreneurship: Strategies and Symbols of Ethnic
    Identity in Chicago, 1900–1965." PhD diss. Harvard University, 1999.

———. "The Origins of Soul Food in Black Urban Identity: Chicago, 1915–1947." *Amer-
    ican Studies International* 37, no. 1 (February 1999): 4–33.

Purkiss, Ava. "'Beauty Secrets: Fight Fat'—Black Women's Aesthetics, Exercise, and
    Fat Stigma, 1900–1930s." *Journal of Women's History* 29, no. 2 (2017): 14–37.

Radway, Janice. Foreword to Gordon, *Ghostly Matters,* vii–xiv.

Ray, Krishnendu. *The Migrant's Table: Meals and Memories in Bengali-American
    Households.* Philadelphia: Temple University Press, 2004.

Reese, Ashanté. *Black Food Geographies: Race, Self-Reliance, and Food Access in
    Washington, D.C.* Chapel Hill: University of North Carolina Press, 2019.

Reese, Ashanté, and Hanna Garth, eds. *Black Food Matters: Racial Justice in the Wake of Food Justice*. Minneapolis: University of Minnesota Press, 2020.

Reid, Debra A. *Reaping a Greater Harvest: African Americans, the Extension Service, and Rural Reform in Jim Crow Texas*. College Station: Texas A&M University Press, 2007.

Renne, Elisha P. 2007. "Mass Producing Food Traditions for West Africans Abroad." *American Anthropologist* 109, no. 4: 616–25.

Rice, Kym, and Martha B. Katz-Hyman, eds. *World of a Slave: Encyclopedia of the Material Life of Slaves in the United States*. Westport, Conn.: Greenwood Publishing Group, 2010.

Riggs, Marlon, dir. *Black Is . . . Black Ain't*. San Francisco: California Newsreel, 1994.

———. *Ethnic Notions*. San Francisco: California Newsreel, 1987.

Rock, Chris. *Chris Rock: Bring the Pain*. First aired June 1, 1996, on HBO.

Romano, Dugan. *Intercultural Marriage: Promises and Pitfalls*. Boston: Nicholas Brealey, 2008.

Romm, Jeffrey M. "The Coincidental Order of Environmental Injustice." In *Justice and Natural Resources*, edited by Kathryn M. Mutz, Gary C. Bryner, and Douglas S. Kenney, 117–38. Washington, D.C.: Island Press, 2002.

Rouse, Carolyn, and Janet Hoskins. "Purity, Soul Food, and Sunni Islam: Explorations at the Intersection of Consumption and Resistance." In Williams-Forson and Counihan, *Taking Food Public*, 175–94.

RZA, dir. *Cut Throat City*. West Hollywood: Patriot Pictures, 2020.

Shardow, Marian. *A Taste of Hospitality: Authentic Ghanaian Cookery*. Victoria, Canada: Trafford Publishing, 2002.

Sharpless, Rebecca. *Cooking in Other Women's Kitchens: Domestic Workers in the South, 1865–1960*. The John Hope Franklin Series in African American History and Culture, edited by Waldo E. Martin Jr., and Patricia Sullivan. Chapel Hill: University of North Carolina Press, 2010.

Shurtleff, William, and Akiko Aoyagi. *History of Macrobiotics (1715–2017): Extensively Annotated Bibliography and Sourcebook*. Lafayette, Calif.: Soyinfo Center, 2017.

Simmons, Scott R. "Red Beans and Rice." In *Foodways*, edited by John T. Edge, 243–44. Vol. 7 of *The New Encyclopedia of Southern Culture*, edited by Charles Reagan Wilson. Chapel Hill: University of North Carolina Press, 2007.

Smith, Barbara. "A Press of Our Own Kitchen Table: Women of Color Press." *Frontiers: A Journal of Women Studies* 10, no. 3 (1989): 11–13. https://doi.org/10.2307/3346433.

Smith, Linda Tuhiwai. *Decolonizing Methodologies: Research and Indigenous Peoples*. London: Zed Books, 2002.

Sobal, Jeffrey, and Carole A. Bisogni. "Constructing Food Choice Decisions." *Annals of Behavioral Medicine* 38, suppl. 1 (2009): s37–s46. https://doi.org/10.1007/s12160-009-9124-5.

Stanonis, Anthony. *Dixie Emporium: Tourism, Foodways, and Consumer Culture in the American South*. Athens: University of Georgia Press, 2008.

Strings, Sabrina. *Fearing the Black Body: The Racial Origins of Fat Phobia*. New York: New York University Press, 2019.

Sullivan, Maureen. "Rozzie and Harriet? Gender and Family Patterns of Lesbian Coparents." *Gender and Society* 10, no. 6 (December 1996): 747–67. doi:10.1177/08912 4396010006005.

Tangney, June Price, and Ronda L. Dearing. *Shame and Guilt*. New York: Guilford Press, 2003.

Tannahill, Reay. *Food in History*. New York: Crown Publishing Group, 1995.

Tate, Greg. *Everything but the Burden: What White People Are Taking from Black Culture*. New York: Broadway, 2003.

Terry, Bryant. *Afro-Vegan: Farm-Fresh African, Caribbean, and Southern Flavors Remixed*. Berkeley, Calif.: Ten Speed, 2014.

———. *Vegan Soul Kitchen: Fresh, Healthy, and Creative African-American Cuisine*. Cambridge, Mass.: Da Capo, 2009.

Thompson, Becky W. *A Hunger So Wide and So Deep: A Multiracial View of Women's Eating Problems*. Minneapolis: University of Minnesota Press, 1996.

Tipton-Martin, Toni. *The Jemima Code: Two Centuries of African American Cookbooks*. Austin: University of Texas Press, 2015.

Trotter, Thomas. "Observations on the Scurvy." In *Observations on the Scurvy: With a Review of the Theories Lately Advanced on that Disease; and the Opinions of Dr. Milman Refuted from Practice*, 17–28. Philadelphia: published by John Parker, 1793. http://resource.nlm.nih.gov/2575040R.

Turner, Patricia A. *Ceramic Uncles and Celluloid Mammies: Black Images and Their Influence on Culture*. Charlottesville: University of Virginia Press, 2002.

Twitty, Michael W. *The Cooking Gene: A Journey through African American Culinary History in the Old South*. New York: Amistad Press, 2017.

Van Andel, Tinde R., Charlotte I. E. A. van 't Klooster, Diana Quiroz, Alexandra M. Towns, Sofie Ruysschaert, and Margot van den Berg. "Local Plant Names Reveal That African Slaves Recognized American Plants." *Proceedings of the National Academy of Sciences* 111, no. 50 (Dec 2014): E5346–E5353.

Walker, Alice. "Everyday Use." In *In Love and Trouble: Stories of Black Women*. New York: Harcourt Brace Jovanovich, 1973.

———. *In Love and Trouble: Stories of Black Women*. New York: Harcourt Brace Jovanovich, 1973.

———. *In Search of Our Mother's Gardens: Womanist Prose*. San Diego, Calif.: Harcourt Brace Jovanovich, 1983.

Walker, Jessica. "Black Women's Food Work as Critical Space: A Research Essay." *Gastronomica: The Journal of Critical Food Studies* 15, no.4 (2015): 34–49.

———. "Nervous Kitchens: Critical Readings of Black Women's Food Practices in the Soul Food Imaginary." Thesis, University of Maryland, 2016. https://doi.org /10.13016/M2751X.

Wallach, Jennifer Jensen, ed. *Dethroning the Deceitful Pork Chop: Rethinking African American Foodways from Slavery to Obama*. Fayetteville: University of Arkansas Press, 2015.

———. *Every Nation Has Its Dish: Black Bodies and Black Food in Twentieth Century America*. Chapel Hill: University of North Carolina Press, 2019.

———. *Getting What We Need Ourselves: How Food Has Shaped African American Life, 2019*. Lanham, Md.: Rowman and Littlefield, 2019.

———. "How to Eat to Live: Black Nationalism and the Post-1964 Culinary Turn." *Study the South*, July 2, 2014, https://southernstudies.olemiss.edu/study-the-south/how-to-eat-to-live/.

Walmsley, Emily. "Race, Place and Taste: Making Identities through Sensory Experience in Ecuador." *Etnofoor* 18, no. 1 (2005): 43–60.

Warner, Mark. *Eating in the Side Room: Food, Archaeology and African American Identity*. Gainesville: University Press of Florida, 2015.

Waters, M. "Ethnic and Racial Identities of Second-Generation Black Immigrants in New York City." *International Migration Review* 28 (1994): 795–820.

Weems, Carrie Mae. *The Kitchen Table Series*. 1990. Series of photographs. 20 platinum prints, 14 letterpress text sheets. Cleveland Museum of Art, Ohio.

Wen, Ming, Xingyou Zhang, Carmen D. Harris, James B. Holt, and Janet B. Croft. "Spatial Disparities in the Distribution of Parks and Green Spaces in the USA." *Annals of Behavioral Medicine* 45, suppl. 1 (2013): S18–27.

White, Monica M. *Freedom Farmers: Agricultural Resistance and the Black Freedom Movement*. Chapel Hill: University of North Carolina Press, 2020.

———. "Freedom Seeds: Collective Agency and Community Resilience: A Theoretical Framework to Understand Agricultural Resistance." *Journal of Agriculture, Food Systems, and Community Development* 7, no. 4 (2017): 17–21.

———. "'A Pig and a Garden': Fannie Lou Hamer and the Freedom Farms Cooperative." *Food and Foodways: Explorations in the History and Culture of Human Nourishment* 25, no. 1 (2017): 20–39. https://doi.org/10.1080/07409710.2017.1270647.

Whitehead, Tony L. "In Search of Soul Food and Meaning: Culture, Food, and Health." In *African Americans in the South: Issues of Race, Class, and Gender*, edited by Hans A. Baer and Yvonne Jones, 94–110. Athens: University of Georgia Press.

Wilk, R. "'Real Belizean Food': Building Local Identity in the Transnational Caribbean." *American Anthropologist* 101, no. 2 (1999): 244–55.

Williams, Andrea. *Dividing Lines: Class Anxiety and Postbellum Fiction*. Ann Arbor: University of Michigan Press, 2013.

Williams, Brett. "Why Migrant Women Feed Their Husbands Tamales: Foodways as a Basis for a Revisionist View of Tejano Family Life." In *Ethnic and Regional Foodways in the United States: The Performance of Group Identity*, edited by Linda Keller Brown and Kay Mussell, 37–65. Knoxville: University of Tennessee Press, 1984.

Williams, Roger Ross, Jonathan Clasberry, and Yoruba Richen, dirs. *High on the Hog: How African American Cuisine Transformed America*. Netflix, 2021–2022.

Williams-Forson, Psyche. *Building Houses out of Chicken Legs: Black Women, Food, and Power*. Chapel Hill: University of North Carolina Press, 2006.

———. "Chickens and Chains: Using African American Foodways to Understand Black Identities." In Bower, *African American Foodways*, 126–38.

———. "The Dance of Culinary Patriotism: Material Culture and the Performance of Race with Food." In *The Larder: Food Studies Methods from the American South*, edited by John T. Edge, Elizabeth S. D. Engelhardt, and Ted Ownsby, 312–34. Athens: University of Georgia Press, 2013.

———. "'I Haven't Eaten If I Don't Have My Soup and Fufu': Cultural Preservation through Food and Foodways among Ghanaian Migrants in the United States." *Africa Today* 61, no. 1 (September 2014): 69–87.

———. "Other Women Cooked for My Husband: Negotiating Gender, Food, and Identities in an African American/Ghanaian Household." *Feminist Studies* 36, no. 2 (Summer 2010): 435–61.

———. "Take the Chicken out of the Box: Demystifying the Sameness of African American Culinary Heritage in the U.S." In *Edible Identities: Food As Cultural Heritage*, edited by Ronda L. Brulotte and Michael A. Di Giovine, 93–107. London: Routledge, 2016.

———. "A Weary Traveler in a Familiar Land." In "The Food Issue," ed. Alice Randall, special issue, *Oxford American* (Spring 2021): 44–51.

Williams-Forson, Psyche, and Carole Counihan, eds. *Taking Food Public: Redefining Foodways in a Changing World*. New York: Routledge, 2012.

Winter, Terence, dir. *Boardwalk Empire*, season 2. HBO Enterprises, 2015.

Witt, Doris. *Black Hunger: Soul Food and America*. Minneapolis: University of Minnesota Press, 2004.

Wolper, Mark, exec. prod. *Roots*. Aired May 30–June 2, 2016, on the History Channel.

Woodard, Vincent, Justin A. Joyce, and Dwight A. McBride. *The Delectable Negro: Human Consumption and Homoeroticism within U.S. Slave Culture*. New York: New York University Press, 2014.

Wright, Nazera Sudiq. *Black Girlhood in the Nineteenth Century*. Urbana: University of Illinois Press, 2007.

Yentsch, Anne Elizabeth. *A Chesapeake Family and Their Slaves: A Study in Historical Archaeology*. Cambridge, UK: Cambridge University Press, 1994.

Zafar, Rafia. *Recipes for Respect: African American Meals and Meaning*. Southern Foodways Alliance Studies in Culture, People, and Place Series, edited by John T. Edge. Athens: University of Georgia Press, 2019.

INDEX

Italic page numbers refer to illustrations.